CHANGING PATTERNS OF PSYCHIATRIC CARE

Bernard L. Bloom
University of Colorado

HUMAN SCIENCES PRESS
SUBSIDIARY OF BEHAVIORAL PUBLICATIONS INC.
72 FIFTH AVENUE, NEW YORK, N.Y. 10011

Library of Congress Catalog Number 74–8850
ISBN: 0–87705–209–3
Copyright © 1975 by Behavioral Publications, Inc.

BEHAVIORAL PUBLICATIONS, INC.
72 Fifth Avenue
New York, New York 10011

Printed in the United States of America
56789   987654321

Library of Congress Cataloging in Publication Data

Bloom, Bernard L
    Changing patterns of psychiatric care.

    Bibliography: p.
    1. Mental health services—Colorado—Pueblo.
2. Mental illness—Colorado—Pueblo—Statistics.
3. Social psychiatry. I. Title. [DNLM: 1. Community mental health services—U.S. 2. Mental disorders—Occurrence—U.S. WM30 B655c]
RA790.65.C6B55   362.2'09788'55   74–8850

Contents

PART III: PSYCHIATRIC CARE IN 1970

PART IV: SERVICE STATISTICS AND EPIDEMIOLOGY

Acknowledgments

In carrying out this project, I am indebted to three sources of grant support. In chronological order, the State of Colorado Department of Institutions, through its discretionary funds available under federal legislation supporting improved community mental health services, awarded me funds to inaugurate the project. Then, the Bio-Sciences Program at the University of Colorado made a continuation grant the following year. Finally, the Center for Epidemiologic Studies at the National Institute of Mental Health awarded funds which enabled me to complete the study.

I am indebted to the citizens of Pueblo, Colorado, to its mental health professionals, and to its psychiatric patients for giving of their time and effort on behalf of this project and for their willingness to share personal information with me. I have learned much from mental health colleagues—from clinical staff, epidemiologists, statisticians, and administrators, all of whom have seen fit to discuss their ideas freely with me. This sharing of ideas was particularly valuable when, in the late summer of 1973, I spent several days in Pueblo with nearly one hundred mental health professionals going over the draft of the manuscript. Their interpretations of the findings were most useful and are referred to throughout the volume. I wish to express special gratitude to Chris Hinz, Jerry Wilson, Wayne Smyer, and Paul Pantleo for their invaluable assistance in preparing the chapter describing Pueblo and its psychiatric service delivery system, and to Bob Abelson, whose unfailing good humor and skill in writing a language a computer could understand yielded the statistical analyses reported in this volume.

Most of the writing was done at the World Health Organization in Geneva between January and June, 1973. It is a pleasure to be able to acknowledge the stimulating friendship of Norm Sartorius and others in the Office of Mental Health and to express my gratitude to the staff at the WHO library, who provided me with a quiet and lovely place to work and with books and journals whenever I needed them.

I wish also to express my gratitude to John A. Baldwin, Bruce P. Dohrenwend, Ruth K. Goldman, Leo Levy, Ben Z. Locke, J. Robert Newbrough, and Morton O. Wagenfeld, who read the draft of this manuscript and shared their critical comments and reactions with me.

And I joyously acknowledge my indebtedness to my wife, Joan, who helped type the manuscript and prepare the index. But even more! For what she did and does is to give so lovingly and devotedly of herself to all of us—to me, the children, our friends, our cats, and our plants—that she brings out the best in us all and makes it possible for us to do our work with some sense of tranquility. Hopefully, we bring her that kind of peace which helps make it possible for her to do her work, too.

Prologue

Just over ten years ago, after having been a professional clinical psychologist for nearly a decade (primarily in public settings) and after spending a year as a Fellow at the Harvard School of Public Health in the Community Mental Health Program, I accepted a position as a mental health consultant in the Denver Regional Office of the U.S. Public Health Service where, as in all other regional offices, staff of the National Institute of Mental Health were deployed. I was not hired as a psychologist, but rather as a "program analyst," a term which was and which has remained creatively ambiguous. Its central characteristic was, however, intended to be empirical and quantitative. Somehow, NIMH program analysts in the regional offices were to begin working with state mental health professionals, particularly in the public sector, to demonstrate how data or information could be used to analyze mental health problems, particularly at the community level, and arrive at rational decisions regarding program planning and resource allocation. Happily, and not coincidentally, a quantitative orientation to clinical psychology was a congenial one to me, and it wasn't very long before I had identified and begun to work with similarly inclined mental health professionals throughout the five states then under the Denver Regional Office jurisdiction—Colorado, Utah, Wyoming, Montana, and Idaho. The group was small and we worked together as colleagues. Among the members of the group there were gifted but, it seemed to me, undervalued staff people, who shared a common conviction that the field of mental health needed to attend more to the facts and figures it should be collecting and less to clinical practice as an art form. I am enormously indebted to these lonely souls who made my task so rewarding, to my colleagues in Denver and in the other regional offices who supported us, and to the central office of NIMH, who gave us the freedom to let our professional instincts take us where they would.

One of the exercises we took on for ourselves during the nearly three years we worked together was to examine some of the information which was then being collected nationwide and which was being published in largely unread volumes by NIMH, by the Bureau of the Census, and by various other federal and state agencies interested in the physical, economic, social, and demographic pulse of the country. We began by looking at various kinds of information being collected at the state level and sought to discover if any of it bore any statistical and perhaps programmatically useful relationship to mental health variables—admission rates into state mental hospitals, costs per patient per day, proportion of state budget allocated to mental health-related activities, manpower in outpatient mental health facilities, etc. Correlations across states were uniformly low and uniformly uninterpretable. Our conclusion was that the "state" was too large a geographic and population unit to characterize meaningfully by single numbers, and such figures often could be understood only in terms of the unique and highly varied histories of each individual state. Furthermore, there was obviously enormous variability among sections of every state, and no figure characterizing a state could do justice to special regional attributes within states.

With this effort behind us, we turned our attention to a single state, Montana, and working closely with the mental health professionals who were then charting Montana's future mental health program plans, we proceeded to collect and tabulate information regarding each of Montana's counties. Across counties within this single state, figures were found which had substantially greater relationships among each other and with mental health variables than we had previously found in looking at the total United States. Our analyses played a useful role in providing the documentary base for mental health plans which were being developed in Montana as the first step in the establishment of community mental health centers, and some of our methodologies were applied in other states within the region.

Heartened by this development and given a sense of directionality by our work until that point, we turned our attention to the possibility of studying a single county and looking at the characteristics of the neighborhoods and subcommunities of which it was comprised. Within a very short time we settled on the county of Pueblo, Colorado, as the object of our study. Our relationships with the mental health agencies in that community had always been productive and pleasant, and the city of Pueblo had a number of attributes which made it ideal to study. The city was relatively rich in mental health treatment resources and was geographically remote from neighboring population centers, and hidden away in a charming structure alongside the railroad tracks were the offices of the Pueblo Regional Planning Commission, which had, among other activities, been collecting and tabulating an astonishing array of variables by census tract. Thus, by selecting Pueblo as a community to study, we would have access to much more census tract information than is ordinarily promulgated by the Bureau of the Census. Coinciding with my last four or five months at the Regional Office, before accepting an appointment on the faculty of the Psychology Department at the University of Colorado, we collected both mental health related information as well as demographic information for the period 1959–1961 about each of Pueblo's census tracts and began the analysis which was finally completed in Boulder.

These analyses were more productive and gained visibility through a series of publications which will be referred to at appropriate times in the pages to follow. I felt we had uncovered little new ground conceptually, but that it had been shown to be possible to describe the demographic anatomy of Pueblo and to identify social and economic factors which were remarkably closely related to treated rates of hospitalized mental disorders. I felt that some of these findings could have implications for mental health programming, particularly those kinds of activities that held the hope of reducing the incidence of mental disorders. I had become persuaded that the census tract was an exquisite geographic and demographic unit for study, and now waited until the 1970 census so that the stability of some of these findings might be examined. By this roundabout route I found the community and its census tracts. But they had not been lost. Sociologists and sociologically-oriented epidemiologists had known about them for nearly fifty years. Such is the price one pays for a substantively parochial education.

Between 1960 and 1970 a virtual revolution took place in the nature, organization, and financing of mental health services. State hospitals had been geographically decentralized, community mental health services had dramatically expanded, mental health manpower had increased, private (nongovernmental, fee-for-service) inpatient and outpatient facilities were being developed, and new modes of prepayment had been introduced which made it possible, in theory at least, for many people, and for all people over age 65, to choose where to obtain psychiatric care. Having some baseline data for the period 1959–1961, another project during 1969–1971 in the same community would tell us much about the impact of these changes on which and where patients were being treated as well as how stable our earlier findings linking census tract characteristics to admission rates would turn out to be. Happily for the research, but unhappily for Pueblo, the decade 1960–1970 saw very little change in that community in terms of population or community characteristics. Thus, whatever changes might be noted in psychiatric care could be attributed to changes in the service delivery system.

This volume thus concerns itself with patterns of psychiatric care and with psychiatric epidemiology during an unusually eventful period in American mental health history from the point of view of a single community—not midtown Manhatten, to be sure, and not rural Nova Scotia, but a city of 120,000 which, like 125 other cities in the United States, comprises a single catchment area, a single area for planning and providing integrated and comprehensive mental health services. Perhaps what we learn will be useful to mental health professionals in these other cities and to those who have long struggled with issues pertinent to the understanding of mental illness at the community level, its character and distribution, and ultimately, its control.

During the first Pueblo study, which retrospectively identified psychiatric inpatients in both public and private facilities by means of a careful search of numerous hospital records, data was restricted to first admission inpatients, that is, to the tabulation of a very limited amount of information about patients with no prior histories of psychiatric hospitalization. Specifically, in addition to name and address, the only information routinely available included age, sex, type of facility (public or private), and diagnosis. Because of the fact that grant support became available for the second project, it was possible to undertake a somewhat more ambitious data collection program. We now collected information on both outpatients as well as inpatients and on patients who had as well as those who did not have psychiatric histories prior to the start of the data collection period. In addition, because the second study was prospective in character, we made an effort, although far from successfully, to collect somewhat more information from patients than had been available retrospectively from the record searches of the first study.

The volume is divided into four sections. The initial section has three objectives: first, to set the stage for the study by reviewing briefly some facts regarding the importance of psychiatric disability as a major social problem and previous efforts to understand how personal and social factors play a role in the development and perpetuation of these disabilities; second, to describe in detail the methodologies employed in the data collection and analyses which form the empirical foundation of the study; and third, to describe the city which was studied, its mental health services in 1960, the changes which took place between 1960 and 1970, and the organization of mental health services at the end of the decade.

The second section concerns itself with those data which allow one to understand and evaluate the consequences of the changes in the mental health service delivery system. In order to develop these comparative analyses, the second section deals only with first admission inpatient rates during the 1960 and 1970 study periods, since it was only these rates which were available for both study periods. Psychiatric hospitalization, particularly when it occurs for the first time in a person's life, can be an enormously significant event both for the patient and for his family, and this phenomenon has received substantial attention in the literature. Since the city and county of Pueblo underwent few important demographic changes during this decade, and since there is no reason to believe that there was any substantial change (increase or decrease) in the incidence of mental disorders, changes in first admission rates are attributed to changes in the organization, financing, and availability of mental health services. The data that are considered in the second section focus on changing admission rates, relationships between these changing rates and characteristics of the neighborhoods from which patients come, differences between the demographic characteristics of first admission inpatients and the total population, and finally, admission rates among the Spanish surnamed, the largest ethnic minority in Pueblo.

The third section deals with the entire mental health service delivery system during the 1970 study period and includes a description and evaluation of how mental health services were used at that time. The data allow us to examine the entire spectrum of formally designated psychiatric services: outpatient as well as inpatient; private as well as public; and readmissions as well as first admissions. Two characteristics of the service delivery system are discussed in special detail: first, length of episodes of care; and second, patterns of collaboration among mental health services.

The final section is concerned with an analysis of the data from the point of view of one particularly important epidemiological problem, namely, the relative contribution of demographic and environmental factors to the observed variations in inpatient admission rates. Since this analysis is based on treated rates and utilizes measures of incidence rather than measures of prevalence, the first part of the final section discusses the place of psychiatric care data in epidemiological investigations and attempts to identify the issues in using treated rates rather than true rates and in using measures of treated incidence rather than treated prevalence. To the extent that variations in admission rates are found to be primarily a function of person characteristics, control programs will need to be aimed at particular high-risk population groups. If, however, environmental factors are found to be more closely associated with variations in admission rates, it may be possible to outline control programs which focus on certain neighborhoods. Thus, it is hoped that the findings of this study will add a small measure of understanding to the social epidemiology of mental disorders and provide some suggestions for additional research oriented toward the development of preventive interventions. The final chapter provides an overview of the findings and considers them in the light of the brief history of the community mental health movement.

LIST OF TABLES

LIST OF FIGURES

Part I

**PSYCHOPATHOLOGY
AND THE COMMUNITY**

1

Psychopathology
as a Community Problem

The problem of mental disorder in the United States can hardly be overestimated. By whatever methods one measures the impact of disease morbidity on the population, mental disorders rank regrettably high. Not only do they appear to occur at a high rate, but their duration is often long and patients accumulate over time, filling to overflowing state mental hospitals, community clinics, private psychiatrists' offices, and the new community mental health centers.

In 1968, the total cost of mental illness was estimated to be nearly $21 billion, of which $4 billion represented treatment and preventive services and $17 billion represented the cost of the reduction in productive activity as a direct consequence of the disability associated with mental illness (Conley, Conwell, and Wellner, 1970). Were this cost to be allocated among the total United States population, it would represent an expenditure of approximately $100 per person per year.

Until after the Second World War, the state mental hospital was the single most important agency devoted to the care of the mentally ill. Year after year, without interruption, a flood of melancholy statistics would emerge. More patients this year than last year. More overcrowding. Staff more overworked. Prior to 1955 the average number of patients on the rolls of public inpatient facilities consistently increased year by year, reaching in excess of half a million. In 1955, however, the number of such patients declined from the previous year and this decline has continued in gradually accelerating fashion ever since. Thus, as of June 30, 1971, there were 308,000 inpatients in public mental hospitals, a drop of over 30,000 from the previous year. Accompanying the gradual decline in the number of patients on the books of public inpatient facilities on any one day, however, there has been a consistent increase in the number of admissions per year. In 1971, nearly 415,000 persons were admitted, an increase of five and one-half percent over the previous year.

Meanwhile, the 255 federally funded community mental health centers which were in operation more than two months in 1970 admitted 335,000 individuals during the year (Taube and Cannon, 1972). Outpatient psychiatric services other than community mental health centers admitted nearly 900,000 patients during 1969 (Taube, 1971). Over 750,000 patients were discharged from general hospitals with a primary diagnosis of mental disorder during that same year (Taube, 1970). Private mental hospitals admitted more than 26,000 patients during 1969 (Witkin, 1972). More than 7500 children were admitted to residential treatment centers (Witkin and Cannon, 1971). In addition, private psychiatrists, halfway houses, nursing homes, and Veterans' Administration hospitals treat psychiatric patients, and it is commonly asserted that a not insignificant proportion of the caseload of primary physicians consists of patients who have a psychiatric component in the conditions which prompt their seeking medical help. Thus, even by considering only formally identified patients, mental disorder represents an enormous repository of morbidity in the United States. What about the general population?

Perhaps the best source of information on the psychiatric status of the general population comes from the
examination of youths for military service. Results of
these examinations are not encouraging. For example, in
1968, local draft boards rejected over four percent of
draft registrants for medical and mental reasons prior to
the physical examinations conducted by the Armed
Forces Examining and Entrance Stations. Of the over
one million draft registrants who received a preinduction physical examination in 1968, over 40 percent were
rejected, and of those young men who were rejected,
nearly 25 percent were rejected because of emotional
problems. To put it another way, about one young man
in ten, having passed his local draft board screening, fails
the preinduction physical examination because of psychiatric reasons (Karpinos, 1969), although some proportion of these rejections may be because of functional
mental retardation.

Once in the military service, psychiatric disability continues to occur. Incidence rates for psychiatric disorders
in the Navy, for example, have been fairly stable during
the past decade, averaging one new case per 100 members of the Navy per year (Gunderson, 1971). Of all
psychiatric patients admitted to naval facilities, only 55
percent are restored to duty, and of those restored to
duty, 22 percent are readmitted to psychiatric facilities
within a year (Gunderson and Arthur, 1967).

CHANGES IN THE MENTAL HEALTH SERVICE DELIVERY SYSTEM

Since the Second World War, a slow but steady change
has been taking place in the locus of psychiatric treatment. First, there is a rapidly expanding role being

played by private inpatient facilities, as opposed to state or county supported inpatient facilities; second, outpatient facilities (both public and private) are becoming increasingly available (see Bloom, 1970, for example). These changes rapidly accelerated during the decade 1960-1970 because of vastly increased governmental and third-party support sources for psychiatric hospitalization and outpatient services and because of a growing manpower pool of mental health professionals. Thus, in a typical community it was not uncommon that, until the 1940's, the major and often sole source of psychiatric services was the state mental hospital, sometimes nearby, but more often some distance away. During the 1940's a child guidance outpatient clinic might have opened, and during the 1950's a local general hospital might have started an inpatient psychiatric ward, in part because of the availability of one or more mental health professionals practicing privately on a fee-for-service basis. Private outpatient facilities would have become available as well. With the arrival of the 1960's and the enactment of federal legislation for the support of community mental health centers (Bloom, 1973) the locally supported child guidance clinic might have been enlarged and might have begun to provide services to a far broader spectrum of the community population. Meanwhile, expanded public and private prepaid insurance programs might be making it possible for persons previously unable to afford it to receive private care, first in inpatient facilities and later as outpatients as well. Thus, what started out as a simple enough plan for providing psychiatric care (the state hospital or nothing) has become a complex "system" involving public inpatient facilities, private inpatient facilities (sometimes exclusively psychiatric, sometimes as part of community general hospitals), comprehensive publicly supported community mental health centers, mental health or mental hygiene clinics, and privately practicing mental health professionals.

The decade 1960-1970 was one of unusually rapid and significant change, and the opportunity to study a single community at the start and end of this decade is an unprecedented one. We are interested in such a study for two reasons, one having to do with issues relevant to the delivery of mental health services, and the other having to do with the further elaboration of ways in which sociocultural factors interact with the development of psychiatric disability. What happens in a community when agencies providing mental health services increase both in number and capacity? Are substantially more patients treated? If so, are they similar to the kinds of patients seen before the expansion of services or are certain types of patients seen with greater increased frequency than other types? What happens to the balance between public sector and private sector services? How do agencies collaborate in the provision of services? Do all agencies treat relatively similar patients, or does some specialization seem to take place? What is the impact of expanded outpatient services for the provision of inpatient services? And if the number of patients increases, does the increase come from all sections of the city, or are certain sections overrepresented?

THE SOCIAL EPIDEMIOLOGY OF MENTAL DISORDERS

As to the interaction of sociocultural factors and psychopathology, efforts to understand these relationships and on the basis of this understanding to reduce the magnitude of the problem of mental disorder have occupied the attention of dedicated social scientists for the last 40 years. Until the early 1950's most studies of psychiatric disability dealt with known psychiatric patients and sought to develop a greater understanding of them as a group and of how they appeared to differ from the general population. Clearly, there were questions of etiology and prevention in the minds of these investigators. With the increasing availability of research support in the early 1950's, it was possible to mount a group of studies whose aim was to extend the understanding of psychiatric disability into the population at large by attempting to identify psychopathology in the community, whether or not persons so identified were officially classified as psychiatric patients.

The pioneering effort in the United States to study social aspects of mental disorders was undertaken by Faris and Dunham based on data assembled at state institutions and private hospitals in the Chicago area for the period 1922-1934 and from the County Psychopathic Hospital for the years 1930-1931. The authors were able to show that when cases of mental disorders were plotted by residence at the time of admission, the resulting rates exhibited a regular increase from the more affluent and better organized peripheral portions of the city to the central poorer, more socially disorganized parts of the city. The correlation between private hospital and public hospital admission rates was very low, but because only 17.5 percent of patients were admitted into private hospitals, public hospital admission rate and total admission rate were almost perfectly correlated. After showing certain differences in this general spatial pattern for various diagnostic categories, the authors proceeded to derive some hypotheses in an effort to account for their findings. It should be noted that the spatial pattern found for schizophrenic patients was quite similar to the pattern found for all patients combined.

First, the authors examined the possibility that, as a consequence of previously existing mental disorder, persons drift into the central slum areas of the city. If this hypothesis were true, argued the authors, the distribution of older cases should show a closer relationship with geographic area than the distribution of younger cases (since younger persons would presumably have had less time to drift). Upon test, this hypothesis was rejected. Older and younger cases showed roughly the same concentration in the central city. The alternative hypothesis, namely that social conditions in central areas of the city were somehow a cause of the high rates of mental disorder found there, was then examined and found worthy of further study, particularly in the context of the extensive social isolation found in the central city. That is, in the authors' words, "extended isolation of the person produces the abnormal traits of behavior and mentality" [Faris and Dunham, 1939, p. 173]. In arriving at the assertion that social causation seemed a more likely explanation for their findings than social selection, the authors noted other research which documented that conditions producing isolation are more frequent in disorganized communities and that, from their own data, admission rates for Negroes, foreign-born, and native-born are all significantly higher in areas not primarily populated by their own members, that is, in areas where each group might be more isolated by virtue of its minority status.

Nineteen years later, the results of the study conducted in New Haven, Connecticut, attempting to link social class and mental illness, were published. In this study, Hollingshead and Redlich (1958) again dealt with identified psychiatric patients, considering as a patient any person who had been in treatment with a psychiatrist or under the care of a psychiatric clinic or mental hospital between May 31 and December 1, 1950, and who was a resident of the greater New Haven area at the time he entered treatment. Data about these patients were abstracted from the patient's clinical record. In addition, social and demographic data were collected by means of a household interview from a five percent stratified random sample of the New Haven community. This sample served as a comparison group for the data collected from patient's records. Social class for patients and for the community sample was determined on the basis of area of residence, occupation, and education. Supplementary information was collected about the characteristics of psychiatric practice and about fee practices of agencies and private practitioners.

It is important to note how the Hollingshead and Redlich study contrasts with the earlier Faris and Dunham study. First, both studies were based on data collected about identified psychiatric patients. The Faris and Dunham study calculated treated incidence rates (based on a count of patients admitted for care in a specified time interval), while the Hollingshead and Redlich study calculated period prevalence rates (rates based upon all patients known to be in treatment on a certain date plus all patients entering treatment during the next six months). Faris and Dunham were concerned solely with place of residence and collected only minimal data beyond that. Hollingshead and Redlich were interested in specific information about patients themselves, notably social class, and collected residential data as part of a much larger questionnaire. Faris and Dunham were interested primarily in the distribution of patients in space, and while they did not explicitly state their hypothesis, they certainly believed that psychiatric patients were not randomly distributed in the Chicago area. Hollingshead and Redlich were more explicit about their hypothesis, and in their volume deal with three fundamental assertions: first, that treated prevalence is related to social class; second, that diagnosis is related to social class; and third, that the type of treatment received by a patient is related to social class.

Hollingshead and Redlich were able to document that with decreasing social class there is an increasing use of coercion and compulsion to induce patients to enter treatment, that treated prevalence is inversely related to social class, with psychiatric disorder being especially prevalent in the lowest class, and that while the prevalence of neurotic disorders is directly related to social class, the reverse is true in the case of psychotic disorders, again especially in the case of the lowest class. As to the character of treatment, their data indicated significant differences in where, how, and for how long patients were treated—always favoring the highest social classes —and that expenditures for treatment were linked to social class as well. Thus the three hypotheses were supported by the data. Hollingshead and Redlich examined their data in terms of the drift (social selection) hypothesis advanced by Faris and Dunham and came to the same conclusion as did the earlier authors, namely that psychotic patients from slum areas do not, in fact, drift into such areas as a consequence of their illnesses, and that neither geographic nor downward social mobility can account for the sharp differences found in the distribution of psychosis among varying social classes.

One final point bears mentioning regarding the comparison of the Faris and Dunham project with the more recent Hollingshead and Redlich study. In spite of the fact that the studies were separated by 19 years in time, and took place in very different communities, and in spite of the fact that incidence rates were used in one study and prevalence rates used in the other, the relationship between social class and severe mental disorder was constant—mental disorder was found to be most common among the lowest social class and the most run-down, socially disorganized, and poverty-stricken sections of the two metropolitan areas.

In the time between these two major projects, a number of other communities had been studied in terms of the distribution of mental disorder. Especially important were the studies conducted in Baltimore, Maryland, by Lemkau and his colleagues (see Lemkau, Tietze, and Cooper, 1941 and 1943, and Lemkau, 1955), by Gruenberg among the elderly in Syracuse, New York (who found in the center of the city an area characterized by high first mental hospital admission rates for psychoses in general and for cerebral arteriosclerotic and senile psychoses in particular, and by a high concentration of multiple family dwellings, and by high percentages of people living alone), by Eaton and Weil (1955) among the Hutterites in Northwestern United States and Southwestern Canada (who found that a simple and relatively uncomplicated way of life does not provide immunity from mental disorders), and by Clausen and Kohn (1959, 1960) in Hagerstown, Maryland (who indicted a form of internally imposed social isolation or faulty socialization as a precursor of schizophrenia).

Two ambitious studies based upon community surveys of mental disorder rather than upon psychiatric patients known to treatment agencies were mounted in the early 1950's and reported in a series of volumes in the 1960's. The first of these studies was based upon a survey of a sample of 1660 men and women between the ages of 20 and 59 in an area of Manhattan, New York, and is commonly referred to as the Midtown Manhattan Study (see Srole et al., 1962, and Langner and Michael, 1963). The second project was undertaken in a rural area in Nova Scotia with a survey sample of about one thousand persons in both socially integrated and disintegrated communities by Leighton and his colleagues and was reported in three volumes (see Leighton, 1959, Hughes et al., 1960, and Leighton et al., 1963). This project is commonly referred to as the Stirling County Study. While the two studies differed somewhat on how they defined a psychiatric case, their estimates of the extent of psychiatric impairment in the general population were staggering. In the Stirling County Study it was concluded that "at least half of the adults . . . are currently suffering from some psychiatric disorder defined in the APA Diagnostic and Statistical Manual" [Leighton *et al.*, 1963, p. 356]. In the Midtown Manhattan Study, using a more limited definition of psychiatric impairment, nearly one-quarter of the sample was judged to be significantly psychiatrically impaired. These two studies reported measures of prevalence at a particular moment in time, rather than rates at which psychiatric disorders appeared to be generated in the communities studied, and both studies sought to identify factors which might bear an etiologic relationship to the development of psychiatric disability.

It is now ten years since these two studies were published, and nearly twenty years since the data upon which they were based was collected. Their startling assertions as to the high prevalence of psychopathology in the general population undoubtedly served as a significant impetus for the development of increased federal resources to deal with problems of mental disorder. There is some evidence that some of these studies had an impact on training in the mental health professions by providing organized information enabling students to look at psychopathology in a far broader sociocultural context than had been the case previously. The critiques of these studies served to identify the kinds of more basic research which needed to be undertaken and thus, indirectly, these studies served as a stimulus for better research.

The authors of the Stirling County study articulated a series of hypotheses, all of which related to the more general concept of social disintegration. They concluded that disintegrated social systems produce disintegrated personalities, but as to what aspects of a disorganized social system were specifically instrumental in the production of disintegrated personalities, they could not be very specific. Their data led them to reject physical insecurity, the frustration of sexual or aggressive impulses, and interference with a person's orientation to his place in society or sense of membership in a definite human group. The authors felt that the most harmful aspects of social disintegration were those affecting the achievement of love, recognition, spontaneity, and the sense of belonging to a moral order and of being right in what one does.

In the Midtown Manhattan Study, ten stress factors were studied as to their relationship to subsequent mental disorder in three socioeconomic status groups. The authors found the effect of these stress factors to be additive and increasingly influential on subsequent mental disorder with decreasing socioeconomic status. Included were such stress factors as broken homes in childhood, poor health of parents or of study subjects while children, economic deprivation and parental conflict, poor health as adults, inadequate interpersonal affiliations, and socioeconomic, marital, and parental worries. As can be seen, these two major studies organized their hypotheses and presented their findings at very different levels of conceptualization, but both had little difficulty in identifying social or demographic factors which might be related to the prevalence of psychiatric disorder.

In one of the very few studies of factors associated with the incidence of mental disorder, Hagnell (1966) examined the entire population of two villages (population 2550) in southern Sweden ten years after they had been examined as part of another project (see Essen-Möller, 1956). On the basis of this reexamination, Hagnell was able to identify cases of mental disorder which had not been judged to be present ten years earlier and was thus able to calculate incidence rates and to identify factors which appeared to be associated with the development of mental disorders. Using as the criterion of mental disorder his own diagnosis based upon clinical examination plus evidence that the subject had consulted a physician (not necessarily a psychiatrist) for the condition, Hagnell found the average annual incidence of mental disorder per 100 population at risk to be 0.88 in men between ages 15 and 59 and 2.27 among women in the same age range. Approximately 15 percent of these identified cases had at some time been admitted to a psychiatric hospital, and about one-half had at some time consulted a psychiatrist. Thus, about half of the cases identified by Hagnell had never consulted a mental health specialist.

As to demographic factors which appeared to predispose persons to develop mental disorders, Hagnell identified as a particularly vulnerable group the wives of skilled workers and craftsmen. In contrast to most other studies, Hagnell found that neither income nor marital status was associated with the development of mental disorder. Persons who complained of somatic and aesthenic symptoms at the start of the ten year period (specifically, sleep disturbances and headaches) were significantly more likely to develop mental disorders, as well as persons who had complained of fatigue, nervousness, strain, and the feeling of being harassed. Finally, those persons judged ten years earlier as listless or torpid or otherwise possibly pathological or abnormal were found upon reexamination to be overrepresented among persons judged as having some form of mental disorder. These findings rest on the reliability and validity of the diagnosis of mental illness as made by the author. Not only is validity an imponderable, but no provision was made for assessing reliability of the diagnosis. We bring this overview full circle by noting that in commenting on Hagnell's work, Dunham was moved to say: "Perhaps it might be more desirable in future epidemiological studies to depend primarily on such operational definitions of a case as going to a psychiatrist, entering an outpatient clinic, or entering a mental hospital. The definition of a case by the 'author's diagnosis' as used by Dr. Hagnell in his study may present more difficulties than utilizing the social process as the selective agent" [1970, p. 226].

Low socioeconomic level and high social disorganization repeatedly have been shown to be associated with mental disorder. This association has been found in studies based on treated incidence, treated prevalence, and on community surveys of the general population and in studies based on ecological assessments of environments as well as on demographic assessments of patients contrasted with some type of nonpatient comparison group.

In a recent review of the literature linking social class and psychopathology (with particular reference to schizophrenia), Kohn has outlined and evaluated six hypotheses which have been advanced to account for these associations. We have already mentioned some of these hypotheses—low social integration, minority status, and high social isolation. Genetic differences associated with social class have been suggested, but no convincing data has yet been presented. Differences in parent-child relationships associated with social class have been suggested, but "there has not been a single well-controlled study that demonstrates any substantial difference between the family relationships of schizophrenics and those of normal persons from lower and working class backgrounds" [Kohn, 1968, p. 167]. Finally, excess stress in lower social classes has been postulated and this line of approach is currently being followed by Dohrenwend and his colleagues (see Dohrenwend and Dohrenwend, 1969, and Dohrenwend, 1969). Dohrenwend,

distinguishing between relatively enduring symptomatology and short-lived symptomatology, suggests
that field studies of mental disorder may overestimate
the extent of psychopathology in lower classes by their
failure to make this distinction. He states the research
issue as follows: ". . . in lower status groups, to what
extent is the excess of symptomatology generated by
personality defects, of whatever origin (for example, genetic, childhood deprivation), and to what extent does
such symptomatology consist of normal reactions to unusually harsh and numerous stressors in the contempo-
rary situations?" [1969, p. 147].

This brief overview serves to illustrate the variety of
studies that have been undertaken to identify social and
demographic factors that might be implicated in the development of psychiatric disability. The data from the
current project has the potential to contribute to the
further understanding of these factors for two reasons.
First, we have studied a single community across a
decade in which many changes have been made in the
availability and variety of mental health services. Will
similar findings emerge in Pueblo as have been reported
elsewhere and will the findings remain stable? Second,
our data is available at two different levels of abstraction.
We have some data whereby it is possible to contrast
patients with the total population; we also have data
characterizing environments rather than people. If the
data is analyzed and interpreted skillfully, we may develop a greater understanding of the interaction of personal and environmental characteristics in the
development of psychopathology.

2

Methodological Details

The empirical basis of this volume consists of patient and census tract data collected at two different points in time. The first data collection period included the three years 1959, 1960, and 1961, and is referred to throughout this volume as the 1960 study. Patient data were actually tabulated during 1964 by a retrospective search of the records of eight inpatient psychiatric facilities in Pueblo, Las Animas, Colorado Springs, and Denver, Colorado. The attempt was made to identify all Pueblo residents who had a first psychiatric inpatient admission during this three-year time period and to tabulate census tract of residence, type of inpatient facility (public or private), age, sex, and diagnosis for every identified patient. Since only first admissions were tabulated, a patient was tabulated only once, and the resulting rates are probably most accurately considered measures of treated incidence. All reported rates are calculated as annual rates per 1000 population at risk, thus making the figures directly comparable to those reported in the second study, whose period of data collection was only two years in length.

It will be seen that few outpatient services, public or private, were available during the 1960 study period, so that while we do not have any information on patients receiving outpatient care, we still have substantial information on identified psychiatric disability. Perhaps the more important area in which information is lacking is regarding hospitalized patients who had had psychiatric episodes requiring hospitalization prior to the start of the 1960 study period. But because our interest was primarily in treated incidence, those patients newly identified as requiring psychiatric services were our major concern.

The 1970 study is based on data collected between September 1, 1969, and August 31, 1971, and in contrast to data collected for the 1960 study, it was collected, in part, prospectively. The intent of the 1970 study went through two distinct phases. Initially, it was planned to replicate the original study and, in addition, to collect information on psychiatric inpatients who had had histories of prior hospitalization. Because financial resources were limited, staff members were identified at each of the participating inpatient facilities and were then trained in the use of the survey schedule rather than assigning a (nonexistent) research project staff member to this task. An attempt was made to complete a questionnaire on every admitted patient regardless of his prior psychiatric history, although the nature of this history was one item on the questionnaire. Because data were collected directly from patients, it was possible to secure more information than had been available for the 1960 study (see Appendix A).

About midway through the two-year data collection period, additional resources became available, and it was then decided to collect information on outpatients as well. Outpatient data could not be collected prospectively and thus the 1960 study model, of collecting retrospective data by means of record searches, was used for outpatients (see Appendix B).

In summary, the 1960 study is based on patient data collected from existing records and is concerned only with first admission psychiatric inpatients of all public and private facilities within commuting distance of Pueblo. In the case of the 1970 study, information was collected directly from patients who were hospitalized and from agency records in the case of outpatients. Not only are data available on first admission inpatients in the 1970 study but also data on inpatients with prior histories of psychiatric hospitalization and on outpatients with and without priot outpatient histories. Our wish, in both studies, was to collect information on all Pueblo residents who received psychiatric treatment at any facility within a reasonable distance of Pueblo. We believe that virtually no Pueblo residents receive psychiatric treatment at locations other than those where data were collected.

Because in 1970 data were collected on all psychiatric admissions throughout the two-year data collection period, in the case of those patients for whom more than one episode of care was reported, it has been possible to identify the patterns of interagency collaboration and the pathways of care through the service delivery system.

STUDY DEFINITIONS

As to the critical definitions, we have attempted to be entirely consistent in both studies. A Pueblo resident is defined as someone who has lived at a Pueblo address for a minimum of 30 days. An episode of care is defined by the reporting agency and begins with an admission and ends with a discharge. In the case of outpatients, it was required that there be at least one face-to-face contact in the professional setting. Diagnosis was determined by the individual mental health professional in each setting, and no attempt was made to confirm the validity or reliability of the diagnosis. All patients otherwise eligible were included if the official primary diagnosis was psychiatric in character, or if there was a secondary psychiatric diagnosis made in consultation with a mental health professional.

The problems of diagnostic reliability are well known in the research literature, and in order to avoid this type of problem as much as possible, all diagnoses were categorized into four groups. The first group, labeled "psychoneuroses and psychosomatic disorders," includes these two categories plus all neurotic depressions and the milder transient reactions. The second group, "personality disorders," includes all character disorders, sociopathies, and all forms of alcoholism and other drug abuse, even if accompanied by transient brain syndromes. The third group, "functional psychoses," includes all schizophrenias and psychotic manic or depressive reactions. The fourth group, "acute or chronic brain syndromes," includes all organic disorders except, as already mentioned, those accompanying excess alcohol or other drug intake. In practice, assigning patients to one of these four major diagnostic groups was not difficult, and resolution of problem diagnoses was easily made by examining clinical records or discussing cases with clinical staff. As a matter of practice, all patients admitted following suicide attempts (by drug overdose or other means) were placed in the "psychoneurotic" diagnostic group, unless the clinical staff considered the patient to be psychotic. Cases of drug abuse were assigned to the "personality disorder" category when the problem related to habituation to any of the host of drugs (soft or hard) of current concern to mental health professionals.

No patients seen only for evaluations in conjunction with vocational rehabilitation programs or insurance claims were included, and no patients with the sole diagnosis of mental retardation were included. Our rationale was to allow for reasonably easy entrance into the patient pool without complicating our understanding of who was included in the pool. Thus, we required that there be an official psychiatric diagnosis and permitted non-psychiatric physicians to make such diagnoses, but did not include the host of patients with such diagnoses as "(1) coronary artery disease; (2) anxiety" unless a mental health professional had been involved in the diagnostic process.

Psychiatric facilities, outpatient as well as inpatient, are considered as public or private according to whether there is a cost to the patient (or to a third party) necessarily associated with their care. Thus, the state hospitals, the VA hospitals, and the University Psychiatric Hospital are considered public facilities, while the psychiatric wards in the Pueblo general hospitals and the proprietary psychiatric inpatient facilities are considered private. The outpatient service at the state hospital (to which patients can be directly admitted) and the community mental health center outpatient program are considered public, while fee-for-service mental health professionals to whom Pueblo residents go for outpatient treatment are considered private.

In the 1960 study, five public and three private inpatient facilities were included in the data collection pool. These included the state hospital in Pueblo, the VA hospitals in Las Animas and in Denver, the state hospital in Denver, where for a short time in 1961 certain Pueblo residents received inpatient care, and the psychiatric hospital at the University of Colorado Medical School as the five public facilities, and one general hospital psychiatric unit in Pueblo, one private psychiatric hospital in Pueblo, and one in Denver as the three private facilties. In the 1970 study, 17 facilities participated in the study, including six private inpatient facilities, four public inpatient facilities, five private outpatient settings, and two public outpatient settings. The private inpatient facilities included two psychiatric units in Pueblo general hospitals, a psychiatric unit in a general hospital and a private psychiatric facility in Colorado Springs, and two private settings in Denver. Between 1960 and 1970, one private psychiatric facility in Pueblo had closed, and new facilities had opened in Pueblo, Colorado Springs, and Denver. As for public inpatient facilities, they included all of the 1960 group except the state hospital in Denver, which prior to the 1970 study had ceased accepting Pueblo residents for care. The private outpatient settings in the 1970 study included three psychiatrists in full-time or near full-time practice and two psychologists with part-time practices. Public outpatient settings included the local community mental health center and the outpatient program at the state hospital in Pueblo. It should be noted that both studies took place at times integrally related to the regular U.S. population census.

The least complete data pool is in the private outpatient sector because of our failure to obtain data from one psychiatrist who was no longer in Pueblo and who could not be located. We have no reason to believe, however, that his patients came from any more selected portions of the city than did private patients in general, so relationships between treated rates and census tract characteristics for private sector care can be examined with reasonable confidence.

Patient data, in the case of inpatient facilities, were collected by regular employees especially trained prior and during the 1970 data collection period. Data collection went reasonably smoothly, although there was a certain amount of staff turnover at some of the facilities. Each inpatient setting was visited biweekly during the first year of data collection and monthly during the second year. We were aware that we would not be entirely successful in collecting complete protocol data on every inpatient, particularly at the general hospital psychiatric wards. From time to time a patient would refuse to participate, although this happened remarkably infrequently. What occurred more often was that a patient would be discharged while the staff member in charge of data collection was off duty (on weekends, for example) or on vacation and before information had been collected. In order to be certain that we had identified each patient, the assistance of the central record room personnel at the two general hospitals in Pueblo was secured following the end of the data collection period in identifying all eligible patients. By this means we located those patients on whom no data had been collected during the data collection period and obtained the minimal information from the hospital records. Nearly 30 percent of patients had been missed during the regular data collection period, some because of failure to collect information on the psychiatric ward, but most because they had been admitted to nonpsychiatric wards. We had not anticipated the magnitude of this latter problem, and the failure to secure complete information from a larger proportion of private inpatients represents a weakness in the empirical basis of the study.

Comparison of age, sex, and diagnosis of patients who were missed with those on whom data were obtained reveals that while there are no sex differences, the aged and those with diagnoses of acute or chronic brain syndromes are overrepresented among patients who were missed, among whom, as has been mentioned, were patients admitted to nonpsychiatric wards. While five percent of patients on whom data was obtained were in the age category 65 and above, and six percent were diagnosed as having acute or chronic brain disorders, the comparable figures for patients who were missed were 14 percent and 13 percent.

SOURCES OF DATA

In developing the schedule of questions which would be asked of hospitalized patients at the time of their admission, it was clear that some type of reference group would be needed with whom it might be possible to contrast the patients. Again because of limited resources it seemed realistic to use the 1970 census as a comparison group, that is, to use the only comparison group for whom reliable data could be assembled without cost. Thus, the total Pueblo population constitutes the group with whom patients are contrasted. The difficulty of this approach is that one is limited to asking patients those questions which were asked in the 1970 census. The set of questions in the census is, unfortunately, not the most pertinent to a social analysis of psychiatric care, but we have obtained some patient data which, when contrasted with population data, help us develop a useful view of how psychiatric patients differ from the total population.

The questionnaire used with all inpatients is shown in Appendix A. After some initial questions regarding the patient and the hospitalization, there is a series of questions taken directly from the draft versions of the 1970 census form. At the end of the brief questionnaire, space was provided for the staff member to record length of hospitalization. Some minor changes were made in the final census form distributed to the total population in comparison with the draft form from which we worked, but these changes do not significantly interfere with the possibility of contrasting psychiatric patients with the total Pueblo population.

Census tract data came from two sources—first, the reports issued by the U.S. Bureau of the Census, and second, data collected and tabulated locally by census tract. Our interest was to identify census tract characteristics which would be available and directly comparable for both the 1960 and 1970 censuses.

A group of 35 different census tract characteristics was selected for analysis. Criteria for selection included, first, that no necessary mathematical relationship exist between any of the variables. Thus, we had to decide, for example, between a measure that indicated the proportion of married couples with children under age 6 and another measure that indicated the proportion of married couples with children under age 18. Although both figures are available from census tract reports, the first measure is actually a subset of the second and thus bears a necessary mathematical relationship to it. The second criterion was to attempt to tap those characteristics which might give clues as to the sociocultural organization of the city without, at the same time, including measures which had high redundancy. The variables selected for analysis are shown in Table 2-1. The brief title is given and is defined in complete detail along with an indication of the source of the data. In the following pages, only the brief title will be used to identify a specific variable. As can be seen, of the 35 variables, eight were based on data collected and tabulated locally. These include library card holders, YMCA members, golf club members, public health nursing visits, families receiving Aid to Dependent Children, delinquency rate, suicide rate, and school dropout rate. As will be described in detail below, a cluster analysis of the 35 variables yielded three separate clusters, and scores were assigned to each census tract for each of these clusters.

Pueblo was, in 1960, divided into 34 census tracts, each with an average population of about 3400. One of the tracts is the Colorado State Hospital, and in fact the property line of the hospital grounds constitutes the boundary of the tract. Because residents in this tract are made up almost exclusively of hospitalized psychiatric

Table 2-1

DEFINITIONS AND SOURCES OF DATA FOR CENSUS TRACT VARIABLES

Brief Title	Definition	Source* 1960	Source* 1970
Demographic Characteristics			
1. Population	Total population	P-1	P-1
2. Median Age	Male median age	P-2	P-1 (calc.)
3. Sex Ratio	Females per 100 males	P-2 (calc.)	P-1 (calc.)
4. Foreign Born	Percent foreign born	P-1 (calc.)	P-2 (calc.)
5. Spanish surname	Percent Spanish surname (1960); Percent persons of Spanish language plus other persons of Spanish surname (1970)	P-1 (calc.)	P-2 (calc.)
6. Fertility Ratio	Number of children under age 5 per 100 females age 15–44	P-2 (calc.)	P-1 (calc.)
7. Education	Median school years completed—persons age 25 and above	P-1	P-2
Community Participation			
8. Library Card Holders	Public library card holders per 1000 population—age 5 and above	PRPC	PRPC
9. YMCA Members	YMCA members per 1000 population—age 3 and above	PRPC	PRPC
10. Golf Club Members	Municipal golf club members per 1000 population—age 21 and above	PRPC	PRPC
11. Public Health Nursing Visits	Public health nursing caseload per 10,000 population	PRPC	PRPC

Family Characteristics

12.	Household Population	Population per household	P-1	P-1
13.	Young Children	Percent married couples with own children under age 6	P-1 (calc.)	P-3 (calc.)
14.	People Living Alone	Percent occupied housing units occupied by one person	H-1 (calc.)	H-1 (calc.)
15.	Household Population Density	Percent occupied housing units occupied by more than one person per room	H-1 (calc.)	H-1 (calc.)
16.	Residential Stability	Percent of population age 5 or above in census year living in same house as 5 years earlier	P-1 (calc.)	P-2 (calc.)
17.	Married Women in Labor Force	Percent nonseparated women in labor force	P-3 (calc.)	P-3 (calc.)
18.	Children Living With Both Parents	Percent population 18 and under living with both parents	P-1 (calc.)	P-1

Housing Characteristics

19.	Single Homes	Percent of all structures containing one housing unit	H-1 (calc.)	H-2 (calc.)
20.	Rooms Per Housing Unit	Median number of rooms per housing unit	H-1	H-1
21.	New Housing	Percent of all housing units built in ten year period prior to census year	H-1 (calc.)	H-2 (calc.)
22.	Housing Unit Value	Median value of owner-occupied housing unit	H-2	H-1

Table 2-1 (cont'd)

DEFINITIONS AND SOURCES OF DATA FOR CENSUS TRACT VARIABLES

Brief Title	Definition	Source* 1960	Source* 1970
Housing Characteristics (continued)			
23. Owner-Occupied Housing	Percent occupied housing units owner-occupied	H-1 (calc.)	H-1 (calc.)
24. Housing Lacking Plumbing	Percent all year-round housing units lacking some or all plumbing facilities	H-1 (calc.)	H-1 (calc.)
25. Central Heating	Percent all year-round housing units with central heating	H-1 (calc.)	H-2 (calc.)
26. Vacant Housing	Percent of year-round housing units available and vacant	H-1 (calc.)	H-1 (calc.)
27. Household Fires	First-response household fire runs as percentage of total housing units	PRPC	PRPC
Socioeconomic Characteristics			
28. Family Income	Median family income	P-1	P-4
29. Unemployment	Percent of male civilian labor force unemployed	P-3	P-3

54

30. White Collar Workers	Percent employed males in professional, technical, and kindred occupations	P-3 (calc.)	P-3 (calc.)
31. Families Receiving ADC	Percent of families receiving Aid to Dependent Children federal assistance	PRPC	PRPC
Personal Disruption			
32. Delinquency	Juvenile delinquents per 100 population age 18 and under	PRPC	PRPC
33. Suicide Rate	Suicides (accumulated over 6 years) as proportion of total population	PRPC	PRPC
34. School Dropouts	School dropouts per 1000 population age 18 and under	PRPC	PRPC
35. Marital Disruption	Number of divorced and separated males per 1000 married nonseparated males	P-2 (calc.)	P-1 (calc.)

*1960: Designated Tables in: *U.S. Censuses of Population and Housing—1960; Census Tracts: Pueblo, Colorado.* PHC(1)–123. Bureau of the Census, U.S. Department of Commerce. Washington: USGPO, 1961.
1970: Designated Tables in: *1970 Census of Population and Housing; Census Tracts: Pueblo, Colorado.* PHC(1)–168. Bureau of the Census, U.S. Department of Commerce. Washington: USGPO, 1972.
PRPC: Pueblo Regional Planning Commission.

patients, the tract is highly atypical demographically, and it has been excluded in all census tract analyses reported in this volume. Fortunately, for the purposes of this study, only minor changes were made in census tract boundary lines in preparation for the 1970 census. In those tracts where substantial population growth had occurred, they were simply subdivided, thus making it possible to reconstitute them for purposes of comparative analysis.

Between 1960 and 1970, there was a change made by the Bureau of the Census in its definition of "persons of Spanish surname." In the 1960 census, 25,437 white native and foreign-born persons of Spanish surname were enumerated in Pueblo. The Bureau of the Census prepared a list of Spanish surnames and anyone with a name on the list was counted. In the 1970 census, however, the definition is "persons of Spanish language or Spanish surname" and a total of 37,088 were enumerated. Persons of Spanish language "comprise persons of Spanish mother tongue . . . and all other persons in families in which the head or wife reported Spanish as his or her mother tongue" [Bureau of the Census, 1972, p. App. 4]. In the five Southwestern states (including Colorado) persons with Spanish surnames are identified but, unfortunately, in a manner which does not permit direct comparison with 1960 figures. Separate statistics are presented for persons of Spanish language and "other persons of Spanish surname," and it is not possible to extract from 1970 census tract publications the number of persons in each census tract with Spanish surnames regardless of their mother tongue. The correlation across census tracts between number of Spanish surnamed persons in 1960 and number of persons of Spanish language or Spanish surname in 1970 is +0.85, however. Accordingly, while it will be difficult to interpret traditionally calculated changing admission rates among Spanish Americans in Pueblo between the 1960 and 1970, correlational analysis comparisons between the two study periods may be made with a good deal of confidence. Numerator data (numbers of patients with Spanish surnames) were consistently tabulated in the two study periods by reference to the official list of Spanish surnames (Bureau of the Census, 1970).

EXTENT AND NATURE OF MISSING DATA

The data collected in 1960 is entirely complete. Address (converted to census tract), age, sex, Spanish surname, diagnosis, and type of facility is available for each of the 919 patients identified during the three-year data collection period. This same data is available on all inpatients in the 1970 study and, with the exception of diagnosis which could not be obtained for eight cases, available for all outpatients.

With regard to the inpatient questionnaire data, in 1970, the situation is not as satisfactory. As already indicated, the greatest difficulty in data collection took place in the private inpatient facilities. Of the 739 private facility first admissions, complete data are available for 415 patients (56 percent). Of the 314 private inpatients who had been psychiatric inpatients at some time prior to the start of data collection, complete information is available on 222 cases (71 percent). The situation with respect to public facility inpatients is far more satisfactory. Of the 299 first admissions, complete data are available on 261 cases (87 percent). Of the 476 public inpatients with histories of prior psychiatric hospitalizations, complete data are available on 420 cases (88 percent). The difference between the completeness of data collection at public facilities as contrasted with that of private facilities is related, in part, to who was responsible for data collection. On the private general hospital psychiatric wards, a specific ward staff person was responsible for data collection. At the state hospital and the VA hospital, personnel in the central record room took responsibility for collecting data during their off-time hours by visiting the wards and interviewing patients there. But the major reason for missing data in private inpatient facilities was that there was a large number of patients with psychiatric diagnoses who were hospitalized on nonpsychiatric wards. Fully two-thirds of the missing cases were accounted for in this way.

Our efforts to examine hospital records in an effort to obtain missing data bore little fruit. The data we needed were rarely to be found. We have little alternative but to examine the data we have and draw our conclusions in an appropriately tentative manner.

Census Tract Cluster Scores

While it is appropriate to relate admission rates directly to each of the 35 census tract characteristics under study, modern computer technology makes it possible to attempt to reduce these 35 variables to a smaller set, each of which would then include several variables which are so highly interrelated as to be considered as differing measures of the same underlying dimension.

By means of statistical analyses developed by Tryon and Bailey (1970), it was possible to determine if such clusters of census tract characteristics could be located and if they were sufficiently stable so that the identical clusters would be found in the 1970 as well as the 1960 census. It is not necessary for census tract characteristics to remain stable across the decade in order for them to appear in the same cluster for two different censuses. Rather, it is necessary that if changes occur, such changes occur in the same way for all variables in a cluster. That is, median family income and education, for example, can appear in the same cluster provided that census tracts high in one are high in the other, and can reappear in a cluster ten years later provided that those tracts which have changed with respect to one of these variables change in a similar and comparable direction with respect to the other. In the cluster analysis method used in this research, a variable appears in only one cluster, and if it appears, it appears fully weighted (see Bloom, 1968).

Analysis of the patterns of interrelationships among the 35 census tract characteristics in 1960 and in 1970 revealed that it was possible to identify three stable clusters utilizing 26 of the 35 variables. Each cluster was composed of the same set of variables for both 1960 and 1970, and thus it was possible to compare individual census tracts directly on each cluster score for the two censuses. The first cluster, accounting for the greatest proportion of the communality of the matrix, has been labeled "Socioeconomic Affluence" and accounted for 48 percent of the correlation matrix communality based on the 1960 data and 47 percent based on the 1970 data. The 12 variables comprising this cluster, along with their pattern of intercorrelations in 1960 and 1970, are shown in Table 2-2. The average intercorrelation of the 12 variables comprising this cluster was 0.66 in 1960 and 0.57 in 1970 (without regard to sign, since some of the variables were phrased in such a way that they correlated negatively with others in the matrix).

This cluster identifies census tracts along a dimension that includes direct measures of affluence and a variety of indices highly associated with affluence. The correlation between 1960 and 1970 scores on this cluster is +0.91. Census tracts high on the socioeconomic affluence cluster are characterized by high median family in-

Table 2-2

INTERCORRELATIONS OF VARIABLES COMPRISING THE "SOCIOECONOMIC AFFLUENCE" CLUSTER: 1960 AND 1970

Census Tract Characteristic	Census Year	Census Tract Characteristic										
		1	2	3	4	5	6	7	8	9	10	11
1. Housing Unit Value	1960											
	1970											
2. Family Income	1960	+.93										
	1970	+.87										
3. White Collar Workers	1960	+.90	+.87									
	1970	+.80	+.72									
4. Education	1960	+.89	+.84	+.87								
	1970	+.81	+.74	+.71								
5. Golf Club Members	1960	+.88	+.84	+.73	+.74							
	1970	+.79	+.70	+.59	+.58							

		1	2	3	4	5	6	7	8	9	10	11
6. Spanish Surname	1960	-.79	-.70	-.71	-.87	-.66						
	1970	-.74	-.70	-.69	-.86	-.58						
7. Central Heating	1960	+.81	+.70	+.76	+.71	+.67	-.63					
	1970	+.59	+.58	+.51	+.61	+.65	-.56					
8. Families Receiving ADC	1960	-.63	-.64	-.62	-.71	-.55	+.76	-.45				
	1970	-.57	-.64	-.47	-.55	-.44	+.70	-.29				
9. Library Card Holders	1960	+.66	+.66	+.62	+.62	+.53	-.44	+.53	-.33			
	1970	+.50	+.45	+.55	+.39	+.32	-.43	+.36	-.15			
10. Married Women in Labor Force	1960	+.62	+.54	+.61	+.75	+.37	-.74	+.50	-.51	+.27		
	1970	+.65	+.62	+.55	+.72	+.35	-.70	+.42	-.43	+.47		
11. Unemployment	1960	-.40	-.49	-.42	-.52	-.30	+.61	-.27	-.18	-.60		
	1970	-.45	-.54	-.42	-.45	-.23	+.54	-.16	-.05	-.62		
12. Household Population Density	1960	-.74	-.65	-.71	-.75	-.65	+.79	-.76	+.58	-.39	-.61	+.33
	1970	-.58	-.48	-.61	-.63	-.66	+.61	-.78	+.38	-.33	-.28	+.13

come and high value and good condition of owner-occupied housing; high level of education and high proportion of employed males in professional, technical, and kindred occupations; large numbers of library card holders and golf-club members; high proportion of married women in the labor force; and low proportion of Spanish surnamed people, low unemployment, low household population density, and few families receiving Aid to Dependent Children assistance. Of the 12 variables, the one that might be the most surprising relates to married women in the labor force. Contrary to what one might suspect, namely, that it is in the poorer families that a second income is needed and therefore where one might find wives gainfully employed, it is in fact among the more affluent census tracts that married women can be found in the labor force in greatest number.

The second cluster which was identified in both the 1960 and 1970 census data has been labeled "Social Disequilibrium" and consists of 10 variables whose inter-correlations for both 1960 and 1970 are shown in Table 2-3. Scores were assigned to this cluster so that a census tract high in social disequilibrium was one which was characterized by high marital and familial disruption, delinquency, and school dropouts; many vacant housing units, people living alone, and frequent household fires; and few single homes, few rooms per housing unit, and few homes owner-occupied. The correlation of the 1960 and 1970 scores on this cluster is $+0.94$. What is seen in this cluster in Pueblo, as in all other cities studied in the United States, is that personal disruption is highly associated with environmental disruption. The average inter-correlation of the variables comprising the social disequilibrium cluster is 0.64 based on 1960 data and 0.73 based on 1970 data. This second cluster accounts for an additional 30 percent of the correlation matrix

Table 2-3
INTERCORRELATIONS OF VARIABLES COMPRISING THE "SOCIAL DISEQUILIBRIUM" CLUSTER: 1960 AND 1970

Census Tract Characteristic	Census Year	Census Tract Characteristic								
		1	2	3	4	5	6	7	8	9
1. Rooms Per Housing Unit	1960									
	1970									
2. Marital Disruption	1960	−.84								
	1970	−.85								
3. People Living Alone	1960	−.78	+.89							
	1970	−.87	+.88							
4. Owner-Occupied Housing	1960	+.86	−.81	−.84						
	1970	+.87	−.85	−.92						
5. Delinquency	1960	−.77	+.73	+.69	−.63					
	1970	−.65	+.43	+.54	−.52					
6. Single Homes	1960	+.63	−.69	−.89	+.73	−.61				
	1970	+.79	−.81	−.94	+.94	−.51				
7. Vacant Housing	1960	−.69	+.61	+.50	−.48	+.51	−.30			
	1970	−.68	+.71	+.53	−.63	+.44	−.52			
8. Children Living with Both Parents	1960	+.62	−.67	−.78	+.70	−.67	+.76	−.26		
	1970	+.83	−.70	−.83	+.87	−.79	+.83	−.52		
9. Household Fires	1960	−.69	+.64	+.63	−.32	+.70	−.57	+.48	−.54	
	1970	−.65	+.74	+.62	−.57	+.57	−.56	+.59	−.61	
10. School Dropouts	1960	−.46	+.45	+.48	−.40	+.63	−.51	+.33	−.47	+.44
	1970	−.78	+.64	+.74	−.72	+.85	−.71	+.60	−.87	+.65

communality in the 1960 data and an additional 32 percent in the 1970 data. That is, between these two clusters, a total of nearly 80 percent of the correlation matrix communality has been accounted for in both the 1960 and 1970 data. Those census tracts high in socioeconomic affluence tend to be low in social disequilibrium, although the degree of this relationship is smaller than one might suppose. The correlation between the first two cluster scores is –0.45 based on the 1960 data, and –0.60 based on the 1970 data (see Bloom, 1966).

The third cluster, made up of only four variables, has been labeled "Young Marrieds." The pattern of intercorrelations of these variables for 1960 and 1970 is shown in Table 2-4. The average intercorrelation of the four variables in 1960 was 0.77 and in 1970 was 0.50. Census tracts high on this cluster score are characterized by low median age, a high proportion of families with children six years of age or younger, high population per household, and high proportion of new housing. 1960 scores on this cluster correlate +0.90 with the 1970 scores. On the 1960 data, an additional 14 percent of the correlation matrix communality is accounted for by this

Table 2-4

INTERCORRELATIONS OF VARIABLES COMPRISING
THE "YOUNG MARRIEDS" CLUSTER: 1960 AND 1970

Census Tract Characteristic	Census Year	Census Tract Characteristic		
		1	2	3
1. Young Children	1960			
	1970			
2. Household Population	1960	+.80		
	1970	+.55		
3. Median Age	1960	–.84	–.92	
	1970	–.61	–.78	
4. New Housing	1960	+.74	+.56	–.55
	1970	+.20	+.39	–.31

cluster. On the 1970 data, an additional 11 percent has been accounted for. Thus, between the three cluster configurations, more than 90 percent of the communality has been identified for both the 1960 and 1970 census data. Regarding the relationship between this third cluster and the two preceding ones, in neither 1960 nor 1970 was there a significant relationship between socioeconomic affluence and young marrieds. In contrast, young marrieds and social disequilibrium were significantly negatively correlated both in 1960 and 1970 (1960 $r =$ -0.48; 1970 $r = -0.45$). Census tracts characterized by a high proportion of young married families range very widely in socioeconomic affluence, but tend to be characterized by relatively low scores on the measure of social disequilibrium.

Examination of the intercorrelations of variables in each cluster score reveals that the variables included in the socioeconomic affluence cluster and in the young married cluster are not as closely related to each other in 1970 as they were in 1960. In contrast, the variables comprising the social disequilibrium cluster are more closely interrelated in 1970 than they were in 1960. That is, while there has been some leveling off of census tract differences in socioeconomic affluence, and while there is less clustering of young married people, the variables making up the social disequilibrium cluster have become increasingly interrelated. Furthermore, social disequilibrium as an environmental characteristic is more definitively associated with low socioeconomic affluence in 1970 as contrasted with 1960.

3

The Setting: Pueblo and Its Mental Health Services During a Decade of Change

Pueblo County is located in south-central Colorado at the foot of the eastern slope of the Rocky Mountains and at the confluence of the Arkansas and Fountain Rivers, geographically removed from other population centers by 35 miles in every direction. The city of Pueblo is the only urban area within the county and accounts for nearly 85 percent of the county population. Pueblo is the third largest urban area in Colorado and comprises one of the 241 standard metropolitan statistical areas in the United States.

The city had its beginning in 1792 when a small trading post was established by French fur trappers on the east bank of the Fountain River. In 1806 the first "American" structure was erected by Zebulon M. Pike. In 1842 the establishment of a permanent trading post and fort marked its beginning as an urban area. The trading post and fort were incorporated as a town with a population of approximately 700 inhabitants in 1871. The railroad arrived one year later, and in 1873 Pueblo was incorporated as a city. In 1886, the three communities of Pueblo, South Pueblo, and Central Pueblo were consolidated. The physical and geographic patterns of this consolidation are still present today and follow the geographic barriers of the two rivers and the railroad terminals.

Pueblo enjoys a mild, semiarid climate with a mean annual temperature of 55 degrees ranging from a July average of 80 degrees to a January average of 31 degrees. It is 4690 feet above sea level and has a mean annual rainfall of 11.85 inches. The general climate conditions result in clear, cool nights with a high percentage of warm sunny days.

The total land area of the city is 24.05 square miles, within a total county area of 2,400 square miles. Until 1960, growth in Pueblo County had been rapid and predominantly urban. Between 1960 and 1970, however, growth in Pueblo came to a virtual standstill. By contrast, Denver and Colorado Springs, the two largest cities in Colorado, boomed phenomenally. The 1970 census revealed that the State as a whole grew in population 25.8 percent since 1960, at a rate far above the national growth average. Pueblo was the state's only large urban area that failed to show an increase in population during the decade.

Pueblo is often described as a "blue collar town" because of the industrialized nature of its economy. The major employer is the C F and I Steel Corporation which operates one of the largest steel mills in the West. The Pueblo Army Depot is a major regional ordinance center which employs a large number of skilled and semiskilled workers. The third largest employer is the Colorado State Hospital which, in addition to its professional staff, employs a number of subprofessional and limited skill workers. The three employers account for nearly 40 percent of the urban employment. The overall employment picture has been rather poor in comparison to state and national trends and the local unemployment rate was 6.4 percent of the working force for the five-year period 1962–1967. The number of welfare recipients increased from 6704 to 15,932 during the last four years of the decade, reflecting not only poor economic conditions in

Pueblo, but also the even worse economic conditions in the surrounding rural regions of Southern Colorado and Northern New Mexico, from which a certain amount of immigration took place.

The ethnic and racial breakdown has remained quite constant over the past decade. The black population numbers about two percent of the city. Mexican-Americans comprise 31 percent of the total population. The majority Anglo population is in itself quite mixed with a strong representation of foreign-born persons, primarily those of Italian and Slovenian descent.

As might be expected from the static economy and population, physical and social characteristics in the past decade have changed little, with the exception of those social changes resulting from the influx of a large number of professional persons brought in by the State Hospital and the local college. During approximately the same part of the decade that Colorado State Hospital greatly expanded its professional staff, the facility of Pueblo Junior College also grew rapidly as it became a full four-year institution (Southern Colorado State College). Because of the changes in these two major institutions and their importation of more affluent and better educated families, there has been some moderate increase in Pueblo's cultural activities and facilities, and it is no longer as limited to the "blue collar" life style attributed to it in the past.

A somewhat unusual feature of Pueblo is the lack of a suburban community structure. The other population centers in Pueblo County are very small, old towns that do not function as bedroom communities, although two planned communities are in the developing stage.

Pueblo County has a traditional governmental structure. The county operates with a three-member elected commission. The Pueblo city structure is the council-manager type. A professional city manager has the administrative duties as outlined by the legislative body, the City Council. The President of Council performs the mayoral duties. The partisan political dynamics of Pueblo County occur within a one-party system. Unlike most of the state, which is heavily Republican, Democrats have dominated local politics for many years.

The presence of a forceful steel union gives labor a very strong voice within the Democratic Party hierarchy. In fact, labor groups might well control Pueblo politics if the old AFL versus CIO split were not still present. The AFL craft trades and the CIO steel group, however, have divided on enough occasions so that nonlabor labels often appear to be an asset for election victory. Nonlabor is not to be construed as antilabor. Rather, it is commonly asserted that both labor groups find it easier to support an outside friend over an inside enemy.

Demographic characteristics of Pueblo and comparison figures for the State of Colorado and for the United States in 1960 and 1970 are presented in Table 3-1. As can be seen, even though there has been an improvement in Pueblo's socioeconomic status in the past decade, it still tends to be in a disadvantageous position when contrasted either with the State of Colorado or the United States as a whole. Especially noteworthy in contrast to the state or nation as a whole are Pueblo's lack of population growth, relatively low median family income, high unemployment, low proportion of employed males in professional level positions, low value of owner-occupied housing, and striking lack of population mobility.

In Table 3-2 will be found the ranges, means, standard deviations, and 1960–1970 correlations of the census tract characteristics employed in this study. Slight discrepancies will be noted between figures reported in Table 3-1 and Table 3-2, because of the manner in which means were calculated. Figures presented in Table 3-1 are based upon the entire county, while figures presented in Table 3-2 are means derived from figures calculated separately for each of the 33 census tracts. In this latter analysis, each census tract is given equal weight regardless of its population.

Given that so few changes have taken place in Pueblo between 1960 and 1970, it should not be surprising that correlations between census tract characteristics across the decade are generally quite high. Five variables, however, have been quite unstable; specifically, residential stability, library card holders, nursing visits, suicide rate, and fertility ratio. Of these five variables, only one (library card holders) appears in a cluster score.

Careful inspection of Table-3-2 will give a vivid portrayal of the changes in Pueblo in the decade between 1960 and 1970. But perhaps the most astonishing characteristic of the city, in 1960 as well as in 1970, is the degree of variability among census tracts on so many of the variables. There are 50 times as many Spanish-surnamed people in the census tract highest on this variable compared with the census tract lowest on this variable. The ratio between highest and lowest census tract is on the order of 30 to 1 for fertility ratio, 25 to 1 for public health nursing visits, 50 to 1 for people living alone, 10 to 1 for household population density, 4 to 1 for residential stability, 16 to 1 for central heating, 17 to 1 for delinquency, and 60 to 1 for marital disruption.

In examining the changes in census tract characteristics between 1960 and 1970, one can see the consequences of the passage of time. Even though the median age has not changed substantially, the older 1960 residents have been the victims of the age-related mortality rate and have been replaced by a new cohort of youngsters. We see the effects of this replacement in the reduction in numbers of foreign-born on the one hand and in the consequences of the reduction in birth rate on the

Table 3-1

Selected Demographic Characteristics for Total United States, State of Colorado, and Pueblo, Colorado: 1960 and 1970

Variable	Total United States			State of Colorado			City and County of Pueblo		
	1960	1970	Percent Change	1960	1970	Percent Change	1960	1970	Percent Change
Population[1]	179,324	203,212	+13.3	1,754	2,207	+25.8	118,707	118,238	- 0.4
Median Age	29.5	28.1	- 4.7	27.9	26.2	- 6.1	28.1	27.5	- 2.1
Percent Population Under Age 5	11.3	8.4	-25.7	11.9	8.4	-29.4	12.2	8.2	-32.8
Percent Population Age 65+	9.2	9.9	+ 7.6	9.0	8.5	- 5.6	9.4	9.4	0.0
Percent Males Age 14+ Married	69.1	65.8	- 4.8	70.1	65.0	- 7.3	67.9	63.6	- 6.3
Percent Males Age 14+ Divorced	2.1	2.7	+28.6	2.8	3.3	+17.9	3.8	3.7	- 2.6
Percent Males Age 14+ Widowed	3.6	2.9	-19.4	3.0	2.3	-23.3	3.7	3.0	-18.9
Median School Years Completed	10.6	12.1	+14.2	12.1	12.4	+ 2.5	10.2	12.0	+17.6
Median Family Income	$5660	$9590	+69.4	$5780	$9555	+65.3	$5450	$8445	+55.0

72

Percent of Male Civilian Labor Force Unemployed	5.0	3.9	− 22.0	3.9	3.9	0.0	5.0	5.6	+12.0
Percent of Male Civilian Labor Force in Professional, Technical and Kindred Occupations	10.3	13.5	+31.1	12.4	16.9	+36.3	8.8	12.1	+37.5
Percent of Married Women in Labor Force	30.7	39.2	+27.7	31.0	40.2	+29.7	26.9	34.1	+26.8
Median Value of Owner-Occupied Housing Units	$11,900	$17,000	+42.9	$12,300	$17,300	+40.7	$9,700	$12,600	+29.9
Median Number of Rooms per Housing Unit	4.9	5.0	+ 2.0	4.6	4.9	+ 6.5	4.3	4.7	+ 9.3
Percent of Occupied Housing Units Owner-Occupied	61.9	62.9	+ 1.6	63.8	63.4	− 0.6	66.7	69.0	+ 3.4
Percent of Population Age 5 and above Living in Same House as 5 Years Ago	49.9	53.0	+ 6.2	40.4	42.9	+ 6.2	49.9	59.9	+20.0

[1]Population figures for United States and the State of Colorado in thousands.

Table 3-2

RANGES, MEANS, STANDARD DEVIATIONS, AND INTERCENSUS CORRELATIONS OF CENSUS TRACT VARIABLES: 1960 AND 1970

Census Tract Variable	1960				1970				r
	Low	High	Mean	S.D.	Low	High	Mean	S.D.	
Demographic Characteristics									
1. Population	828	6303	3406.2	1268.3	624	9280	3522.5	1935.1	+0.86
2. Median Age	15.7	37.2	26.6	6.4	19.6	41.0	26.8	5.1	+0.88
3. Sex Ratio	83.0	126.0	103.4	7.6	82.8	121.1	104.7	8.3	+0.76
4. Foreign Born	0.8	12.2	3.4	2.8	0.4	8.3	2.5	2.1	+0.93
5. Spanish Surname	1.3	62.9	22.4	17.3	6.6	84.5	35.1	20.7	+0.85
6. Fertility Ratio	3.2	90.6	57.3	19.0	27.3	51.5	40.7	6.1	+0.18
7. Education	8.0	12.6	10.3	1.6	8.5	12.7	11.1	1.2	+0.84
Community Participation									
8. Library Card Holders	0.0	459.2	247.0	131.0	113.6	452.9	259.4	92.4	+0.34
9. YMCA Members	0.0	132.8	39.2	34.2	0.0	25.8	6.6	5.8	+0.51
10. Golf Club Members	0.0	50.4	11.5	11.9	0.0	27.8	5.0	6.0	+0.94
11. Public Health Nursing Visits	19.0	474.0	87.1	87.5	0.0	120.8	31.5	32.8	-0.13
Family Characteristics									
12. Household Population	2.08	4.65	3.5	0.6	1.9	4.1	3.2	0.5	+0.96
13. Young Children	19.0	61.0	36.3	11.9	12.2	40.3	26.1	5.5	+0.65
14. People Living Alone	0.7	50.9	13.5	10.6	3.5	57.1	18.0	11.2	+0.95
15. Household Population Density	4.0	39.6	18.5	9.9	3.0	27.7	12.7	6.4	+0.94
16. Residential Stability	15.2	67.2	50.9	12.0	38.0	78.9	60.3	10.3	+0.38

17. Married Women in Labor Force	14.9	44.8	27.8	7.1	16.1	48.4	32.4	7.0	+0.58
18. Children Living with Both Parents	69.8	96.9	87.1	7.1	58.5	93.5	80.1	8.2	+0.87
Housing Characteristics									
19. Single Homes	29.6	99.7	85.8	17.1	21.2	100.0	83.4	18.0	+0.93
20. Rooms Per Housing Unit	2.2	5.2	4.3	0.6	2.8	5.5	4.6	0.5	+0.84
21. New Housing	1.8	100.0	29.8	30.0	0.7	50.0	15.7	13.8	+0.74
22. Housing Unit Value	$5000	$16500	$8993.9	$3177.0	$7000	$20600	$11538.6	$3276.9	+0.86
23. Owner-Occupied Housing	16.6	93.1	66.9	17.0	18.0	92.8	71.4	15.0	+0.84
24. Housing Lacking Plumbing	0.0	66.3	23.0	21.5	0.3	30.9	7.5	8.2	+0.87
25. Central Heating	6.5	100.0	57.0	27.6	23.0	100.0	70.2	22.3	+0.89
26. Vacant Housing	0.5	19.2	2.8	3.1	0.6	8.3	3.2	2.2	+0.56
27. Household Fires	0.0	5.2	1.8	1.3	0.0	2.2	0.6	0.5	+0.59
Socioeconomic Characteristics									
28. Family Income	$3793	$8353	$5467.5	$1123.8	$5707	$12112	$8060.0	$1602.9	+0.85
29. Unemployment	0.0	11.8	5.1	3.1	0.0	14.4	6.2	3.6	+0.50
30. White Collar Workers	1.7	23.4	8.2	5.9	1.7	29.2	10.4	7.5	+0.67
31. Families Receiving ADC	0.0	11.0	3.1	2.6	0.0	25.8	10.2	7.4	+0.67
Personal Disruption									
32. Delinquency	0.5	8.5	3.6	2.1	0.0	8.7	4.4	2.1	+0.71
33. Suicide Rate	0.0	3.05	1.1	0.8	0.0	3.2	0.6	0.7	-0.11
34. School Dropouts	0.0	80.0	30.2	20.6	0.0	36.0	16.8	9.9	+0.57
35. Marital Disruption	5.92	341.1	59.3	67.0	12.8	508.7	91.7	96.3	+0.96

other hand; fewer families with young children, and reduced population per household and household population density.

Second, a certain amount of homogenation has taken place among the census tracts. This phenomenon can be seen in the instances of reduced variability in the absence of comparable reductions in mean values. Particularly noteworthy in this connection are median age, fertility ratio, school years completed, library card holders, young children, centrally heated housing, and vacant housing. On these variables the census tracts are more nearly like each other in 1970 than they were in 1960. On only one variable, children living with both parents, has a meaningful increase in variability among census tracts taken place at the same time that there has been a decrease in mean value.

Third, there are numerous instances of improved sociocultural, economic, and housing characteristics in the decade. Educational level has increased, value of housing has increased, there are fewer housing units lacking plumbing facilities or central heating, household fires have decreased in frequency, median family income has increased, and dropping out of school has become less common. In comparison with the State of Colorado, however, these improvements are not enough. Pueblo still lags behind the state as a whole in educational level, median family income, and value of owner-occupied housing (see Table 3-1).

Finally, there is quantitative evidence of a generalized stagnation and, at the risk of being inappropriately clinical, a kind of ecological depression having taken place during the decade. There are fewer YMCA members and golf club members. Public health nursing visits have decreased. More people lived alone in 1970 than did in 1960. There is substantially less new housing. Vacant housing has increased. There has been a decrease in in- and out-migration. Unemployment is up. Three times as many families received financial assistance in 1970 as did in 1960. Delinquency is up, and marital disruption has shown more than a 50 percent increase in the decade with its inevitable consequence of greater numbers of children living in homes with only one parent.

A useful view of the city and county of Pueblo is afforded by examining the geographic distribution of census tract cluster scores. In each of the figures to follow, we have divided census tracts into thirds, according to each cluster score, and have portrayed these groups of census tracts by easily distinguishable patterns. In one case (social disequilibrium for 1960) a minor adjustment was made in the division of census tracts into groups because of a tie score. The cluster score limits for each census tract grouping are shown on each figure. It is well to keep in mind that while the census tracts within the city are drawn according to their relative location and approximate size, all census tracts outside of the city have had to be significantly compressed in size.

Several general observations about the interrelationships of cluster scores should be made by way of background. Socioeconomic affluence cluster scores range from a low of 31.7 to a high of 68.5. These and all other cluster scores are directly interpretable in standard deviation units with a mean of 50.0 and a standard deviation of 10.0. Examination of Figure 3-A will assist in developing a view of the index of socioeconomic affluence in the Pueblo census tracts. As can be seen, the most affluent tracts form two groupings, one in the north-central portion of the city and the other in the southwestern portion of the city. Tracts with moderate scores on the index of socioeconomic affluences are located in the northeastern quadrant of the city and the southern portion as well. Two of the southern rural tracts are included in the moderately affluent group. Those tracts with the lowest

Figure 3-A
Socioeconomic Affluence Cluster Scores — 1960

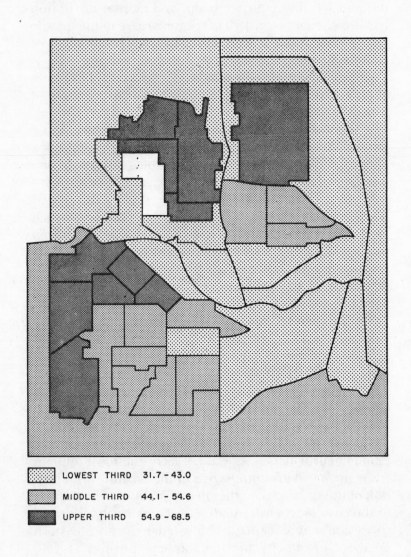

LOWEST THIRD   31.7 - 43.0

MIDDLE THIRD   44.1 - 54.6

UPPER THIRD   54.9 - 68.5

level of affluence are located in the central portion of the city and in the rural sections to the north, east, and southeast. Little change had taken place by 1970 in the census tract indices of socioeconomic affluence. The range was from 32.5 to 72.1 and the correlation across tracts between 1960 and 1970 was +0.91. Three of the least affluent tracts and three of the moderately affluent traded places; and one of the moderately affluent and one of the high affluent likewise traded places. The result of this realignment, as can be seen in Figure 3-B, left somewhat more of the inner city as well as the surrounding rural tracts to the north in the lowest affluence category while the southern, more rural area outside of the inner city had grown in affluence.

The index of social disequilibrium ranged from a low of 38.8 to a high of 82.5 in 1960 and from a low of 36.2 to a high of 82.9 in 1970. Census tract scores on the social disequilibrium index for 1960 are shown in Figure 3-C and the concentration of high scores in the central area of the city is readily apparent. Changes in cluster scores between 1960 and 1970 were minor—two pairs of census tracts exchanged contiguous rankings, and the correlation across census tracts between the 1960 and 1970 indices of social disequilibrium was +0.94 (See Figure 3-D). The skewed character of these cluster scores can be seen. In 1960 and 1970, approximately two-thirds of the census tracts had scores below 50. The correlations between the measures of social disequilibrium and socioeconomic affluence are significantly negative—somewhat more so in 1970 than in 1960—but the two measures are in no sense redundant. Two census tracts in the inner city, for example, are high on both measures, and the rural tracts surrounding the central city tend to be low on both measures.

The young married index ranged from 33.5 to 70.7 in 1960 and from 32.5 and 69.2 in 1970 and the 1960 and

Figure 3-B
SOCIOECONOMIC AFFLUENCE CLUSTER SCORES — 1970

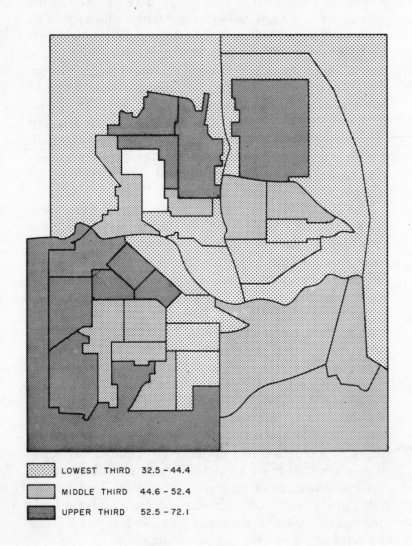

```
▒▒  LOWEST THIRD   32.5 – 44.4
▢   MIDDLE THIRD   44.6 – 52.4
▓   UPPER THIRD    52.5 – 72.1
```

Figure 3–C
Social Disequilibrium Cluster Scores — 1960

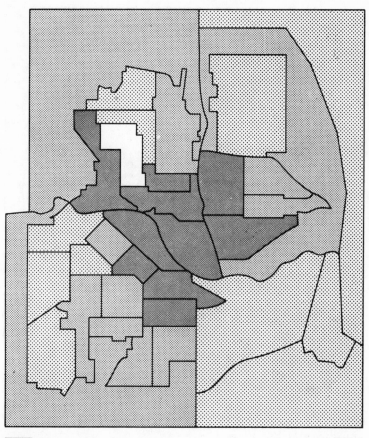

LOWEST THIRD   38.8 – 45.8

MIDDLE THIRD   46.0 – 49.0 (N = 12)

UPPER THIRD   50.0 – 82.5 (N = 10)

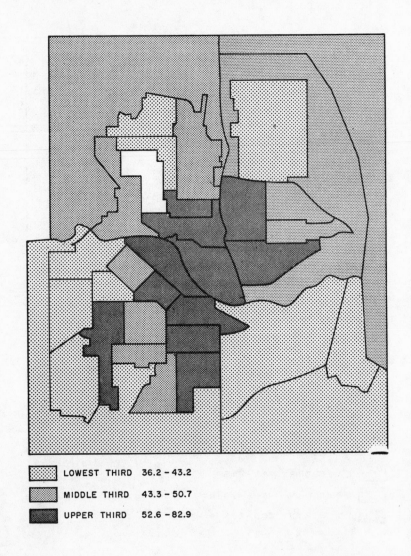

Figure 3-D
SOCIAL DISEQUILIBRIUM CLUSTER SCORES — 1970

LOWEST THIRD   36.2 – 43.2

MIDDLE THIRD   43.3 – 50.7

UPPER THIRD   52.6 – 82.9

1970 indices correlated +0.90 with each other. The high correlations of all three of these census tract cluster scores across the decade is, in part of course, a consequence of how the variables comprising the indices were chosen. Since high stability of cluster scores during both study periods was desired, variables which were themselves unstable were not accepted into clusters. As was already mentioned, the young married index was entirely unrelated to the measure of socioeconomic affluence and significantly negatively related to the index of social disequilibrium. Census tracts high on the young married index appeared both in areas of high and low affluence. The distribution of census tract scores on the young married index is shown in Figure 3-E for 1960 and 3-F for 1970. The general absence of large numbers of young married families in the central inner city is readily apparent and is perhaps more striking in 1970 than in 1960.

Throughout the decade, the inner portion of the central city could be characterized as low in affluence, high in social disequilibrium and low in proportion of young married families. As one examines census tracts between the inner city and the rural surrounding countryside, one finds decreasing social disequilibrium, increasing affluence, and increasing proportions of young married families. In the rural areas surrounding the city, affluence generally decreases as does social disequilibrium, while the proportion of young families increases. Pueblo is clearly large enough to be geographically and demographically stratified, and we will be interested in how this stratification is associated with the measures of treated mental disorder which have been derived by the analysis of the caseloads of agencies comprising the mental health service delivery system.

Figure 3-E
YOUNG MARRIEDS CLUSTER SCORES — 1960

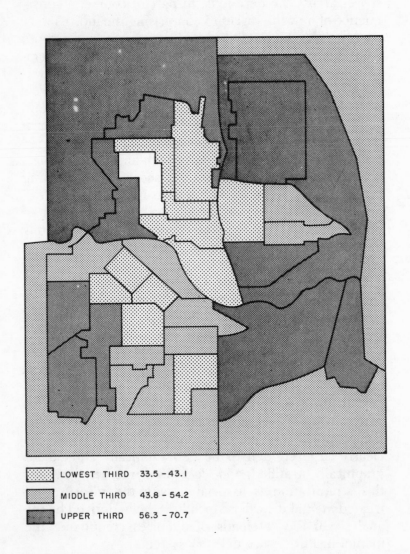

LOWEST THIRD 33.5 – 43.1

MIDDLE THIRD 43.8 – 54.2

UPPER THIRD 56.3 – 70.7

Figure 3-F
YOUNG MARRIEDS CLUSTER SCORES — 1970

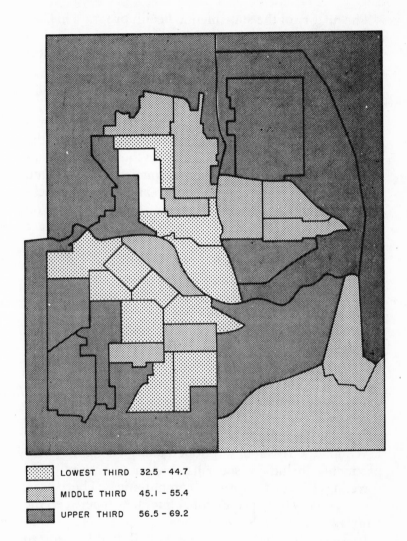

LOWEST THIRD   32.5 – 44.7

MIDDLE THIRD   45.1 – 55.4

UPPER THIRD   56.5 – 69.2

AN OVERVIEW OF THE COLORADO STATE MENTAL HEALTH PROGRAM

The history of the state mental health program in Colorado is both interesting and important background to this review of Pueblo in the sixties because it is so typical of developments in other states and because events at the state level contributed so directly to the developments in Pueblo.

The State General Assembly assumed major responsibility for public mental health services in 1879 with the creation of Colorado State Hospital at Pueblo. This institution, like many other state hospitals in the United States, grew in patient population year after year, reaching a maximum of over 6000 patients being cared for on any given day. Patients were well cared for but were seldom discharged.

In 1925 the Board of Regents established Colorado Psychopathic Hospital at the University of Colorado Medical School in Denver. This hospital stressed intensive treatment for acute illnesses thought likely to respond quickly. It was, and remains, under its university auspices, a training hospital and could therefore afford to be selective in its admissions and generous with its staff-patient ratios. But it soon provided a forum and demonstration area for some remarkable members of the Department of Psychiatry to suggest better programs that might be undertaken for the mentally ill. Colorado Psychopathic Hospital developed a large outpatient department, including specialized clinics, and initiated traveling clinics to various communities. There was, however, very little professional interaction between the University and the State Hospital.

In 1951, the plight of the mentally ill had become so noticeable that the Governor convened the first of a series of special Citizens' Conferences on the Care of the

Mentally Ill. Members of the conference, which included faculty of the Medical School Department of Psychiatry, recommended a state mental health program incorporating nearly all the ideas which later came to be recognized nationally as the hallmarks of good community mental health planning. They stressed that the state should plan for all types of patients and their particular needs rather than just for the needs of institutions. They emphasized prevention and community consultation. They recommended that responsibility for statewide mental health program planning and operation be located in one department and that a community approach be taken in education, prevention, and treatment. Furthermore, they recommended the hiring of trained mental health professionals and better inservice training of present employees, expansion of outpatient services and development of aftercare services, the establishment of a second state hospital, to be located in Denver, creation and expansion of intensive treatment programs at Colorado State Hospital, establishment of outpatient clinics and psychiatric wards in general hospitals, and research to help identify the factors responsible for mental illness.

In the meantime a handful of mental hygiene clinics were getting started with help from grants-in-aid supplied by the National Mental Health Act of 1946. The Colorado Department of Public Health was named as the mental health authority and established a Mental Health Section in its Preventive Medical Services Division. It organized a traveling clinic team which provided services to remote communities once or twice a month.

The State Hospital, as other state institutions, was at various times placed under nominal supervision of various boards or the Department of Public Welfare. In 1951, the Department of Institutions was created to incorporate Colorado State Hospital, the prisons, the schools for the retarded, and other state institutions. It was, however, funded only for a director and secretary, attached to an advisory board, and given no real function beyond advising the Governor. It was never part of the Department of Public Health and thus the State Hospital was administered separately from the community mental hygiene clinic program.

A second Governor's conference in 1955 reported continuing serious deficiencies in the Colorado mental health program and in 1958, the Governor brought in a team from the National Institute of Mental Health to survey the psychiatric needs of the state. The survey concentrated heavily on Colorado State Hospital and among other recommendations urged that the state mental health program be headed by a full-time, fully qualified psychiatrist. In 1959 a reorganization act was passed which greatly broadened the scope and authority of the Department of Institutions. The Director of Institutions was then able to develop a central office staff of assistants and to organize the Department into program area divisions headed by career professionals. The Governor secured a qualified psychiatrist from the Medical School as Director of Institutions in December, 1960. A few months later, he brought in a second psychiatrist from the Medical School as Chief of Psychiatric Services.

In 1961, two other momentous actions were taken. First, Fort Logan Mental Health Center was established to provide community-oriented state hospital services to the Denver area. Fort Logan quickly became a nationally recognized model for hospital-based, modern, intensive, comprehensive and community-oriented mental health services. Second, in Pueblo, one of the most dramatic transformations in American mental health program history was begun. Mass programs for hiring new professional staff and training nursing personnel were initiated. Release policies and procedures were completely redesigned and those patients who could be returned home or placed in foster families or nursing homes were released. In March 1962, the hospital was decentralized into eight general units, each of which began to relate to geographic catchment areas of the state. Intensive treatment, rehabilitation programs, and aftercare services were now provided, and the teams of the geographic divisions began getting acquainted with local community groups and resources.

In 1962 the State Mental Health Authority designation was transferred from the Department of Public Health to the Department of Institutions and a Coordinator of Community Mental Health Services was hired to assist the local mental hygiene clinics, which were also transferred from Health Department auspices. This transfer was vital to the development of a unified state program but was not an unmixed blessing. The former Mental Health Section in the Health Department of two staff members had grown into a Division of Community Mental Health Services with nine professionals, a staff larger than the Department of Institutions Division of Mental Health has yet been able to develop. This staff had been providing real assistance in the formation of community clinics and was espousing broader conceptions of community programming and improved mental health training for public health nurses and other caretakers. Under its auspices the first program of after-care services for state hospital patients had been established. There was considerable anxiety and tension in many quarters that much might be lost in the transfer, but with improving state and federal funding for community clinics, they grew to twenty-one in number by 1965, making area services potentially available to nearly all of the population of the state.

The next major step to further community services was taken in 1963 when Colorado became the sixteenth state to pass a Community Mental Health Services Act. The Act specifically supported services for outpatients, rehabilitation, prevention, consultation, education, study and training, and mental retardation services. Clinics under control of Boards of Health, nonprofit corporations, or political subdivisions were eligible for support. The 1963 funding provisions were on a 50 percent state matching basis, not to exceed 25 cents per capita in the area being served. A liberalization of matching provisions of up to 75 percent was allowed for clinics less than three years old. In 1965 the legislature raised the per capita allotment to 40 cents and allowed 60 percent matching contribution from the State for older clinics.

A unified state mental health program was now pumping life into a new state hospital in Denver and into many community programs, but perhaps the most important of all, for developments in Pueblo, was the total change wrought in the Colorado State Hospital. From that agency had always come the bulk of the services for Pueblo's major mental illness but, from 1960 to 1970, those services and their community impact would take an entirely new form.

THE MENTAL HEALTH SERVICES DELIVERY SYSTEM IN PUEBLO

Before examining the individual agencies in detail it will be helpful to take an overview of Pueblo programs as they appeared in 1960. Considerable progress was being made at national and state levels to support the development of new forms of treatment for mental illness. Graduates of medical schools, departments of psychology, and schools of social work were embarking on their careers with ideas and techniques unknown to earlier generations. Legislators and professional associations were just beginning to grapple with competing conceptual models for the ways in which services should be organized, programmed, and funded.

Not many options were available in Pueblo to someone in search of professional mental health care at the opening of the 1960's. Private care was very limited even for those who could afford to pay. There were no qualified professionals in full-time private practice, although some evening or weekend psychiatric care was available. A small private psychiatric hospital which had opened some years earlier had closed in 1959, and the nearest remaining ones were 40 or more miles away. One of the two general hospitals had psychiatric beds, but the ward was staffed by regular nursing personnel and used mainly by physicians in general practice.

Public outpatient services were, for the most part, limited to evaluation or to marital or school counseling, and there were long waiting lists. The local mental hygiene clinic was relatively small. The social work agencies did not yet employ any graduate social workers and thus their counseling services were not of fully professional quality. In the public sector, most of Pueblo's psychiatric patients had only one resource, namely the state's only mental hospital.

The major treatment approach which was used was custodial care. It grew, of course, out of the national condition in which most mental illness was handled in poorly funded state hospitals with enormous ratios of patients to professional staff. Most patient-staff contact was with nursing attendants and maintenance employees. Any given patient might see a psychiatrist for a few minutes a month—and then again, he might not.

The only use of what might be called a problem-solving approach to emotional problems was in the diagnosis and referral services or in the counseling services mentioned above. Ancillary therapies were just beginning to be used at the state hospital, but they did not involve a large proportion of patients. Even the "work therapy" then in use did not touch the vast majority of patients. Somatic therapies were the treatment of choice. Chemotherapy was heavily used, although the new psychotropic drugs which appeared in the mid-fifties were still unfamiliar to many physicians. Control of the "difficult" psychotic in any hospital was likely to be managed with repeated electroshock, and insulin shock was also being utilized. Most of one large building at the state hospital was devoted to hydrotherapy, a form of treatment which was equally popular with physicians who admitted their patients to the general hospitals. Happily, psychosurgery was never popular in Pueblo, and its citizens were spared the rage of prefrontal lobotomies which swept through numerous public and private psychiatric hospitals in the United States.

In short, intensive treatment for the average person in Pueblo was impossible to obtain. One could get assistance for minor problems if he could wait for intake. If the disturbance was major, one either healed with time or generally grew senile and immobile in a benign but custodial public inpatient setting.

It is apparent, then, that in 1960 Pueblo lacked any real delivery system for mental health services. What little planning existed was focused on individual agency growth rather than upon meeting the community's needs. Nor did planning include any significant community participation outside of various efforts to enlist the support of the business sector or middle class women's groups behind individual agency planning. Interagency relationships consisted mainly of referral of clients who could not be served because of the agency's limited treatment resources or the client's limited financial resources. Federal financing of services was still quite meager and not directed toward identified community needs. No one was delegated responsibility to study what the community's needs were, what treatment methods might be employed to be more effective, or what resources were necessary to support new programs.

Under these circumstances, it was inevitable that the public attitude toward mental illness should be characterized by guilt and stigma and the image of mental health services should be one of uselessness or horror. Psychiatric personnel were viewed more as agents of social control than caregivers, and it was not uncommon for parents to threaten to send children who misbehaved to the state hospital, for which numerous pejorative terms had been coined.

THE AGENCIES AND THEIR CHANGING SERVICES

Colorado State Hospital

With the appointment of a new superintendent who took office in March, 1961, a thorough reorganization of the hospital's administration and clinical program was begun. The tremendous obstacles he faced were foreseen in the 1958 Survey Report by a team from the National Institute of Mental Health, who felt that improvement within the hospital would require a total change in the philosophy of care, of administration, of staff utilization, of patient-staff relationships, and of hospital-community relationships, and that this change would need to be total and far-reaching. Furthermore, as with any change which would have such wide impact, it could not occur all at once, but rather over a period of time and in a series of carefully conceived phases.

As with many other state hospitals, the "establishment" was organized in such a way as to be quite resistive to change. The release of patients was at the discretion of one psychiatrist, who made sure that no one who might come to public attention, or who would cause offense to families who thought they had their troublesome relative safely "put away," could leave the institution. This cautious policy was effectively abetted by a host of procedures which insured that the paperwork required for release clearance might consume weeks. The patient even had to have the librarian certify in writing that all books charged out to him had been returned before he could be released.

Centralization of authority was complete in other matters as well. All patient privileges were approved and all letters were signed by the Assistant Superintendent. Physicians and other professionals were discouraged from getting involved in the ward life. Supervision of the wards, and therefore of the treatment program, was the responsibility of the nursing personnel—partially trained aides supervised by nurses under the very tight control of the director of nursing, who brooked no interference with her domain.

This well ordered *status quo* enjoyed the support of the town's own *status quo* through a variety of close ties with influential community people. A large proportion of the county medical society enjoyed paid consultant appointments to the hospital. Local politicians had patronage leads into the personnel office of the hospital. Local businessmen had close ties with the hospital administration. There were few on the hospital staff who wished to see change or who could be expected to perceive change as other than a disruptive interference with a perfectly satisfactory routine.

The new superintendent came imbued with the ideas of the Stantons at Boston's McLean Hospital, where he had been Assistant Superintendent, and was also much impressed by the growing therapeutic community fostered by a 1957 reorganization at neighboring Utah State Hospital.

His principle task was to find a way to bring patients into contact with intensive and effective treatment so that they could be rehabilitated and returned to community living. The major obstacles in the path were extreme overcrowding, a custodial environment which was often alleged to be antitherapeutic in its effect, and a staff unprepared for conducting an intensive treatment program oriented toward release.

The new superintendent's strategy of reform began with various efforts at decentralizing authority and decision making from the top administration to the staff levels. These decisions involved a number of small but important matters, which, taken together, placed responsibility for patients and their treatment and release planning in the hands of the professional staff who knew the patients best. At the same time, a number of new young professionals were brought in who did not have quite so much unlearning to do.

The creation of a therapeutic community environment would remain impossible in such overcrowded conditions, so an immediate objective became the reduction of the patient population. New intensive treatment units, organized around the concept of a clinical team responsible for its own patients and program, were established for the patients newly admitted to the hospital. A special team was created whose sole function was to evaluate elderly patients, prepare them for release, and locate or develop community placement situations for them. In the first year, many hundreds of elderly patients who were not receiving any special benefit from psychiatric hospitalization were released to their families, boarding homes, or nursing homes.

For many years, the Colorado statutes had permitted voluntary admissions to the State Hospital, but this opportunity had seldom been used. Within two months the new superintendent had published a policy of actively encouraging voluntary admissions, because it fostered a more positive attitude by the patient toward the hospital and his treatment program, avoided loss of self-esteem and of certain civil rights, encouraged a more effective working relationship with the family and the family physician, and made discharge easier when the patient was ready to go home. This policy quickly became a great asset to the intensive treatment approach for new admissions.

As authority was being decentralized to the wards and new approaches were being introduced to treatment and hospital-community relationships, training programs for the basic ward personnel were provided which led eventually to the upgrading of nursing attendants to skilled psychiatric technicians. Registered nurses also received training or were given educational leave for graduate work in psychiatric nursing.

A new clinical director joined the hospital staff in November, 1961, and was given the task of planning for the total reorganization of the clinical activities of the hospital. A charismatic leader with a proven record of implementing innovation, he came well equipped for this task. As Assistant Superintendent of the Clarinda Mental Health Institute in Iowa, he had decentralized that hospital with the Clarinda Plan in 1959. The unit system concept of decentralization had already been developed in 1951 by Karl Menninger and applied in Kansas, Utah, and New York. The Clarinda Plan, which would now be applied in Colorado, advanced the decentralization concept with several very important features.

First, the semiautonomous units of the hospital were converted to serving patients from a particular geographic region of the state, rather than from the state as a whole. The regions themselves were defined according to certain social-ecological characteristics of the areas, such as natural regional identities, common services networks, topographical barriers and highway systems, population densities, and county admission rates to the hospital.

Responsibility for only one regional area allowed the unit staff to develop special knowledge of and working relationships with the community they served and the helping agencies located there. The unit staff had the responsibility of establishing after-care programs in the areas they served and, because of differences in locally available services, that function varied from coordination of existing community resources to assisting actively in the development of such resources.

Whereas the original unit system involved only a portion of the hospital in its decentralization, the new plan decentralized much of the central organization of the hospital. The unit or division team operated much as a regional hospital and responsibility for patient care was lodged with it.

In addition to the geographical divisions, four specialty divisions were established to serve the special program needs of the alcoholic, the elderly bedridden, the dangerous criminal, and the medical-surgical patient. Children and adolescents were, at that time, housed within their respective geographical divisions and bused to a day care center. Later this center became a full-time special division.

In July, following the geographical decentralization, a most fortunate new development occurred which contributed immeasurably to the success of the reorganization. A new program, referred to as the Career Residency, was established in cooperation with the University of Colorado Medical School and its psychiatric hospital. A number of third-year residents in psychiatry at the Medical School became full-time staff members of Colorado State Hospital for one year, in return for stipends about double that of a normal resident's stipend. These new staff members were well trained psychiatrists eager to apply their learning and energies to this institutional revolution. Assigned as both division directors and team leaders to most of the newly created units, they quickly provided vigorous and creative leadership.

One of the geographical units which had been created was the Pueblo Division. Because of this radical new system, Pueblo now had for the first time a major mental health facility which focused its services directly upon that community. Within a short time, the Pueblo Division developed day care and outpatient programs as well as expanded inpatient and aftercare services. A revolutionary reorganization of the hospital had now taken place and Pueblo was perhaps its principal beneficiary.

Obviously, a crucial ingredient in the mental health scene from 1960 to 1970 was the massive increase in financial support from public sources. While President Kennedy and the Congress led the way with federal legislation and appropriations, the Colorado legislature responded to its own executive branch leadership with large increases in its own appropriations. In addition, large numbers of qualified professionals of all types were brought to the hospital during the decade. The social work staff, for instance, increased from four to 20 in less than a year. The development of the clinical team concept for operating the decentralized units necessitated full complements in each division of psychiatrists, psychologists, social workers, occupational therapists, and recreational therapists, in addition to nurses and psychiatric technicians. Bringing new professionals to the hospital usually meant bringing new professionals into Pueblo itself. The hospital staff thus served as a principal source of manpower for other agencies' recruitment, part-time work in private practice, and sometimes for full-time private practice.

The increased emphasis on the development of pre-service and inservice training programs for nursing personnel was crucial to the hospital's reorganization. Many, of these training programs were formalized and transferred to the auspices of Southern Colorado State College. Hospital buildings were used by the College for on-site instruction and field experience. A considerable academic curriculum was developed for mental health nurses, B.A. degree mental health workers, psychiatric technicians, and a variety of paramedical technologists; a basic behavioral science program with considerable psychiatric content was inaugurated.

In 1960 only inpatient service had been provided, but by 1970, less than 60 percent of the hospital's enrollment was in inpatient care. Nearly every inpatient in 1970 was in some form of group therapy. Individual psychotherapy was employed wherever it was deemed appropriate, and all patients received some measure of individual counseling and attention. Pueblo patients, in particular, were often found in marital or family therapy groups.

In part as a consequence of these changes, there has been a dramatic reduction in length of stay. In 1960 some 70 percent stayed in the hospital more than two years, many for their remaining years. In 1970, 75 percent were discharged in under 90 days, and 40 percent left in under 30 days. The hospital census is now just over 1000.

The success of the geographical decentralization and intensive treatment was recognized in 1966 with the Silver Award of the American Psychiatric Association. The Bronze Award was granted two years later for creation of a new special division, the Mental Retardation Center, in which all the nonpsychotic retarded patients were removed from the psychiatric divisions and placed in a carefully tailored program of rehabilitation and training for their specific needs. This division was removed from the hospital organization in 1969 and became an independent State Home and Training School within the State's Division of Mental Retardation.

Spanish Peaks Mental Health Center

The Spanish Peaks Mental Health Center was established in 1958 as the Pueblo Guidance Center, under the sponsorship of the Pueblo Mental Health Association. In 1961 it was incorporated as a private, nonprofit, outpatient clinic, and in 1964 its name was changed when services were inaugurated in Las Animas and Huerfano Counties (two counties to the south of Pueblo).

Its initial budget in 1958 enabled the Spanish Peaks Mental Health Center to provide the equivalent of one-and-a-half clinical psychologist days per month and four hours of psychiatry per month, plus a half-time secretary. From this initial start a mental health clinic has been developed which by 1970 included 18 full-time staff, seven part-time staff, and a small number of volunteers.

Its history is not atypical of mental health clinics in general during the past decade. As treatment availability was expanded, so was the base of treatment facilities. Services continued to be delivered primarily at the center offices until 1968, when initial efforts were made in working in poverty neighborhoods. With the advent of a contractual school program in 1969 additional services were taken to the community. As increased efforts were made toward working in and with the community, changes began to occur in the type of patient population served. The Pueblo Guidance Center had served primarily the white middle class, of which a significant majority were female. The age of clients in 1960 was fairly equally distributed between children under twelve and middle-aged females. By 1970 more emphasis was being placed on serving adolescents and young adults and on serving persons from disadvantaged areas.

As more services were made available, an increased case load was developed. During the last five years of the decade attention had also shifted to include an increasing amount of community consultation. In order to provide these indirect services, direct patient care was increasingly restricted to patients who had been referred because of acute psychiatric emergencies. Even so, by the middle of 1969, a six-month waiting list for routine referrals had developed. It was only when federal funds became available to expand the number of staff that the waiting list could be eliminated.

In 1968, the Spanish Peaks Mental Health Center joined with several divisions of the state hospital to create the Southern Colorado Comprehensive Mental Health Center. Participating units from the Colorado State Hospital included the Southern Colorado Psychiatric Center (formerly the Pueblo Division), the Children's Treatment Center, and the Alcoholic Treatment Center. Inpatient services, partial hospitalization services, and emergency services were provided at the state hospital, while outpatient services and consultation and education services were based in the Spanish Peaks Mental Health Center. These services were to be provided in a coordinated manner under the direction of an administrative board which included representatives of both the Spanish Peaks Mental Health Center and the Colorado State Hospital.

With the establishment of the Southern Colorado Comprehensive Mental Health Center, two types of federal grants were obtained. The initial grant was for remodeling of Spanish Peaks Mental Health Center office space, and the remodeling of two buildings at the Colorado State Hospital, one for the Alcoholic Treatment Center and the other for the Southern Colorado Psychiatric Center. This money supplemented state money already allocated for these improvements. Remodeling was initiated in the summer of 1969 and completed early in the spring of 1970.

The second funding request was for a staffing grant which affected the Spanish Peaks Mental Health Center and the Children's Treatment Center of the Colorado State Hospital. In addition to enabling the Spanish Peaks Mental Health Center to double their staff, the grant enabled the Children's Treatment Center of the Colorado State Hospital to build new facilities and to establish a new treatment team of approximately 20 staff members.

The establishment of the Southern Colorado Comprehensive Mental Health Center enabled a greater degree of cooperative programming to be developed between the two agencies. There was greater opportunity to coordinate treatment programs and provide continuity in the care of the mentally ill.

By 1970 the impact of this new delivery system was only beginning to be felt, but already significant changes were underway. These changes included a much more aggressive effort in taking services to the people, particularly to those in the poverty areas of town. Increased emphasis on continuity of care enabled patients to continue in treatment with the same therapist, regardless of the location or type of treatment.

A further outgrowth of the Southern Colorado Comprehensive Mental Health Center was the establishment of a Human Services Center to serve six census tracts on the south side of Pueblo. The purpose of this Human Services Center was to bring together a variety of helping services (including but not limited to mental health) to serve a geographically defined neighborhood from a common facility in a coordinated and cooperative manner.

Private Sector Services

In 1960, as has already been mentioned, private care facilities for inpatient psychiatric treatment in Pueblo consisted primarily of a small psychiatric ward in one of the two large general hospitals within the city. Low income groups were generally unable to utilize this facility, except perhaps while awaiting transfer to the state hospital.

St. Mary-Corwin Hospital is the larger of the two general hospitals in the Pueblo area, and is a church-operated, nonprofit agency providing general medical services and short-term treatment. There are 460 beds, of which 24 comprise the psychiatric ward. Medical coverage in 1960 was provided by a part-time psychiatrist and by several primary physicians in the community. By 1970, the staff had increased dramatically and now included, in addition to more psychiatrists, an expanded number of nurses, psychiatric technicians, and a social worker. As a result, it was possible to inaugurate a variety of therapeutic programs.

In the early 1960's the psychiatric unit was a locked ward with a high utilization of hydrotherapy and heavy reliance on restraint and seclusion; in the latter part of the decade, the ward was opened and the use of the somatic therapies decreased. While psychopharmacological agents were used extesively, the use of restraints, electroshock, and insulin had been considerably reduced. Furthermore, the staff had begun to establish formal collaborative relationships with other caretaking agencies and had begun a small school consultation program.

St. Mary-Corwin provides treatment for those types of psychiatric disorders that are most often found in private treatment facilities—acute psychotics, a fairly high percentage of neurotics, and a generally low percentage of alcoholics, organic brain syndromes, and senile disorders.

The greater use of inservice education by professionally trained staff was initiated during this decade, and the roles and responsibilities of the staff have changed considerably. There has been an increasing referral from the community of suicidal patients, psychotics, drug overdoses, and more severe psychiatric disorders. The change in treatment philosophy has been quite marked with the addition of milieu therapy, group psychotherapy, music therapy, and recreational and occupational therapy.

Parkview Episcopal Hospital is a large, general hospital located in the city of Pueblo. It, too, is church affiliated and operates as a nonprofit corporation, providing general medical and surgical services. The total bed capacity is 248. At the beginning of the decade, there was no established psychiatric unit, and psychiatric admissions were limited to emergency "holding" services or were treated on the general medical wards. In 1966, a psychiatric ward with 18 beds was established. It was staffed part-time by a local psychiatrist and full-time by two registered nurses and a varying number of nursing attendants. Later, the unit was moved to another area of the hospital as an 18-bed ward which could be expanded to 24 beds. By 1970, two professional level social workers had been added, along with three psychiatrically trained registered nurses and ten fully trained psychiatric technicians, and an active treatment program was begun. There is no waiting list for admission, although in the last few years the number of admissions has begun to tax the available beds. Spanish-speaking staff members have been added to facilitate the treatment of this minority group, and the professional staff are now making intake visits to the patients' homes and other locations as appropriate.

As a result of the increased subsidy for private treatment, the patient load has changed with a higher percentage of psychiatric treatment of the indigent, minorities, and the lower socioeconomic levels, although the major portion of the patient population is still in the middle-class group. A marked change in the patient population has occurred as a consequence of a structured and active program which was established in the latter part of the decade for adolescents.

Private practitioners were uncommon in the Pueblo area in 1960. Two psychiatrists offered limited service on a part-time basis consisting mostly of a few hours a week of coverage at St. Mary-Corwin Hospital. These psychiatrists were employed full-time either by the public facilities or were providing part-time service in other areas of the state as well. Most of the medical coverage for private psychiatric patients was provided by local physicians whose specialty was in other fields of medicine. Private practice by other mental health professionals was almost nonexistent and consisted of a few hours per week by social workers and psychologists who were employed full-time in the public agencies. The area failed to attract well trained private practitioners, as the vast majority of these mental health professionals preferred to practice in the larger and more economically attractive areas of the state, mainly Denver and its suburbs.

With the changes at the State Hospital already mentioned, and the expansion of the community mental health center, a larger number of mental health professionals came into the community and many then moved into part-time and then full-time private practice. By 1970, there were three full-time and five part-time psychiatrists practicing in the Pueblo area in addition to four psychologists and several social workers who were doing part-time private work.

Supportive Services

There are six district vocational rehabilitation offices located throughout the State of Colorado supported by federal and state funds. The Southern District office is located in Pueblo and its basic purpose is to restore and develop the dormant human resources of the disabled. In 1959, the Colorado General Assembly enacted a ruling which expanded the services to include the psychiatrically disabled. In 1960, the Pueblo office of the agency added one full-time counselor who was to provide services to the psychiatrically disabled.

In 1962, a well equipped and well staffed rehabilitation center was opened on the Colorado State Hospital grounds. The establishment of this center and the increase in staff resulted in a tremendous boost in the provision of this form of supplementary psychiatric services. In 1963, approximately 18 percent of the 1229 clients of the State Vocational Rehabilitation had been psychiatric patients. By 1970, 40 percent of the persons in the state who were receiving rehabilitation services were mentally disabled. As a result of the center being established in Pueblo, a high proportion of Pueblo patients availed themselves of the variety of rehabilitative services that were developed by the center. These services include an evaluation and diagnostic center, a formal school program, a sheltered workshop, and a halfway house.

In the year 1960, the nursing home program in Colorado was in its infancy. Pueblo had only one nursing home with a total of 60 beds. These facilities were used primarily as placements for those needing extensive and ongoing physical care services. There were no adult boarding homes.

In 1962 the Colorado State Hospital began its decentralization program and began placing long-term patients in the community, many of them in nursing homes.

To facilitate these placements, a Supportive Placement Team was established by Colorado State Hospital in 1963 whose purpose was to review the patient load and place those individuals deemed appropriate in nursing and boarding homes throughout Colorado.

The Pueblo Welfare Department assigned a caseworker to the Southern Division in December of 1967, which greatly facilitated cooperation between the two agencies. In January, 1968, the responsibility for the supportive placement program was delegated to each geographic division including the one serving Pueblo.

The increased cooperation between the public welfare department and the Colorado State Hospital resulted in the provision of more follow-up services to released patients living in supportive placement facilities. Teams composed of nursing staff from the Colorado State Hospital and caseworkers from public welfare jointly visited the boarding and nursing homes to provide ongoing services to released Colorado State Hospital patients. This role was expanded to include all residents of the facilities with an emphasis on preventing unnecessary hospitalizations at the Colorado State Hospital.

Diagnostic Services

The two major diagnostic service agencies in Pueblo include the Mental Evaluation Clinic and the Psychology Department of the local school district. Both of these agencies provide diagnosis and evaluation of children's problems.

The Mental Evaluation Clinic provides psychological, physical, social, and neurological evaluation of children for the age group between preschool and nineteen. It is supported by the Department of Health, Education, and Welfare through the State Department of Health. The clinic was established in Pueblo in 1958 with a part-time staff of three professionals: a pediatrician, a neurologist, and a psychologist. In 1970, the staffing pattern had increased to include a full-time social worker and a full-time secretary. The primary services provided include the definitive evaluation of children with suspected mental disability. All of these services are on an outpatient basis. No treatment is done by the clinic, except for some use of chemotherapy where required and counseling with parents. A good deal of consultation is done with the schools and other public and private facilities concerned with children. The major trend in the delivery of this service over the past decade revolves around the screening and evaluation of children at an increasingly early age. Approximately 30 percent of the children seen suffer from some form of prenatal trauma, while about 40 percent have some form of genetically caused mental retardation. The other 30 percent exhibit disorders stemming from emotional or behavioral disturbances. The great majority of the patients come from the lower socioeconomic levels, with a ratio of four boys to one girl.

The Psychology Department of the school district provides psychological diagnostic evaluation for approximately 30,000 students. It is now staffed by four school psychologists, two clerks, and four liaison counselors—in contrast to 1960, when the staff consisted of one psychologist and one clerk.

Referrals are made by local schools, and over the past decade there has been a tremendous increase in their number. By 1970 there was a backlog of nearly 150 referrals, with a waiting list up to four months in length. The socioeconomic level of the clients has remained essentially unchanged—predominantly middle class.

Auxiliary Services

Social Service United is one of the major auxiliary services in the mental health field of Pueblo. In 1960, two separate agencies, Catholic Charities and Family Services, were providing more or less duplicate services including family counseling, individual counseling, and general information and assistance in the area of social functioning. In 1964, these two agencies combined under the auspices of a community board to provide a wide range of general social and family counseling to the Pueblo residents. This agency, Social Services United of Pueblo, is funded locally by the United Fund Agency and by several local charitable organizations.

All of the casework services are on an outpatient basis. Approximately 40% of the counseling done is of a psychotherapeutic nature and includes individual, group, and marital counseling. The clients are primarily from the middle class with fairly sizeable representation of Spanish-surnamed people. The majority of the clients seen for mental health reasons are in the middle-age group and are experiencing problems of family or marital discord. The most significant change within the agency since its formation has been the addition of better trained social workers and the upgrading of staff functioning through inservice education. The combining of two separate agencies into a larger, more efficient, and better staffed agency has resulted in the provision of more adequate services to the community with none of the previous duplication of effort.

Pueblo Mental Health Association, an office of the Colorado Association for Mental Health, Inc., was initiated in 1953 as a citizen nonprofit organization and promotes citizen activity and interest on behalf of the mentally ill. The primary purpose of the organization is to improve public attitudes toward the mentally ill, to improve services for the mentally ill, and to develop programs to prevent mental illness.

In 1958 the association was instrumental in establishing the Pueblo Guidance Center and it has also been a consistent supporter of the Colorado State Hospital.

During the sixties, the organization was very involved in supporting local mental health programs and in 1969 hired a full-time director based in Pueblo for Southern Colorado.

Emerging Services

There have been three new mental health services that have emerged in the Pueblo area over the past decade. They are the Pueblo Suicide Prevention Center, the community drug programs, and the informal establishment of student psychological services for the local college students. These services were established to cope with particular problem trends that had become more and more prominent in the community.

The Suicide Prevention Center was established in early 1968 and was organized by several staff members of the state hospital and a number of volunteers from the community. The center is operated and administered by volunteer mental health professionals and community lay people. It provides twenty-four hour, seven-day-a-week telephone service. Approximately 30 percent of the calls are judged to involve significant suicidal potential. Aside from the direct counseling telephone service, the center also provides an ongoing training program for its volunteer staff. In the two-year period 1968–69, the center handled almost 2000 calls and provided considerable counseling with individuals in crisis and a large number of referrals to other agencies.

Recently, community drug programs have emerged as drug abuse has increased in prevalence. It is estimated that there are between 75 and 200 heroin addicts in Pueblo. The use of the softer drugs has increased in the adolescent and young adult groups as well. As a result of this increase, several programs were initiated in the latter part of the decade in an effort to cope with the problems of drug abuse in the Pueblo area.

The state hospital began two programs for drug abuse problems. A methadone maintenance program was organized in early 1970 for the purpose of providing an outpatient methadone service to the surrounding community, and a drug program was established in the Division of Forensic Psychiatry. Several of the hospital professional staff and a number of lay volunteers from the community began weekly outpatient groups for the younger drug abusers in the community. The local police department, in cooperation with the public schools, began an intensive drug education program for the elementary through high school levels. The joint efforts of the state hospital staff and the local college produced a series of educational television programs devoted to the problems of drug abuse.

When Pueblo Junior College became a four-year college in the early part of the decade, the number of students with emotional problems greatly increased as the college attracted a larger enrollment. In response to this increased need, the psychology department established informal counseling services with a staff composed of faculty members specializing in clinical or counseling psychology. The majority of the students being seen for counseling are freshmen and sophomores with adjustment problems. Those students that have a more severe form of psychiatric disorder are referred to private psychiatrists or to the local mental health clinic.

THE PUEBLO SCENE IN 1970

Options for psychiatric care in 1970 were much less limited than they were in 1960. More money had brought more and better staff to Pueblo and more mental health services were being offered. The two principal differences between 1960 and 1970 are that major mental illness has a far more effective treatment resource at the state hospital and that a far larger network of early case finding and therapeutic services exist throughout the county for less severe emotional disturbances. Four overlapping features of these developments can be noted. First, two new problems arose on the national scene: drug abuse and adolescent rebellion. Although these problems did not reach the same proportions in Pueblo as they did in more metropolitan areas, there was an increase in the prevalence of addiction and adolescent difficulties. Some older problems came to new awareness and received the kind of special attention that resembles the emergence of new categories of treatment. Among these are children's learning disabilities, marital and family discord, and the social oppression and alienation of ethnic minorities.

Second, expansion and specialization of old programs brought increased emphasis and more effective rehabilitation to certain groups such as the alcoholic, the senile, the offender, and the schizophrenic. The benefits of this special attention were a higher rate of return to community living and a foundation of new hope for these groups.

The third developmental feature is the introduction of new policies and approaches in the delivery of psychiatric services. Here we find a deliberate attempt to enlist the patient's cooperation in setting treatment goals and participating in the program, to the end that he may *expect* to resume normal functioning quickly. The old method of dealing with disorders by means of civil court commitment was largely replaced by voluntary admission or short-term involuntary hospitalization. Intensive treatment was then provided through a variety of modalities and support was given the patient on his resumption of normal living patterns. Another aspect of the new approach is that of reaching directly into the neighborhood, the school, and the job in order to make services more accessible and readily accepted.

The fourth feature of the 1960's developments is a new pattern of financing care. Welfare funds and medicare/medicaid contributed to the development of nursing homes as a replacement for the lifetime storage of the aged in hospital back wards. The growth of private health insurance coverage for mental illness contributed to the growth of private psychiatric practice by increasing the number of persons able to purchase private care. And, finally, federal funds provided the people of Pueblo with a new comprehensive community mental health center.

It is evident that the state hospital had a major impact upon the delivery of mental health services in Pueblo. Colorado State Hospital was responsible for establishing the first intensive treatment program for Pueblo's mentally ill; for bringing well trained mental health professionals into the Pueblo community, including those who also worked part-time in other agencies or later went into private practice; for establishing the use of the newer therapeutic approaches to treating mental illness, such as group psychotherapy, the various ancillary therapies, after-care services, day care or partial hospitalization, and training, consultation, and educational services to community care-givers; for the expansion of inservice training programs; and for establishing formalized training programs for mental health nurses, mental health workers, and psychiatric technicians at the Southern Colorado State College.

The Human Services Center on Pueblo's south side represents the local development of a neighborhood-based service delivery system by a comprehensive team. It is the first local attempt to carry out the full concept of a community program in mental health. It is also the first attempt to go beyond mental health professions alone and encompass comprehensive health and welfare services.

Frequent comment is heard in Pueblo that mental illness is losing some of its stigma. The mental health professional now enjoys a much better public image, and is considered more approachable and a more likely source of help for personal difficulties. This movement toward public acceptance of mental illness as a community problem, the improved understanding of mental illness as a common "human" problem without personal shame, and the perception of the mental health professional as a helpful person appear to be interrelated. The changes appear to be due in part to increasing experience of receiving appropriate therapy both quickly and effectively.

But one should not overlook another very basic factor in producing such changes. The tremendous increase in funding of mental health services during the sixties has meant that many more mental health professionals were in contact with the general public than ever before. It has meant new opportunity to discover fellow citizens and neighbors and to replace whatever caricatured misconceptions one might have held before. Perhaps, in the final analysis, the most beneficial result of the new money has been simply to bring people together, providing the opportunity to share what skills and insights they have.

With the possible exception of private sector outpatient services, mental health programs changed so significantly during the decade that they were qualitatively different in 1970 compared with 1960. The state hospital was a custodial faculty in 1960, accepting committed patients and providing extremely limited services, both in terms of amount and variety. As with most state hospitals at that time, the single most therapeutic aspect of the program was that patients were provided a protected setting in which their own restitutive potentials could continue to function, sometimes more effectively than was the case when they were in their own homes. By 1970, as a consequence of the dramatic reduction in numbers of patients and the equally dramatic increases in number of staff combined with the programmatic and geographic decentralization, it was possible to raise the level of treatment, develop an entirely new legal relationship between the hospital and its patients, and begin to view psychopathology in a larger community context. The state hospital in 1970 was, for all practical purposes, not the same institution that it was in 1960. An entirely new relationship was established between the hospital and the communities it served. Entirely new services were established. Not only were there more staff, but they came to the hospital better trained and able to implement a whole series of innovative programs. Morale among patients and staff increased to such an extent that the spirit of the hospital underwent a qualitative change. Both staff and patients were younger, and both brought with them a greater optimism and a greater willingness to experiment with less authoritarian modes of treatment and interaction. Major changes took place in the physical plant, so that the hospital became more attractive, more modern, and more appealing. With these changes and the development and skillful utilization of psychopharmacological agents, the hospital looked less like an institution for chronic deteriorated psychiatric patients than it had in 1960. Interaction with the community, particularly with the Pueblo community, increased. Patients spent less time in the hospital and more time in the city with the advent of day care programs and outpatient programs. Members of the community participated more in intramural programs, and a gradual change began to take place in the attitude of the community to the hospital, its staff, and its patients. In 1960, the state hospital was located in Pueblo, but it was not part of Pueblo. By 1970, the hospital had begun to become an integral part of the Pueblo community.

Public outpatient programs likewise changed in size and in concept, so that they too came to be viewed in an entirely different light. The most visible consequences of the expansion in staff size were, first, the growing ability to provide service when needed in contrast with the prior practice of maintaining a long and forbidding waiting list, and second, the movement of staff into the community by means of a whole network of expanding consultative relationships. Public outpatient programs, of course, were never as psychologically isolated from the community as was the state hospital, but what isolation there was underwent a significant reduction during the decade.

Evidence has been presented to indicate that private inpatient facilities underwent major changes during the decade. New programs were established for groups of patients previously underserved, and enough salaried staff were added so that programs essentially independent of but in collaboration with those instituted by the privately practicing physicians could be developed. Until the addition of new staff, the psychiatric wards in the general hospitals were little more than an administrative convenience for private sector medicine. What special treatment existed was limited to the daily visits of the attending physicians. While patients tended to interact with each other, this interaction was never formalized or deliberately utilized for its therapeutic value. In fact there was the feeling that attending physicians would be uneasy if staff did more than provide traditional nursing services. As new psychiatrists came into Pueblo, there was a greater readiness to exploit the therapeutic potential of the psychiatric ward and programs were developed which depended more on permanent nursing staff and less on the psychiatrists who were present a relatively small proportion of each day. At the same time it became possible for staff to begin limited contact with the greater community by means of home visits and new consultative relationships.

Least of all is known about private sector outpatient services. It is known that such services became increasingly available during the decade, and there is reason to believe that most of the mental health professionals who began full-time or part-time private practice were well trained. Furthermore, since so many of them gained entry into the community by means of their affiliations with public sector programs, much more was known about them than would have been the case had they come into the community directly into private practice. Because these mental health professionals were already known to the community, it was possible for referrals to be made in a more knowledgeable fashion. Little is known about the character of individual private practices and about how this practice may have changed over the decade. The general impression in the community, however, is that most of the private practitioners are competent and ethical. Because of the fact that private practitioners had worked in public agencies, relationships between public and private agencies were probably more cordial and productive than is the case in other communities, and this fact helped maintain the generally positive attitude toward psychiatry which had grown during the decade.

Part II

First Psychiatric Hospitalizations: 1960–1970

4

The Changing Character
of Hospitalized Psychiatric Patients

We have seen that in the decade 1960–1970 vastly increased mental health services became available in Pueblo for potential psychiatric patients. With expanded financial resources and staff in public facilities, expanded and more varied programming became possible. With the arrival of increased numbers of mental health professionals, new private sector services were created, both for inpatients and for outpatients. With the geographic decentralization of the large public hospital it became feasible to inaugurate a new array of services designed to meet the needs of the community of Pueblo. Outpatient and partial hospitalization programs were developed at the state hospital as totally new services. The level of collaboration among services appeared to increase. While our data from the 1960 study dealt only with inpatient facilities, there were, in fact, few outpatient services from which data could have been obtained, and what services did exist were relatively small.

The data which permit us to examine most directly the consequence of an expanded service delivery system consist of information on first-admission inpatients. It is these data which are available for both the 1960 and 1970 study periods and they bear reasonably detailed examination.

1960 FIRST INPATIENT ADMISSIONS

In the three years of data collection for the 1960 study, a total of 919 individuals were identified who had been hospitalized for the first time in their lives for a psychiatric condition. This number represents an annual admission rate of 2.73 cases per 1000 population at risk (see Bloom, 1968). More than 90 percent of these patients were hospitalized in Pueblo.

Admission rates are shown in detail in Tables 4-1 and 4-2 for 1960 and in Tables 4-3 and 4-4 for 1970, specific for age, sex, diagnosis, and type of facility. For persons unaccustomed to viewing the flow of psychiatric patients from the vantage point of the admitting office, the analysis of this data may yield some surprising results. First, in spite of the fact that a very large public inpatient facility was located in the community and private inpatient facilities were few in number and small in size, approximately two-thirds of these patients were hospitalized in private facilities. While public facilities were responsible for providing service to large numbers at any one time, admissions and discharges were relatively infrequent during the 1960 study period. In contrast, private facilities, never serving very many patients at any one particular time, maintained a very rapid movement of patients in and out of their units.

While the overall admission rate was slightly higher for males than for females, this was actually the consequence of the fact that there was a considerably higher admission rate for males than for females into public facilities, and a somewhat higher admission rate for females than for males into private facilities. Of all males hospitalized during the three years of the 1960 study, 40 percent were hospitalized in public facilities. In contrast, of all females hospitalized during this same period of time, only 29 percent were admitted into public facilities.

Table 4-1

INPATIENT FIRST ADMISSIONS AND FIRST ADMISSION RATES BY TYPE OF FACILITY, AGE, AND SEX: 1960 STUDY PERIOD

Age[1]		Type of Facility and Sex									
		Public			Private			Total			
		Male	Female	Total	Male	Female	Total	Male	Female	Total	
Under 21	N[2]	24	6	30	28	30	58	52	36	88	
	R[3]	0.32	0.08	0.20	0.38	0.40	0.39	0.70	0.48	0.59	
21–34	N	31	13	44	54	90	144	85	103	188	
	R	1.13	0.43	0.77	1.98	2.98	2.50	3.11	3.41	3.27	
35–64	N	78	27	105	151	145	296	229	172	401	
	R	1.53	0.52	1.02	2.95	2.78	2.87	4.48	3.30	3.88	
65+	N	56	82	138	48	56	104	104	138	242	
	R	4.40	5.74	5.11	3.77	3.92	3.85	8.17	9.66	8.96	
Total	N	189	128	317	281	321	602	470	449	919	
	R	1.14	0.75	0.94	1.69	1.87	1.79	2.83	2.62	2.73	

[1] Population at risk: Male—Under 21 = 24890; 21-34 = 9111; 35-64 = 17037; 65+ = 4242; Total = 55280
Female—Under 21 = 24913; 21-34 = 10069; 35-64 = 17378; 65+ = 4764; Total = 57124
Total—Under 21 = 49803; 21-34 = 19180; 35-64 = 34415; 65+ = 9006; Total = 112404

[2] Three-year total
[3] Annual admission rate per 1000 population at risk

Table 4-2

INPATIENT FIRST ADMISSIONS AND FIRST ADMISSION RATES BY TYPE OF FACILITY, DIAGNOSIS, AND SEX: 1960 STUDY PERIOD

Diagnosis[1]		Type of Facility and Sex								
		Public			Private			Total		
		Male	Female	Total	Male	Female	Total	Male	Female	Total
Psychoneuroses	N[2]	17	7	24	82	195	277	99	202	301
	R[3]	0.10	0.04	0.07	0.49	1.14	0.82	0.60	1.18	0.89
Personality Disorders	N	80	17	97	128	37	165	208	54	262
	R	0.48	0.10	0.29	0.77	0.22	0.49	1.25	0.32	0.78
Functional Psychoses	N	21	15	36	22	51	73	43	66	109
	R	0.13	0.09	0.11	0.13	0.30	0.22	0.26	0.39	0.32
Brain Syndromes	N	71	89	160	49	38	87	120	127	247
	R	0.43	0.52	0.47	0.30	0.22	0.26	0.72	0.74	0.73
Total	N	189	128	317	281	321	602	470	449	919
	R	1.14	0.75	0.94	1.69	1.87	1.79	2.83	2.62	2.73

[1] Population at risk: Male = 55280; Female = 57124; Total = 112404
[2] Three-Year Total
[3] Annual admission rate per 1000 population at risk

124

Table 4-3

INPATIENT FIRST ADMISSIONS AND FIRST ADMISSION RATES BY TYPE OF FACILITY, AGE, AND SEX: 1970 STUDY PERIOD

Age[1]		Type of Facility and Sex									
		Public			Private			Total			
		Male	Female	Total	Male	Female	Total	Male	Female	Total	
Under 21	N[2]	39	21	60	74	130	204	113	151	264	
	R[3]	0.78	0.43	0.61	1.49	2.68	2.07	2.27	3.11	2.68	
21-34	N	77	20	97	72	112	184	149	132	281	
	R	4.18	1.00	2.52	3.91	5.59	4.78	8.08	6.59	7.30	
35-64	N	98	33	131	131	200	331	229	233	462	
	R	2.73	0.86	1.77	3.65	5.24	4.47	6.38	6.10	6.24	
65+	N	25	19	44	22	46	68	47	65	112	
	R	2.65	1.57	2.05	2.33	3.80	3.16	4.99	5.38	5.21	
Total	N	239	93	332	299	488	787	538	581	1119	
	R	2.10	0.78	1.43	2.63	4.11	3.39	4.74	4.89	4.81	

[1] Population at risk: Male—Under 21 = 24917; 21-34 = 9218; 35-64 = 17951; 65+ = 4713; Total = 56799
Female—Under 21 = 24286; 21-34 = 10020; 35-64 = 19093; 65+ = 6046; Total = 59445
Total—Under 21 = 49203; 21-34 = 19238; 35-64 = 37044; 65+ = 10759; Total = 116244

[2] Two-year total
[3] Annual admission rate per 1000 population at risk

Table 4-4

INPATIENT FIRST ADMISSIONS AND FIRST ADMISSION RATES BY TYPE OF FACILITY, DIAGNOSIS, AND SEX: 1970 STUDY PERIOD

Diagnosis[1]		Type of Facility and Sex								
		Public			Private			Total		
		Male	Female	Total	Male	Female	Total	Male	Female	Total
Psychoneuroses	N[2]	33	24	57	157	366	523	190	390	580
	R[3]	0.29	0.20	0.25	1.38	3.08	2.25	1.67	3.28	2.50
Personality Disorders	N	169	37	206	101	43	144	270	80	350
	R	1.49	1.31	0.89	0.89	0.36	0.62	2.38	0.67	1.51
Functional Psychoses	N	17	9	26	19	36	55	36	45	81
	R	0.15	0.08	0.11	0.17	0.30	0.24	0.32	0.38	0.35
Brain Syndromes	N	20	23	43	22	43	65	42	66	108
	R	0.18	0.19	0.19	0.19	0.36	0.28	0.37	0.56	0.47
Total	N	239	93	332	299	488	787	538	581	1119
	R	2.10	0.78	1.43	2.63	4.11	3.39	4.74	4.89	4.81

[1] Population at risk: Male = 56799; Female = 59443; Total = 116244
[2] Two-year total
[3] Annual admission rate per 1000 population at risk

126

Thus, whether a person was admitted to a public or private facility was, in part, a function of his sex. As will be seen, however, the likelihood of being hospitalized in a private facility is also related to age and diagnosis.

In the 1960 study, private facilities admitted approximately two-thirds of patients under the age of 21, 77 percent of patients between the ages of 21 and 35, 74 percent of patients between the ages of 35 and 64, but only 43 percent of patients aged 65 and above. Of all patients with diagnoses of psychoneuroses or psychosomatic disorders, 92 percent were hospitalized in private facilities; of patients with the diagnosis of personality disorders, 63 percent were hospitalized in private facilities; of patients with the diagnosis of functional psychoses, 69 percent were hospitalized in private facilities; and of patients with the diagnosis of acute or chronic brain syndromes, 36 percent were hospitalized in private facilities. Thus, not only did women in general have a greater likelihood of being hospitalized in private rather than public facilities, but so did the young and those with what are traditionally thought of as non organic conditions. In 1960 the elderly psychiatric patient, typically with a diagnosis of some type of brain syndrome, had a far more likely chance of being hospitalized in a public facility than did younger patients.

In 1960, admission rate increased with age, being less than one case per thousand in the under-21 age group, between three and four cases per thousand in the 21-64 age group, and nearly nine per thousand in the age 65 and above group. This generally increasing admission rate with age characterized both sexes, and was found in private as well as public facilities. Regarding diagnosis, what might be most surprising is the fact that the most common diagnosis of hospitalized psychiatric patients is in the mildest category—psychoneurosis and psychosomatic disorder. Of all patients admitted to inpatient facilities during the 1960 study, nearly 33 percent were given this diagnosis. Patients with personality disorders constituted another 29 percent, patients with acute or chronic brain syndromes 27 percent, and less than 12 percent of patients were given diagnoses of functional psychoses. This distribution of diagnoses stands in sharp contrast to the experiences one would have if visiting the wards of a typical public or private psychiatric hospital. Here one would get the distinct impression that a very large proportion of patients was psychotic. Patients with functional psychoses typically have the longest hospital stays (see Chapter 9) and thus accumulate on hospital wards, giving the erroneous impression that most patients admitted into psychiatric facilities are psychotic. The facts are quite the opposite.

In 1960, while males and females had approximately the same admission rate for acute or chronic brain syndromes and for functional psychoses, diagnoses of psychoneuroses were twice as common for females as for males, and diagnoses of personality disorders were four times as common for males as for females. While psychoneuroses and psychosomatic disorders constituted less than eight percent of admissions into public facilities, such patients constituted nearly 46 percent of admissions into private facilities. In contrast, while patients with acute or chronic brain syndromes constitute less than 15 percent of admissions into private facilities, they made up virtually half of the admissions into public facilities.

1970 FIRST INPATIENT ADMISSIONS

So much for the pattern of first inpatient admissions for the 1960 study period. During the two years of the 1970 study, a total of 1119 individuals were hospitalized for the first time in their lives with a psychiatric diagnosis, representing an annual admission rate of 4.81 cases per 1000 population at risk, substantially higher than the 1960 rate. The increased availability of outpatient services clearly did not result in a reduction of admissions into inpatient facilities. Of these 1119 patients, 70 percent were hospitalized in private facilities and 30 percent in public facilities. Total admission rates were very similar for males and females, but there was a sharp differentiation by sex as to type of facility where treatment took place. While 55 percent of males were hospitalized in private facilities, 85 percent of females were hospitalized in private facilities.

Private facilities in 1970 admitted nearly 78 percent of all patients under 21, 66 percent of all patients between ages 21 and 34, 72 percent of all patients ages 35-64, and 61 percent of all patients aged 65 and above. Of all patients given a diagnosis of psychoneurosis or psychosomatic disorder, 90 percent were hospitalized in private facilities; of patients with personality disorders, 41 percent were hospitalized in private facilities; of patients with functional psychoses, 69 percent were hospitalized in private facilities; and of patients diagnosed as acute or chronic brain syndromes, 61 percent were hospitalized in private facilities. Thus, during the 1970 study period, women were far more likely than men to be admitted to private facilities for care, age seemed to play relatively little role in determining the type of facility to which patients were admitted, and patients with personality disorders were far less likely than patients with any other diagnosis to be admitted into private facilities.

During the 1970 study period, admission rate was related to age in a two step fashion. The admission rate for patients under age 21 was lower than for any other age group, and it doubled in the age group 21-34 and remained relatively stable through age 35-64, dropping slightly in the age 65 and above group. The age-related admission rates pattern was stable for both sexes and for both public and private inpatient facilities. As for the relation of admission rate to diagnosis, the mildest condition, psychoneurosis and psychosomatic disorder, again included the largest number of patients, making up 52 percent of all first admissions. Personality disorders constituted 31 percent of all cases; patients given a diagnosis of functional psychosis made up seven percent of all the cases, and patients with acute or chronic brain syndromes made up the remaining ten percent.

While admission rate for functional psychosis was similar in men as in women, in all other diagnostic categories there were again substantial sex differences in diagnosis in 1970. The admission rate with the diagnosis of psychoneurosis and psychosomatic disorder was twice as high for women as for men, while the admission rate for personality disorders was nearly four times as high for men as for women. As for the diagnosis of acute or chronic brain syndrome, admission rates for women were nearly twice as high as admission rates for men. Psychoneurotics and patients with psychosomatic disorders constituted 66 percent of admissions into private facilities but only 17 percent of admissions into public facilities. In contrast, patients with personality disorders constituted 62 percent of admissions into public facilities but only 18 percent of admissions into private facilities.

CONTRASTING 1960 and 1970 STUDY PERIODS

Regarding the statistical significance of the differences of various admission rates between 1960 and 1970, a conservative rule to follow in examining the data in Tables 4-1 through 4-4 is that differences approaching one case per thousand are significant. The difference in total first-admission rate between 1960 and 1970 (2.73 versus 4.81) is more than eight times its standard error. The difference in first admission rate in the 35-64 age group between the two study periods (1.02 versus 1.77) is more than two and one-half times its standard error. By contrast, the difference in first admission rate for functional psychosis between the two study periods (0.32 versus 0.35) is not statistically significant. Following this one case per thousand general rule, it can be seen that each age-specific admission rate for the total population changed significantly between the two study periods (increasing significantly in all age groups below 65 and decreasing significantly in the age group 65 and above).

Regarding diagnosis-specific first admission rates, the increases in the case of the psychoneuroses and personality disorders were statistically significant. Differences in the inner cells of the parallel tables may be similarly interpreted.

Striking similarities and dissimilarities are thus seen when the pattern of first inpatient admissions for 1960 is contrasted with 1970. First, the total first admission rate rose from 2.73 per 1000 to 4.81 per thousand, representing a 76 percent increase. Female admission rate increased more than male (87 percent vs. 68 percent), and private admission rate increased more than public (89 percent vs. 52 percent). That these changes in admission rates by sex and by type of agency should have occurred in this specific pattern is not surprising given that the chances of being treated in a private facility are substantially better for females than for males.

This overall admission rate increase is not constant across the various age groups or across diagnoses. Regarding age, the increase is greatest in the youngest age group and gets smaller with increasing age. The admission rate for patients under 21 years of age increased by more than 400 percent between 1960 and 1970; for the age group 21-34 the admission rate doubled; in the age group 35-64 the admission rate increased by only 60 percent; and in the group age 65 and above, the admission rate actually decreased—by 43 percent. For patients with the diagnoses of psychoneuroses and related relatively mild disorders, the admission rate nearly tripled; patients with personality disorders nearly doubled in number; the admission rate for patients with functional psychoses remained unchanged; and there was a decrease of 37 percent in the admission rate for patients with a diagnosis of acute or chronic brain syndrome. These two patterns of change in admission rate, by age and by diagnosis, are obviously related, since there is a close relationship between age and diagnosis, the diagnosis of acute or chronic brain syndrome being restricted largely to patients age 65 and above.

In examining the changes in the two sexes separately, it can be seen that the increase in admission rate between 1960 and 1970 in the under-21 age group is substantially higher for females than for males and in the 21-34 age group the increase in admission rate is somewhat higher for males than for females. While there are no substantial differences in the patterning of admission rates by diagnosis, it is noteworthy that while in 1960 the majority of patients with personality disorders were admitted into private inpatient facilities, in 1970 the majority were admitted into public inpatient facilities. In contrast, while in 1960 most patients with acute and chronic brain syndromes (and most patients over age 65) were admitted into public facilities, in 1970 it was the private inpatient facility which admitted such patients in greatest numbers.

The distribution by diagnosis within each of the four age categories is presented in Table 4-5 and indicates a generally stable pattern in the two study periods. The only major shift occurs in the under-21 age group, where

Table 4-5

DISTRIBUTION OF DIAGNOSES WITHIN AGE GROUPS: FIRST INPATIENT ADMISSIONS, 1960 AND 1970 STUDY PERIODS

Study Period and Diagnosis	Under 21		21-34		35-64		65+		Total	
	N	%	N	%	N	%	N	%	N	%
1960										
Psychoneuroses	36	40.9	96	51.1	150	37.4	19	7.9	301	32.8
Personality Disorders	27	30.7	48	25.5	172	42.9	15	6.2	262	28.5
Functional Psychoses	18	20.5	35	18.6	49	12.2	7	2.9	109	11.9
Brain Syndromes	7	8.0	9	4.8	30	7.5	201	83.1	247	26.9
Total	88	100.1	188	100.0	401	100.0	242	100.1	919	100.1
1970										
Psychoneuroses	181	68.6	159	56.6	226	48.9	14	12.5	580	51.8
Personality Disorders	65	24.6	97	34.5	174	37.7	14	12.5	350	31.3
Functional Psychoses	15	5.7	20	7.1	41	8.9	5	4.5	81	7.3
Brain Syndromes	3	1.1	5	1.8	21	4.5	79	70.5	108	9.7
Total	264	100.0	281	100.0	462	100.0	112	100.0	1119	100.1

the diagnosis of psychoneurosis or psychosomatic disorder was given in 41 percent of the cases in 1960 and in 69 percent of the cases in 1970. Since it is in the under-21 age group that the greatest increase in admission rate occurred between the two study periods, this suggests that the largest portion of that increase can be attributed to young people who, being admitted into psychiatric inpatient facilities, received the diagnosis of psychoneurosis, psychosomatic disorder, or transient situational reactions of childhood or adolescence. In all other age groups distribution of diagnosis seems within the same general range when the two study periods are contrasted.

As can be seen from Table 4-6, where age-specific admission rates are shown for each of the major diagnostic groupings, admission rates for psychoneuroses peaked in the 21-34 age group both in 1960 and 1970. Admission rates for patients with personality disorders were highest in the 35-64 age group in 1960, but during the 1970 study period enough younger patients were given the personality disorder diagnosis so that the age group 21-34 had the highest admission rate. As for functional psychoses, admission rates are not high in any age category, and perhaps the most prudent interpretation of the data is that admission rates are higher during the adult years than during the years either of childhood or senescence. Admission rates for brain syndromes, of course, are extremely low below age 65 and relatively high in the 65 and above age group.

What has occurred, then, with regard to first-admission rates into inpatient facilities between 1960 and 1970 has been a sharp but nonuniform increase, surely not due to an increase in the incidence or severity of mental disorders in the community. Rather these increases seem most likely due to increases in the availability and variety of mental health services and to the fact that attitudes

Table 4-6

ANNUAL AGE-SPECIFIC ADMISSION RATES PER 1000 POPULATION AT RISK BY DIAGNOSIS, TOTAL FIRST INPATIENT ADMISSIONS: 1960 AND 1970

Diagnosis	1960 Age Group				1970 Age Group			
	Under 21	21–34	35–64	65 +	Under 21	21–34	35–64	65 +
Psychoneuroses	0.24	1.67	1.45	0.71	1.84	4.13	3.05	0.65
Personality Disorders	0.18	0.83	1.67	0.56	0.66	2.52	2.35	0.65
Functional Psychoses	0.12	0.61	0.47	0.26	0.15	0.52	0.56	0.23
Brain Syndromes	0.05	0.16	0.29	7.45	0.03	0.13	0.28	3.67

toward mental illnesses and the "image" of the service delivery system have both improved during this decade as well.

Regarding admission rates during the two study periods, the following findings seem most noteworthy by way of summary. First, there has been a major increase in admission rate in general but this is actually attributable to a sharp increase in admissions with the diagnosis of psychoneuroses or psychosomatic disorder and to a lesser extent to the diagnosis of personality disorder. Similarly, the general increase seems due primarily to an increased admission rate in the under-21 age group and, to a lesser extent, in the 21-34 age group. In point of fact, admission rates for functional psychoses have remained stable and admission rates for acute or chronic brain syndromes and for persons aged 65 and above have actually decreased. There has been a particularly striking increase in the admission rate of persons under 21 given the diagnosis of psychoneurosis. In 1960, only 12 such cases were hospitalized per year. In 1970, 90 cases in this age-diagnostic category were hospitalized each year.

During both study periods, about two-thirds of all patients were admitted into private facilities, and this proportion was generally higher in females and lower in males. Not only did private facilities serve a stable proportion of patients in total and by sex, but equally stable were the proportion of patients in each age category below age 65 served by private facilities and the proportion of patients diagnosed psychoneurotic or functional psychotic. Furthermore, there was notable stability in the general relationship of sex and diagnosis. Admission rate for psychoneuroses was twice as high for females as for males in both study periods, and admission rate for personality disorders was four times as high for males as for females in both study periods. The changes between 1960 and 1970 beside those already mentioned relate to the site of treatment for patients with personality disorders and with acute or chronic brain syndromes. The former patients, treated primarily in private settings in 1960 were, in 1970, treated primarily in public settings. Exactly the opposite was true in the case of patients diagnosed as having acute or chronic brain syndromes.

Because inpatient first-admission rates were calculated for each census tract both for 1960 and 1970, it is possible to determine whether there has been a more or less generalized increase across the entire city by correlating the various admission rates across census tracts for these two time periods. The correlational analysis (nonsignificant correlations are shown as blanks) presented in Table 4-7 show that while in general those census tracts providing large numbers of patients in 1960 did so again in 1970, the situation is by no means uniform. First, there is much greater consistency regarding public facil-

Table 4-7

CORRELATIONS BETWEEN 1960 AND 1970 INPATIENT FIRST ADMISSION
RATES

	Male	Female	Total
Age Group			
Under 21			
21–34			
35–64	+0.57	+0.61	+0.76
65 and Above			
Diagnostic Group			
Psychoneuroses			
Personality Disorders	+0.76	+0.67	+0.86
Functional Psychoses			
Acute or Chronic			
Brain Syndromes	+0.39		+0.40
Age-Adjusted Rates			
Public Facilities			+0.75
Private Facilities			+0.43
Total			+0.65

ity admissions than private facility admissions, and second, it is really only the age group 35-64 and the personality disorder diagnosis that significantly contribute to this uniformity.

Total age-adjusted admission rates in the Pueblo census tracts in 1960 ranged from a low of zero to a high of 5.88 cases per 1000 population at risk per year. Across the 33 census tracts, the range for age-adjusted public facility admission rates was from a low of zero to a high of 3.53 cases per 1000 and for private facility admissions from a low of zero to a high of 3.90 cases per 1000. One census tract, a rural area with a total population of only 828 persons, admitted no patients into either public or private facilities. In terms of the average admission rate in the county, one would have expected only two or perhaps three cases, and thus the absence of cases is not sufficiently remarkable to justify special attention.

The correlation between public and private admission rates in 1960 was not significantly different from zero ($r = +0.21$). Of the 11 census tracts with the lowest admission rates into public facilities, only three are among the tracts with the lowest admission rates into private facilities, while four are among the 11 tracts with the highest admission rates into private facilities. Of the 11 census tracts with the highest admission rates into public facilities, only three are among the 11 tracts with the highest admission rates into private facilities, while six are included among the 11 tracts with the lowest private facility admission rates. Thus, in 1960 it would not have been possible to predict private facility admission rates knowing public facility admission rates.

Total age-adjusted admission rates in 1970 ranged from a low of zero to a high of 13.18 cases per 1000 per year. The range was from zero to 6.29 for public agency admissions, and from zero to 6.88 for private facility admissions. The census tract from which no patients came in 1960 again produced no cases in 1970, although since by 1970 its total population was only 624, the absence of patients is still within expected limits.

The correlation of public and private age-adjusted admission rates, insignificant in 1960, was significant in 1970 ($r = +0.41$), although the relationship was still not very close. Three of the census tracts with the lowest public facility admission rates were among the tracts with the highest private facility admission rates, and three of the tracts with highest public admission rates were among the tracts with the lowest private facility admission rates.

It has already been noted that total age-adjusted admission rates have a relatively high degree of similarity between 1960 and 1970, but there are some exceptions. Two census tracts, highest in total age-adjusted admission rate in 1960, were among the census tracts with the lowest total admission rates in 1970, and two other tracts, lowest in total age-adjusted admission rates in 1960, were among the highest in 1970. Similar changes between 1960 and 1970 took place in two census tracts with respect to public facility age-adjusted admission rates and in seven census tracts with respect to private facility admission rates.

Thus, as inpatient mental health service facilities expanded their capacity to serve the community, they apparently had little difficulty attracting a larger clientele. Since, in 1970, there were no waiting lists at any facility, we have some reason to believe that most persons seeking help found some place where help was available and that there is little need for further expansion of inpatient services. By implication, large numbers of persons needing inpatient care in 1960, at least by 1970 standards, were unable to be served. Since little in the way of outpatient services was available in 1960, it means that these persons, if served at all, became part of a nonpsychiatric service delivery system. Given this general finding, the lack of change of admission rate for persons diagnosed as functional psychotics and the reduction of admission rate for the elderly are especially noteworthy.

The annual admission rate for functional psychotics was 32 cases per 100,000 population in 1960 and 35 cases per 100,000 population in 1970. Virtually all of these patients were classified as schizophrenics, the avoidance of the diagnosis manic–depressive psychosis in the United States being well-known (see Cooper *et al.*, 1969). If we contrast these admission rates with those reported in the literature for schizophrenia, the general similarity is striking (see Dunham, 1965, pp. 20ff). Not only are the reported incidence (first-admission) rates remarkably constant, but the magnitude of the rates is very comparable to those found at two different points of time in Pueblo. Annual incidence rates for schizophrenia were found to be 32 per 100,000 in Chicago in 1931-33 (See Faris and Dunham, 1939), 47 per 100,000 in Baltimore in 1933 (See Cohen and Fairbank, 1938), 30 per 100,000 in New York State in 1935 (see Malzberg, 1940), 30 per 100,000 in New Haven in 1950 (See Hollingshead and Redlich, 1958), 35 per 100,000 in Texas in 1951-52 (see Jaco, 1957), 19 per 100,000 in Hagerstown, Maryland during the period 1940-1952 (see Clausen and Kohn, 1959) and 28.5 per 100,000 in Chicago in 1961 (see Levy and Rowitz, 1973). The close agreement between the Pueblo figures and those reported in the literature affords us a measure of confidence in the representativeness of our data and underlines the comment made earlier that the first-admission rate increase between 1960 and 1970 is not due to any general increase in incidence.

As to the decreased admission rate for elderly psychiatric patients into inpatient facilities, we are undoubtedly seeing the consequences of the federal Medicare legislation which allows persons aged 65 and above who require hospitalization to receive that care in private or general hospitals without regard to their financial resources or to diagnosis. No such legislation existed during the 1960 study period, and elderly persons requiring hospitalization who were unable to pay for such care often had little alternative other than to use the public psychiatric facility in their community. Once admitted to such a facility, the administrative pressures to provide a psychiatric primary diagnosis were surely operative, even though nonpsychiatric difficulties might also have been present. We have seen in our own data that patients aged 65 or older with psychiatric diagnoses are treated much more commonly in private than in public facilities in 1970 while the opposite was true in 1960. Furthermore, general hospitals have no reason to ascribe psychiatric diagnoses, and when elderly patients are admitted they can be given primary physical diagnoses.

The number of patients aged 65 and above admitted to general hospitals has increased dramatically between 1960 and 1970. During the 1960 study period, the two general hospitals in Pueblo admitted 3145 patients annually in this age category. In contrast, during the 1970 study period these same two hospitals admitted 5128 patients annually, most without psychiatric diagnoses. Many of the patients admitted to general hospitals in 1970, regardless of diagnosis, would have been hospitalized in public psychiatric facilities in 1960 where they would have carried psychiatric diagnoses.

The increase in admissions of young people into psychiatric inpatient facilities noted during the decade in Pueblo is part of a similar nationwide trend (see Kramer, 1967). The lack of availability of inpatient services for young people in need of psychiatric care has long been felt in the United States, and we see in Pueblo the growing provision of inpatient services for this age group in both public as well as private facilities. As can be seen from the Pueblo data, virtually all of this increased service capacity has been utilized by young persons whose psychiatric conditions are relatively mild—transient situational reactions, psychoneuroses, and personality disorders. Inpatient services were apparently available in 1960 for more severe conditions, since no increase in admissions of young persons with diagnoses of functional psychoses or brain syndromes was noted.

Thus, the network of inpatient services had a considerably finer mesh in 1970 than in 1960. Large numbers of mildly disturbed potential patients slipped through it in 1960 but were captured in 1970. In contrast, the more seriously disturbed were not identified in any greater frequency in 1970 than in 1960. It is entirely possible that this change documents a serious defect in the 1960 inpatient service system—not enough capacity to hospitalize patients in need of that kind of care and protected environment which characterizes the psychiatric ward. It is equally possible that the increased availability of inpatient services resulted in a lowered threshold for determining eligibility and appropriateness of hospitalization in 1970. And the extraordinary increase in first psychiatric hospitalizations for young, relatively mildly disturbed individuals raises the possibility that the threshold for hospitalization could have been lowered further than the amount solely dictated by clinical needs. Our data is not responsive to the question, but overutilization of hospital facilities is an issue which might well be explored in interpreting the increase in admission rate identified across the decade. It is difficult to assert that hospitalization was the treatment of choice in all cases in 1970 without raising the question of how hospitalization was apparently successfully avoided in many cases in 1960.

There is no evidence that the "true" incidence of psychoneuroses and personality disorders increased dramatically during the decade, with the possible exception of problems associated with drug abuse. The appearance of this problem during the decade in Pueblo was noted in the previous chapter. But during the 1970 study, only 54 cases associated with drug abuse were hospitalized, far short of the number which might satisfactorily account for the increased admission rate noted. Of these 54 cases, only 25 were patients less than 21 years old, and it is in this youngest age group that the greatest increase in admission rate took place. We are drawn to conclude, therefore, that many young people were hospitalized in 1970 who would not have been hospitalized in 1960 and are raising the question as to what extent this phenomenon necessarily constitutes an improvement in the mental health service delivery system. As Denner and Price have recently stated, "It should be recognized that the community mental health movement is not merely reaching out to clients who have passed their days on waiting lists. The movement has the potential of artificially creating whole new caseloads by transforming the status of large numbers of people" [1973, p. 9; see also Sarbin, 1970]. Perhaps additional study by means of utilization review techniques will provide an approach to resolving this issue.

Both public and private inpatient facilities exhibited a marked increase in admission rates between 1960 and 1970. But while those sections of the city which yielded large numbers of patients into public facilities in 1960 continued to do so in 1970, much less similarity was noted for private facility admissions. There has been a substantial change in which specific census tracts provide private facilities with their first inpatient admissions. Since there has been little significant change in the character of individual census tracts, it is unlikely that patients are continuing to come from the same kinds of neighborhoods. Rather, a different type of patient was apparently being treated in private inpatient units in 1970 as contrasted with 1960.

It is this general problem that we turn to next. What are the characteristics of the census tracts from which come excess numbers of first admission inpatients, and how similar were these characteristics between 1960 and 1970?

5

Admission Rates and Neighborhood Characteristics

Having examined first inpatient admission rates for the two study periods and noted their relationships to age, sex, diagnosis, and type of facility, we can now turn to the linkages between neighborhood characteristics and admission rates. That is, we can now explore the question of what kinds of census tracts yield what kinds of patients. As can be seen from Table 5-1, diagnosis-specific admission rates across census tracts tend to be quite unrelated to each other, not only between the two study periods but within each study period as well. In fact, the 1970 admission rate for functional psychoses is

Table 5-1

SIGNIFICANT INTERCORRELATIONS AMONG DIAGNOSIS-SPECIFIC
TOTAL FIRST INPATIENT ADMISSION RATES: 1960 AND 1970

		1960				1970		
Admission Rate		PN	PD	FP	ACBS	PN	PD	FP
1. 1960 Psychoneuroses								
2. 1960 Personality Disorders								
3. 1960 Functional Psychoses		+.37	+.56					
4. 1960 Brain Syndromes			+.59	+.61				
5. 1970 Psychoneuroses			+.45					
6. 1970 Personality Disorders			+.86	+.57	+.44			
7. 1970 Functional Psychoses								
8. 1970 Brain Syndromes				+.36	+.40			

145

Table 5-2

SIGNIFICANT INTERCORRELATIONS OF MALE WITH FEMALE
ADMISSION RATES: 1960 AND 1970 STUDY PERIODS

Admission Rate	1960			1970		
	Public	Private	Total	Public	Private	Total
Psychoneuroses						
Personality Disorders	+.72	+.58	+.69	+.86		+.72
Functional Psychoses						
Brain Syndromes	+.37				+.36	
Under 21 years old						
21–34 years old	+.56			+.45	+.41	+.55
35–64 years old		+.36		+.53		+.58
65 and above						

not significantly related to any other diagnosis-specific
admission rate for either study period, and all 1970 diagnosis-specific admission rates are independent of each
other. It is possible to calculate a total age-adjusted first
inpatient admission rate for each census tract, and this
figure is useful in indexing the total rate of psychiatric
service provided by inpatient facilities to residents of a
specified census tract, but the proportion of that volume
made up by each of the four diagnostic groups is clearly
quite variable. Thus, we should not be surprised to learn
that census tract characteristics associated with a high
rate of admissions from a specific diagnostic group are
substantially different from census tract characteristics
associated with a high rate of admissions from another
diagnostic group.

Furthermore, as shown in Table 5-2, with the exception of personality disorders, there is relatively little consistency between male and female admission rates either
by diagnosis or by age. That is, knowing the admission
rate of males with the diagnosis of psychoneurosis, for

example, in each census tract would not allow us to predict what the admission rate for females with the same diagnosis might be. Therefore, census tract characteristics associated with male psychoneuroses admission rates might have a considerably different pattern when compared with census tract characteristics associated with female psychoneuroses admission rates. Accordingly, it will be useful to contrast the two sexes in terms of census tract characteristics associated with diagnosis- and age-specific admission rates.

Census Tract Characteristics and Admission Rates

In order to simplify data presentation regarding the associations of census tract characteristics with admission rates, we will deal entirely with census tract cluster scores. It will be remembered that 26 of the 35 census tract characteristics are included in one or another of the three cluster scores, leaving nine variables sufficiently independent of clusters to justify their separate consideration. Of the nine variables, only three are often enough significantly correlated with census tract admission rates to require examination: foreign-born, YMCA members, and housing units lacking plumbing. The other six variables (total population, fertility ratio, residential stability, suicide rate, nursing visits, and sex ratio) are rarely if ever significantly correlated with census tract admission rates.

As regards the three census tract variables not included in cluster scores which are significantly correlated with admission rates, foreign-born (the proportion of census tract residents born outside of the United States) is invariably positively correlated with each admission rate with which it is significantly correlated; that is, admission rates are higher in those census tracts where there is a relatively large proportion of foreign-born. As to why foreign born is not part of any cluster of variables, the reason is that it is unrelated to socioeconomic affluence and lies midway between the social disequilibrium cluster (with which it is correlated +.45 in the 1960 data and +0.50 in the 1970 data) and the young marrieds cluster (with which it is correlated −0.45 in the 1960 data and −0.54 in the 1970 data). That is, it is not unequivocally enough related to either of the two clusters to justify its being included as part of that cluster.

As for YMCA members and the proportion of housing units lacking complete plumbing facilities, these two variables can be considered part of the socioeconomic affluence cluster. Both were extremely closely related to this cluster in 1960 (+0.84 for YMCA members and −0.82 for lacking plumbing) but failed to be included as definers of the cluster because these correlations were substantially smaller in 1970 (+0.47 for YMCA members and −0.49 for lacking plumbing). Thus while neither variable qualified as part of any cluster score, because of the stringent requirements utilized in establishing clusters, we will learn little from examining these variables individually that we do not learn by examining the socioeconomic affluence cluster score.

Results of the analysis of admission rates and census tract cluster scores are presented in Table 5-3. Correlations are shown by sex for total admission rates as well as for admission rates into public and private facilities separately and this information is provided for 1960 as well as for 1970. A correlation coefficient of 0.34 is significantly different from zero at the 0.05 level of confidence. Correlations below this level are indicated as blanks in the table. Even though there are many blanks in the table, the number of significant correlation coefficients is nearly six times as high as would be expected by chance.

Table 5-3

CORRELATIONS OF FIRST INPATIENT ADMISSION RATES WITH CENSUS TRACT CLUSTER SCORES BY TYPE OF FACILITY, SEX, AND STUDY PERIOD

Admission Rate, Sex and Study Period			Socioeconomic Affluence			Social Disequilibrium			Young Marrieds		
			Public	Private	Total	Public	Private	Total	Public	Private	Total
Total Age-Adjusted	1960		-.35	+.38		+.65	+.36	+.64		-.41	-.38
	1970		-.56		-.40	+.78	+.49	+.76			-.43
Psychoneuroses	1960	Total		+.54	+.50	+.40			-.42	-.39	-.43
		Male		+.41	+.32	+.54					
		Female		+.46	+.45					-.46	-.47
	1970	Total									
		Male									
		Female									
Personality Disorders	1960	Total	-.34			+.87	+.62	+.84	-.42	-.46	-.51
		Male	-.34			+.87	+.54	+.80	-.40	-.43	-.48
		Female				+.70	+.60	+.74	-.42	-.42	-.48
	1970	Total	-.50		-.51	+.77	+.57	+.83			-.38
		Male	-.54	-.37	-.57	+.80	+.65	+.87		-.35	-.34
		Female				+.65		+.58			-.44

Table 5-3 (cont'd)

Admission Rate, Sex and Study Period		Socioeconomic Affluence			Social Disequilibrium			Young Marrieds		
		Public	Private	Total	Public	Private	Total	Public	Private	Total
Functional Psychoses										
1960	Total				+.51	+.44	+.55	-.44	-.39	-.49
	Male				+.63	+.53	+.69	-.47		
	Female								-.42	-.39
1970	Total	-.37			+.53		+.38			
	Male				+.55					
	Female									
Brain Syndromes										
1960	Total				+.54	+.41	+.60	-.38	-.50	-.51
	Male				+.48	+.39	+.53		-.39	-.38
	Female				+.39		+.42		-.42	-.44
1970	Total				+.42	+.41	+.49	-.41	-.43	-.49
	Male		+.41		+.41	+.48	+.54		-.42	-.46
	Female									
Under Age 21										
1960	Total	-.37			+.66		+.46			-.39
	Male	-.34			+.61		+.60			
	Female									
1970	Total					+.49	+.48		-.45	-.48
	Male									
	Female					+.50	+.54			-.34

150

Age 21-34	1960	Total	-.36		+.46		+.59			
		Male			+.49		+.59			-.37
		Female					+.42		+.35	
	1970	Total					+.50	-.40		-.58
		Male			+.34		+.45	-.49		-.50
		Female								-.52
Age 35-64	1960	Total	-.46		+.66	+.38	+.71			
		Male	-.35		+.67		+.71			
		Female	-.41		+.36					
	1970	Total		-.39	+.70	+.43	+.76	-.45		
		Male			+.82	+.58	+.76			
		Female		-.39			+.52			
Age 65+	1960	Total								
		Male								
		Female								
	1970	Total				+.36				
		Male			+.36					
		Female							+.42	

Regarding total age-adjusted admission rates, it can be seen that the single most consistent finding in both study periods is the strong association between census tract measures of social disequilibrium and admission rates. Areas of greatest social disequilibrium consistently yield greatest numbers of admissions into both public and private facilities. This relationship, even stronger in 1970 than in 1960, holds true not only with respect to the social disequilibrium cluster score, but generally high relationships of total age-adjusted admission rate with many of the census tract variables that comprise this cluster are found—low proportion of persons under 18 years of age living with both parents ($r = -0.67$ for all facilities combined in 1970), high marital disruption ($r = +0.75$), low proportion of housing units owner-occupied ($r = -0.63$), low number of rooms per housing unit ($r = -0.72$), low proportion of single homes ($r = -0.65$), substantial vacant housing ($r = +0.57$), frequent household fires ($r = +0.62$), high delinquency ($r = +0.61$), high proportion of school dropouts ($r = +0.64$), and a high proportion of people living alone ($r = +0.67$). A chi-squared analysis of social disequilibrium cluster scores and total age-adjusted admission rate (see Tables 5-4 and 5-5) yields significant results, highly significant in the case of the 1970 study period.

With regard to total age-adjusted admission rates from census tracts characterized by varying scores on the index of socioeconomic affluence, the situation has clearly changed between the 1960 and 1970 study periods. During 1960 there was a rather clear demarcation along socioeconomic lines between which census tracts sent most patients to private facilities and which to public facilities, with the more affluent census tracts tending to make heavy use of private facilities and the poorer census tracts tending to make heavy use of public facilities. As a consequence of this pattern of differential utili-

Table 5-4

SOCIAL DISEQUILIBRIUM CLUSTER SCORE AND TOTAL AGE-ADJUSTED
ADMISSION RATE: 1960 STUDY PERIOD

| Social Disequilibrium | Total Age-Adjusted Admission Rate | | | |
Cluster Score	Low	Medium	High	Total
Low	7	3	1	11
Medium	1	6	4	11
High	3	3	5	11
Total	11	12	10	33

$\chi^2 = 9.19; df = 4; P = <.10$

Table 5-5

SOCIAL DISEQUILIBRIUM CLUSTER SCORE AND TOTAL AGE-ADJUSTED
ADMISSION RATE: 1970 STUDY PERIOD

| Social Disequilibrium | Total Age-Adjusted Admission Rate | | | |
Cluster Score	Low	Medium	High	Total
Low	9	2	0	11
Medium	1	5	5	11
High	1	4	6	11
Total	11	11	11	33

$\chi^2 = 18.55; df = 4; P = <.001$

zation, there was no significant relationship between the index of socioeconomic affluence and total admission rates in 1960. Ten years later, this differential utilization pattern had vanished, and a generalized overrepresentation of the less affluent tracts occurred throughout the inpatient service delivery system. It should be noted, however, that the index of social disequilibrium is a far more powerful and consistent guide to census tract admission rate than is the index of socioeconomic affluence.

As for the index of young married persons, while relationships with total age-adjusted admission rates are generally weaker than in the case of the other two cluster scores, it is only necessary to note at this point that the correlations, where significant, are negative. That is, census tracts high on the young marrieds cluster score tend to produce relatively few psychiatric first admission inpatients.

Turning now to diagnosis-specific rates we can identify, insofar as such patterns exist, census tract characteristics associated with high or low admission rates. In the case of psychoneuroses and psychosomatic disorders, in 1960 affluent census tracts tended to yield a disproportionate number of both male and female patients into private facilities, socially disordered census tracts tended to yield a disproportionate number of patients into public facilities, and census tracts in which large numbers of young families lived tended to produce few cases into either public or private facilities. It will be noted that sex-specific admission rates for patients given the diagnosis of psychoneurosis or psychosomatic disorder were differentially related to the social disequilibrium and the young marrieds cluster score. In the case of the significant relationship between the social disequilibrium and high admission rate into public facilities, it is seen that this is due to the male admissions, that is, only male admission rates with diagnoses of psychoneuroses are higher from the census tracts characterized by high social disequilibrium. In the case of the generally significant negative relationship between psychoneurotic admission rate and the young married cluster score, this relationship is attributable to females. It is actually a low female admission rate for psychoneuroses which characterizes those census tracts with large numbers of young married parents. By 1970 all these relationships had virtually disappeared, and no census tract characteristic appeared to be significantly associated with psychoneurotic admission rate.

Regarding patients given diagnoses of personality disorders, census tract measures of social disequilibrium are consistently and powerfully associated with high admission rates. Measures of socioeconomic affluence, only slightly related to admission rate in 1960, are in 1970 negatively associated with high admission rates particularly of males, and those tracts with a relatively high preponderance of young married families generally produce few cases, although, as in the case of the psychoneuroses, the relationship is not as strong in 1970 as it was in 1960. Male patients with functional psychoses tended, in 1960, to come from areas high in social disequilibrium, and the relationship between the young marrieds cluster score and functional psychosis admission rate is sex-linked, being significantly negative for males into public facilities and for females into private facilities. Again, census tract cluster scores are less strongly related to functional psychosis admission rate in 1970 than was the case in 1960. Finally, the pattern for admission of patients diagnosed as having acute or chronic brain syndromes is similar to that just described for functional psychoses. The index of socioeconomic affluence is a poor predictor of admission rate, areas characterized by high social disequilibrium and by few young families tend to produce an overabundance of cases, and these relationships are weaker in 1970 than they were in 1960 (see Bloom, 1969).

We turn next to census tract characteristics associated with age-specific admission rates. It should be remembered that age-specific admission rates are calculated by dividing the number of admissions by the specific population at risk. That is, to calculate the admission rate of persons below age 21, the number of patients admitted from each census tract who are under 21 years of age is divided by the census tract population under 21 years of age. Thus, while diagnostic-specific admission rates are additive, in that the total population in each census tract is used as the denominator for each diagnosis, age-specific admission rates are not additive, since each rate is calculated using a different denominator. Diagnosis-specific rates indicate the chances of having a specified diagnosis regardless of age. Age-specific admission rates, on the other hand, indicate the probabilities, within each age group, of being admitted, regardless of diagnosis. With regard to the admission rates for young persons, that is, persons below age 21, the findings are particularly noteworthy. First, neither in 1960 nor in 1970 were census tract measures of socioeconomic afflu-ence consistently associated with these rates. In both 1960 and 1970, when significant relationships were found, census tracts with high proportions of young fam-ilies produced few patients. And those census tracts high in social disequilibrium, particularly those forms of disequilibrium associated with the young (marital dis-ruption, low proportion of persons under 18 living with both parents, delinquency, and school dropouts) yielded the highest rates of patients. But while in 1960 public facilities played a more important role in treating young people from such areas, in 1970 the role had shifted to private facilities. And while in 1960 these relationships were primarily because of male admissions, in 1970 it was female admissions which were responsible for the significant findings. In this connection, it should be re-membered that among persons under 21 years of age, female admission rate increased twice as much as male admission rate between 1960 and 1970, and admissions into private facilities increased nearly twice as much as admissions into public facilities (see Table 4-1).

With regard to admission rates of patients between 21 and 34, that is, young adults, no census tract characteris-tics are consistently associated with hospitalization in private facilities. But admission into public facilities of young adults, both in 1960 and 1970, was markedly associated with census tract measures of high social disequilibrium and, in 1970 only, with low socioeconomic affluence. Specific census tract characteristics most closely associated with high admission rates into public facilities include high marital disruption, low number of rooms per housing unit, much vacant housing, relatively frequent household fires, high proportion of families receiving financial assistance for dependent children, and high delinquency.

The relationships of census tract characteristics to admission rates seen in the case of young adults are even more pronounced in the case of older adults, that is, persons between the ages of 35 and 64. Measures of social disequilibrium are expecially strongly associated with these admission rates (particularly in the case of males), and of the individual census tract characteristics making up the index of social disequilibrium, marital disruption is strikingly associated with admission rate of older adults ($r = +0.80$ for all facilities combined).

The situation regarding admission rates of persons age 65 and above stands in sharp contrast to all other age groups. For all practical purposes, no census tract characteristic either individually or as part of a defined cluster of characteristics bears a significant relationship to the admission rate of the aged. Furthermore, this striking negative finding holds true for both study periods. Because the age group 65 and above so commonly receives a diagnosis of acute or chronic brain syndrome, it is important to indicate again that while the diagnosis-specific admission rate for acute or chronic brain syndrome indicates the probability of an entire census tract producing such a diagnosis, the age-specific admission rate for persons aged 65 and above represents the probability, within that age group, of being admitted regardless of diagnosis. For example, the annual admission rate for acute or chronic brain syndromes in 1970 for public and private facilities combined was 0.46 per 1000, that is, for every two thousand persons in Pueblo (regardless of age) about one case per year is identified as a first admission. In contrast, the age-specific admission rate for persons age 65 and above is 5.20. That is, *of all persons aged 65 and above*, about five cases per 1000 are admitted annually into psychiatric inpatient facilities for the first time in their lives. It is this latter rate, the probability of admission among persons aged 65 and above, which bears no relationship to census tract characteristics.

We can summarize these findings from the point of view of census tract cluster scores. As for socioeconomic affluence, closely related to what other authors have referred to as social class (see Hollingshead and Redlich, 1958, for example) most studies, whether of treated rates or based upon field studies, have found that the residential areas of lowest socioeconomic status produce an excess number of psychiatric inpatients (see Dohrenwend and Dohrenwend, 1969). This was not the case in Pueblo during the 1960 study but it is so during the 1970 study. The reason for this change is to be found in the admission patterns into private facilities since census tracts low in socioeconomic affluence have consistently produced excess numbers of patients into public facilities. But while in 1960 private facilities admitted an excess number of patients from the more affluent census tracts, that situation no longer prevailed in 1970. In 1960 significant correlations between socioeconomic affluence and admission rates into private facilities were invariably positive and especially so in the case of the psychoneurotics who made up nearly half of all private facility admissions. But by 1970 similarly calculated correlations were generally insignificant and in the case of male personality disorders, negative. In fact, the significant negative correlation between socioeconomic affluence and total age-adjusted admission rate found in 1970 seems clearly due to the contribution made by patients with personality disorders who were admitted from less affluent census tracts at disproportionately high rates, while at the same time the tendency to admit psychoneurotics from the more affluent sections of the city evident in 1960 had disappeared in 1970. But it must be noted again that the socioeconomic affluence of a census tract was not generally a powerful correlate of admission rate, either in 1960 or 1970.

Not so with social disequilibrium. Of the 150 correlation coefficients calculated between the social disequilibrium cluster score and the various admission rates, 79 are significantly different from zero at the 0.05 level. This is ten times the number of significant correlations that would be expected by chance. And what is perhaps more striking is that without exception these significant correlations are all positive, that is, admission rates are highest from those census tracts characterized by high levels of social disorganization. Significant correlations are found not only for total age-adjusted rates but for every age and diagnostic group, although relationships do vary in magnitude. But the great and consistent repository of identified first admission psychiatric inpatients are those census tracts high in measures of social disequilibrium. This measure is most compellingly associated with admission rates for patients with personality disorders, males as well as females, into private as well as public facilities, and for both the 1960 and 1970 study periods. And the index of social disequilibrium is almost as closely related to admission rates for male patients with functional psychoses and for male patients with acute or chronic brain syndromes as it is for patients with personality disorders. Furthermore, the index of social disequilibrium is significantly correlated with age-specific admission rates at all ages except age 65 and above, and is especially highly correlated with admissions in the 35-64 age group. This relationship is particularly noteworthy in view of the fact that only about 40 percent of the patients in this age group receive the diagnosis of personality disorder. In other words, the significant relationship of the social disequilibrium index with the admission rate for older adults cannot be accounted for by an unusual diagnostic distribution within this age group.

Interpretation of the importance of the young marrieds cluster score is somewhat complicated by the fact that census tracts high on this cluster contain large numbers of young people. Accordingly we would expect, on this basis alone, that diagnoses associated with advancing age would be relatively uncommon. Thus, the consistent significant negative correlations with admission rates for acute or chronic brain syndromes hardly bear additional interpretation. But, by the same logic, one might expect the admission rate for psychoneuroses (half of whom are below age 21) to be positively correlated with the young married cluster and this is not the case. Furthermore, age-specific admission rates, which are independent of the proportion of people in each census tract in each age group, are also negatively correlated with the young marrieds cluster score wherever such correlations are significant. Thus, it is clear that census tracts high on this cluster score contribute remarkably few patients to inpatient facilities, particularly patients with personality disorders (of whom more than half are below age 35). There has been a substantial change in the role of the young marrieds cluster score between 1960 and 1970. A low score on this cluster was much more associated with high admission rates in 1960 than in 1970, as in the case of psychoneurotics and functional psychotics. And examination of the data further reveals that it is female admission rates which are most affected by the young marrieds cluster score. Where there are large numbers of young married families, admission rates for females are particularly low.

Private inpatient facilities were admitting a far broader spectrum of patients in 1970 than was the case in 1960 as far as socioeconomic affluence is concerned. During the 1960 study period, the more affluent census tracts were overrepresented, particularly in the case of the large number of patients diagnosed as psychoneurotics. But whether due primarily to the increased availability of third party insurance programs or to some other reason, enough additional patients from less affluent census tracts were admitted during the 1970 study period to eliminate the relationship found in 1960. In fact the most parsimonious explanation for the changes between 1960 and 1970 in the relationship between census tract measures of socioeconomic affluence and admission rate is that larger numbers of patients from poorer tracts were admitted into the entire inpatient system, with the result that the relationships became more negative for both public as well as private facilities.

We have not found that each diagnostic, sex, or age group admission rate has a remarkably different pattern of relationships with census tract characteristics. Rather, the general findings in the case of total age-adjusted admission rates seem to hold true, in greater or less degree, for all subcategories of patients. Those census tracts high in measures of social disequilibrium consistently yield large numbers of patients and could thus be the subject of more intensive investigation. By contrast, those census tracts with large proportions of young married families tend to yield relatively few patients and this finding is not due merely to the fact that there are large numbers of young persons living in these tracts. Thus, these tracts too could profitably be studied in greater depth.

Sex Differences

There are three groupings of findings linking admission rates with census tract cluster scores in which substantial sex differences have been found. First, the positive relationship between census tract measures of social disequilibrium and admission rates tends to be much more remarkable in the case of males than females. Since these are sex-specific admission rates, these findings are not attributable to the fact that more males than females may live in census tracts in which there is a high level of social disequilibrium. Rather, a higher proportion of males living in areas of high social disequilibrium are identified as psychiatric patients than among males living in other parts of the city, and this relationship is not as strong in the case of females. For males, furthermore, the relationship is ubiquitous—applying to nearly every diagnosis and age group and to both study periods. In the case of females, the relationship is much more limited, and with only one exception it never occurs without also occurring in males.

Second, the negative relationship between measures of socioeconomic affluence and admission rates is much more pronounced for males than for females. A higher proportion of males tend to become psychiatric patients if they live in poor areas than in more affluent areas, but in the case of females, little evidence of such a relationship appears to exist. Furthermore, the relationship in the case of males is not limited to any one age group and it occurs during both study periods. Third, areas where there are large numbers of young married families yield disproportionately low numbers of female patients, again in a variety of age and diagnostic groups. This relationship does not hold in the case of male patients.

Thus men appear to be at high risk of being hospitalized for psychiatric conditions if they live in areas characterized by high poverty and social disorder, while females appear to be at high risk if they live in areas in which there are low proportions of young married families.

There are two major groups of patients for whom census tract characteristics bear no stable or significant relationship to admission rates—psychoneurotics and persons over age 65. Possible clues to the origin of these disorders are not to be found in neighborhood characteristics. In the case of persons aged 65 and above, it is likely that attributes of their family setting may be predictive of hospitalization, particularly the presence and nature of alternative social supports within the immediate or extended family. In the case of psychoneurotics, it is far more difficult to identify variables which might be associated with those kinds of problems which result in hospitalization. Yet psychoneurotics constitute such a large proportion of first admissions into public and private inpatient units that continued research is clearly needed. One strategy which might be followed, at least for exploratory study, would be to use the patient as an expert and solicit from him his responses to two kinds of questions. First, what is his own theory of how his life experiences culminated in the development of that degree of discomfort so that hospitalization was deemed necessary; and second, what would have had to have been different in his life so that he would not have required psychiatric care.

The single most important consequence of the results reported in this chapter is that social class (or what we have called socioeconomic affluence), while somewhat related to first inpatient admission rates, is a far poorer predictor of such rates than the environmental measure of social disequilibrium. While socioeconomic affluence and social disequilibrium are not independent environmental characteristics (see Chapter 2), their interrelationship is far from perfect. To the extent that the findings in Pueblo are reasonably typical, it would seem that the most likely avenue for the development of a greater understanding of how environmental factors influence the development of psychopathology would be to explore in greater depth than was possible in this study the variables which comprise the measure of social disequilibrium. A beginning step in this direction will be undertaken in the concluding section.

6

Contrasting Patients
and the General Population

Census tract cluster scores, of course, characterize census tracts rather than people, and it may be quite incorrect to assume that patients admitted from a particular census tract have, as individuals, the same characteristics as are attributable to the census tract as a whole. It is conceivable, for example, that patients admitted from a census tract high in marital disruption are in fact all happily married. Fortunately, we have from the 1970 study period some information which can help interpret the possible relationship of individual characteristics to census tract characteristics. It will be remembered that the questionnaire administered to psychiatric inpatients was patterned after the form utilized in the 1970 census. Using census reports as a source of comparison data allows us the opportunity to contrast patients with the general population and then to compare the results of this analysis with that already developed from census tract cluster scores. We will contrast first admission inpatients with the general population in this analysis, and leave until a later chapter the analysis of differences between first admission and repeat admission inpatients. It is in this analysis that our failure to obtain data from all patients will be most keenly felt. In each of the tables in this chapter evidence is provided regarding the extent of missing data. It will be seen that in some instances substantial data are missing.

In 1970, the index of socioeconomic affluence was found to correlate –0.40 with total age-adjusted admission rate; the index of social disequilibrium correlated +0.76 with total age-adjusted admission rate; and the correlation of the young marrieds cluster score with total age-adjusted admission rate was –0.30, nearly reaching significance at the 0.05 level. Are we justified in concluding, therefore, that first admission inpatients tend to be less affluent, more socially disorganized, and less often young married persons than the total population?

SOCIOECONOMIC AFFLUENCE

Data permitting us to contrast socioeconomic affluence of patients with that of the population as a whole comes from three of the variables included in the cluster score: Spanish surname, education, and white collar males. And as for white collar males, the questionnaire data allow us to examine both normal occupation and present job. The results of these analyses are shown in Tables 6-1 through 6-4. Regarding Spanish surname (see Table 6-1), the chi-squared analysis is significant

Table 6-1
SPANISH SURNAMED PERSONS IN THE PATIENT GROUP CONTRASTED WITH THE TOTAL COUNTY POPULATION: 1970 STUDY PERIOD

Frequency	Spanish Surnamed		
	Yes	No	Total
Observed	298	821	1119
Expected	240.6	878.4	
Cell Chi-Square	11.41	3.75	

$\chi^2 = 15.16; df = 1; P = <.001$

Table 6-2

EDUCATION IN THE PATIENT GROUP CONTRASTED WITH THE TOTAL
COUNTY POPULATION: 1970 STUDY PERIOD

Frequency	School Years Completed: Aged 25 and Above					
	None	11 Years or Less	High School Graduate	Some College	College Graduate	Total
Observed	7	271	134	85	34	531[1]
Expected	9.6	249.6	167.8	61.1	43.0	
Cell Chi-Square	0.70	1.84	6.81	9.35	1.89	

$\chi^2 = 20.59; df = 4; P = <.001$
[1]Information not available for 227 patients

and in the expected direction. There are, as will be described in the following chapter, some difficulties in making this particular analysis, but on the basis of the best assumptions which can be made about the proportion of Spanish surnamed persons in the total population, Spanish surnamed persons appear to be overrepresented in the 1970 first admission inpatient population.

In the case of education, since it is positively associated with the socioeconomic affluence cluster score and since the score is negatively correlated with total age-adjusted admission rate, we would expect educational level to be lower in patients than in the general population. While the chi-squared analysis reveals that the distribution of educational level of patients is significantly different from that of the total population (see Table 6-2), the relationship we would predict does not exist. While there are substantially fewer high school graduates among the patients than among the general population, there are also more patients with some college education than would have been expected.

The variable, white collar males, that is, the proportion of employed males in professional and managerial positions, is positively associated with the socioeconomic affluence score, and thus it would be expected that fewer patients would be in this category than would be the case if rates found in the total county would be applied. There is in this analysis a high level of agreement between individual data and census tract data. Regarding both present employment and usual occupation, patients are underrepresented in higher level jobs and are overrepresented in unskilled and semiskilled positions. The difference between the patient group and the total population is more marked in the case of usual occupation than in the case of present position, suggesting that those patients in lower level jobs may have the greatest difficulty in retaining gainful employment when psychiatric difficulties arise and thus leave the labor force (see Tables 6-3 and 6-4).

In summary, socioeconomic affluence as a census tract characteristic, which was found to be negatively associated with total age-adjusted admission rate, bears a fairly close relationship to individual measures on three variables included in the cluster score. In the case of occupation (both usual and present) and ethnic group, patients are in those categories where they might be expected to cluster. Insofar as education is concerned, patients do not appear to be meaningfully different from the general population.

SOCIAL DISEQUILIBRIUM

Of the variables included in the social disequilibrium cluster score, a score which is powerfully related to total age-adjusted admission rate, individual measures are available for five: male marital status, owner-occupied housing, rooms per housing unit, single homes, and persons per housing unit. Basing our predictions on the census tract cluster score relationship with admission

Table 6-3

USUAL OCCUPATION IN THE PATIENT GROUP CONTRASTED WITH THE TOTAL COUNTY POPULATION: 1970 STUDY PERIOD

Frequency	Usual Job: Males Age 16 and Above—Employed or Student						
	Student	Professional Managerial	Clerical Sales	Agricultural Semiskilled	Service	Unskilled	Total
Observed	47	34	22	161	20	89	373[1]
Expected	42.2	70.9	43.6	128.3	35.8	52.6	
Cell Chi-Square	0.55	19.21	10.70	8.33	6.97	25.19	

$\chi^2 = 70.95; df = 5; P = <.001$
[1] Information not available for 97 patients

Table 6-4

PRESENT JOB IN THE PATIENT GROUP CONTRASTED WITH THE TOTAL COUNTY POPULATION: 1970 STUDY PERIOD

Frequency	Present Job: Males Age 16 and Above—Employed or Student						
	Student	Professional Managerial	Clerical Sales	Agricultural Semiskilled	Service	Unskilled	Total
Observed	37	25	19	97	18	53	249[1]
Expected	28.1	47.3	29.1	85.7	23.9	35.1	
Cell Chi-Square	2.82	10.51	3.51	1.49	1.46	9.13	

$\chi^2 = 28.92; df = 5; P = <.001$
[1] Information not available for 149 patients

rate, we would expect to find more marital disruption, more renter-occupied housing, fewer rooms per housing unit, fewer single homes, and fewer persons per housing unit in the case of patients than in the general population. As seen in Tables 6-5 through 6-10, all these predictions are verified.

Table 6-5

HOUSING UNITS PER STRUCTURE IN THE PATIENT GROUP CONTRASTED WITH THE TOTAL COUNTY POPULATION: 1970 STUDY PERIOD

Frequency	Housing Units Per Structure			
	One	Two	Three or More	Total
Observed	610	29	115	754[1]
Expected	628.8	34.7	90.5	
Cell Chi-Square	0.56	0.94	6.63	

$\chi^2 = 8.13; df = 2; P = <.02$
[1]Information not available for 365 patients

The relationship of housing units per structure is shown in Table 6-5. As can be seen, patients more commonly live in structures containing three or more housing units than would be expected on the basis of general population housing statistics. As for rooms per housing unit (see Table 6-6), patients show a greater likelihood of living in single room apartments than the general population, but at the same time they are overrepresented in very large housing units as well. This latter finding may be the consequence, however, both of young patients and of patients who occupy rooms in large dwellings listing the number of rooms in the entire dwelling. This latter possibility suggests itself because, as will be seen later, patients not infrequently report living in households where they are unrelated to the head of the household. Furthermore, when the analysis

Table 6-6

ROOMS PER HOUSING UNIT IN PATIENT GROUP CONTRASTED WITH
TOTAL COUNTY POPULATION: 1970 STUDY PERIOD

		Rooms Per Housing Unit						
Frequency	One	Two	Three	Four	Five	Six	Seven or More	Total
Observed	30	41	65	174	193	106	156	765[1]
Expected	16.1	31.4	84.2	215.7	212.7	101.7	103.3	
Cell Chi-Square	12.00	2.94	4.38	8.06	1.83	0.18	26.89	

$\chi^2 = 56.28; df = 6; P = <.001$
[1]Information not available for 354 patients

of rooms per housing unit is undertaken just for heads of households among the patient group, the anticipated finding emerges (see Table 6-7). In contrast with expected frequencies, patients who are heads of households are consistently overrepresented in small (three rooms or less) housing units and underrepresented in larger (four rooms or more) housing units.

A similar finding emerges in the case of persons per household. As seen in Table 6-8, among patients who are heads of households, those living alone are significantly overrepresented when contrasted with expected frequencies based upon county household data. Patients are clearly overrepresented as renters and underrepresented as owners of the housing units where they live (see Table 6-9). This relationship is further accentuated when only heads of households are considered. There is an overwhelming relationship between patient status and marital disruption, as shown in Table 6-10. While approximately the same number of patients, age 14 and above, are single or widowed, as would be expected from the statistics of the general population, patients are far less commonly married and living with their spouses, far more often married and living apart, and far more often divorced than would be predicted on the basis of the general population. Of all the variables making up the social disequilibrium cluster score, marital disruption is most striking as both an individual as well as a census tract correlate of patienthood.

YOUNG MARRIEDS

Individual data is available on two of the variables included in the young marrieds cluster—age and year of construction of housing. On the basis of the negative

Table 6-7

ROOMS PER HOUSING UNIT IN PATIENT GROUP HEADS OF
HOUSEHOLDS CONTRASTED WITH TOTAL COUNTY HOUSEHOLDS:
1970 STUDY PERIOD

	Rooms Per Housing Unit					
Frequency	One	Two-Three	Four	Five	Six+	Total
Observed	23	65	72	77	64	301[1]
Expected	6.3	45.5	84.9	83.7	80.7	
Cell Chi-Square	44.27	8.36	1.96	0.54	3.46	

$\chi^2 = 58.59; df = 4; P = <.001$
[1]Information not available for 13 patients

relationship of the young marrieds cluster score to admission rate, one would predict that patients would be
older and would live in older housing than the general
population. The age distribution is shown in Table 6-11
and indicates that, as predicted, patients are underrepresented in the under 21 age category and overrepresented in all other age categories. In the case of year of
construction of housing, as can be seen from Table 6-12,
the distribution of patients is not significantly different
from what would have been expected had total popula-

Table 6-8

PERSONS PER HOUSING UNIIT IN PATIENT HEADS OF HOUSEHOLDS
CONTRASTED WITH TOTAL COUNTY HOUSEHOLDS: 1970 STUDY
PERIOD

	Persons Per Housing Unit				
Frequency	One	Two	Three	Four or More	Total
Observed	83	65	46	114	308[1]
Expected	52.7	87.5	49.9	118.0	
Cell Chi-Square	17.42	5.79	0.30	0.14	

$\chi^2 = 23.65; df = 3; P = <.001$
[1]Information not available for 6 patients

tion rates prevailed. Nor is the relationship significant when only patients who are heads of households are considered.

ADDITIONAL COMPARISONS

Five other comparisons between patients and the general population yield significant results, but these variables are not included in any of the cluster scores and are now presented separately. First, as to the position of the patient with respect to the head of the household, Table 6-13 shows that most strikingly different when patients are contrasted with the general population is the large proportion of patients living in households where the head of the household is unrelated to them. These patients are roomers, lodgers, or boarders, and there are substantially more of them than would be expected. Heads of households themselves are overrepresented and other relatives (brother, sister, son, daughter, etc.) are underrepresented. This latter observation is undoubtedly related to the small number of young persons in the patient population.

Table 6-9

HOUSING TENURE IN PATIENT GROUP (HEAD OF HOUSEHOLD AND WIFE OF HEAD OF HOUSEHOLD) CONTRASTED WITH TOTAL COUNTY POPULATION: 1970 STUDY PERIOD

| Frequency | Housing Tenure | | Total |
	Renter Occupied	Owner Occupied	
Observed	182	277	459[1]
Expected	124.9	334.2	
Cell Chi-Square	26.10	9.79	

$\chi^2 = 35.89; df = 1; P = <.001$
[1]Information not available for 23 patients

Two measures of mobility are shown in Tables 6-14 and 6-15. As can be seen, patients are significantly more mobile than the general population, and this finding is much more remarkable in the case of mobility from one house to another than moves into the county from outside of Pueblo.

Finally data on household population density and number of automobiles is shown in Tables 6-16 and 6-17. Assuming that these variables are associated with socioeconomic affluence, one would expect to find higher household population density and fewer automobiles among patients than among the general population. These hypotheses are supported consistently both in the case of persons per room (our measure of household population density) and in the case of automobiles.

One final comparison between patients and the general population is possible, namely, children ever born to women aged 35-44, a measure of fertility. In the general population of Pueblo in 1970 there were a total of 6693 women between ages 35 and 44 who were married at one time or another. These women delivered 23,836 children or 3.56 children per person. Calculating this figure

Table 6–10

MARITAL STATUS IN PATIENT GROUP CONTRASTED WITH TOTAL
COUNTY POPULATION: 1970 STUDY PERIOD

	Marital Status: Males Age 14 and Above					
Frequency	Single	Married–Living Together	Married–Living Apart	Divorced	Widowed	Total
Observed	107	169	44	61	17	398[1]
Expected	118.0	249.6	3.6	14.7	11.9	
Cell Chi-Square	1.03	26.03	453.38	145.83	2.19	

$\chi^2 = 628.46; df = 4; P = <.001$
[1]Information not available for 111 patients

Table 6-11

AGE DISTRIBUTION IN PATIENT GROUP CONTRASTED WITH TOTAL
COUNTY POPULATION: 1970 STUDY PERIOD

	Age Distribution				
Frequency	Under 21	21–34	35–64	65 and above	Total
Observed	264	281	462	112	1119
Expected	468.8	188.0	356.8	105.3	
Cell Chi-Square	89.47	46.01	31.02	0.43	

$\chi^2 = 166.93; df = 3; P = <.001$

Table 6-12

YEAR OF CONSTRUCTION OF HOUSING UNIT IN PATIENT GROUP
CONTRASTED WITH TOTAL COUNTY POPULATION: 1970 STUDY
PERIOD

	Year of Construction of Housing Unit					
Frequency	1965 or later	1960–1964	1950–1959	1940–1949	Before 1940	Total
Observed	85	79	188	83	311	746[1]
Expected	69.4	76.8	188.0	83.6	328.2	
Cell Chi-Square	3.51	0.06	0.00	0.00	0.90	

$\chi^2 = 4.47; df = 4; P = $ not significant
[1]Information not available for 373 patients

for female first admission inpatients in the same age and
marital history category indicates a very similar result—
3.60 children per ever married female aged 35-44.

SUMMARY

It is time now to develop a summarizing overview of
patient characteristics with special reference to how they
differ from characteristics of the total county population,
again remembering that we have had to assume that

Table 6-13

RELATION OF PATIENT TO HEAD OF HOUSEHOLD IN PATIENT GROUP
CONTRASTED WITH TOTAL COUNTY POPULATION: 1970 STUDY
PERIOD

	Relation to Head of Household				
Frequency	*Head of Household*	*Wife of Head*	*Other Relative*	*Not Related*	*Total*
Observed	314	168	275	41	798[1]
Expected	246.6	174.8	366.3	9.6	
Cell Chi-Square	18.42	0.26	22.76	103.70	

$\chi^2 = 144.14; df = 3; P = <.001$
[1]Information not available for 321 patients

patients for whom data were available were representative of the total patient population. We have compared, as a single group, all first admission inpatients on whom data was available with the relevant county data, and have not separately contrasted private or public patients with total population or male or female patients with appropriate county data. Conducting the analysis in this manner allows us to deal with the question at its most fundamental level, namely, how do patients as a group differ from the total population and how do the results

Table 6-14

LENGTH OF TIME AT PRESENT ADDRESS IN PATIENT GROUP
CONTRASTED WITH TOTAL POPULATION: 1970 STUDY
PERIOD

	Length of Time at Present Address		
Frequency	*Under Five Years*	*Five Years or More*	*Total*
Observed	433	351	784[1]
Expected	314.4	469.6	
Cell Chi-Square	44.74	29.95	

$\chi^2 = 74.69; df = 1; P = <.001$
[1]Information not available for 335 patients

of this type of analysis contrast with the correlational analysis at the census tract level.

First, let us examine those patient characteristics in which analyses at the individual level and at the census tract level yield parallel results. These include ethnic group, more commonly Spanish surnamed among patients; present and usual occupation, more commonly unskilled or semiskilled inpatients than in the general population; proportion of persons living in single homes, lower among patients than in the general population; rooms and persons per housing unit, fewer among patients; proportion of persons renting, higher among patients than in the general population; disrupted marital status, higher among patients than among the general population; and age distribution, with significantly fewer young people among patients than among the general population. That is, when patients are contrasted with the total county population they both are and live in census tracts characterized by a high frequency of low level occupations; high proportion of Spanish surnamed; apartment renters, as opposed to single home owners; relatively older age groups; higher frequency of living alone in small households; and high proportion of disrupted marriages.

Second, there are some findings which are significant at the individual level but are not significant at the census tract level. Patients are clearly more mobile (especially from house to house in Pueblo) than the general population, even though there is no tendency for them to come from census tracts in which there is a generally high level of mobility. Patients live in high population density households significantly more often than the general population, although such overcrowding is not a census tract characteristic of those areas producing high admission rates.

Finally, there are some findings significant at the census tract level which are nonsignificant at the individual level. While census tracts in which the educational level is low produce an excess number of patients, patients as a group are not consistently less well educated than the total population. And while census tracts in which there is relatively new housing produce unusually few patients, the difference between patients and the total population in age of housing unit is not significant. In no case,

Table 6-15

LENGTH OF TIME IN PUEBLO COUNTY IN PATIENT GROUP
CONTRASTED WITH TOTAL COUNTY POPULATION: 1970 STUDY
PERIOD

	Length of Time in Pueblo County		
Frequency	Under Five Years	Five Years or more	Total
Observed	153	630	783[1]
Expected	123.7	659.3	
Cell Chi-Square	6.94	1.30	

$\chi^2 = 8.24; df = 1; P = <.01$
[1]Information not available for 336 patients

Table 6-16

PERSONS PER ROOM IN PATIENT GROUP CONTRASTED WITH TOTAL
COUNTY POPULATION: 1970 STUDY PERIOD

	Persons Per Room			
Frequency	1.00 or Less	1.01 to 1.50	1.51 or More	Total
Observed	626	89	37	752[1]
Expected	663.3	66.2	21.8	
Cell Chi-Square	2.10	7.85	10.60	

$\chi^2 = 20.55; df = 2; P = <.001$
[1]Information not available for 367 patients

however, is a failure of confirmation due to a significant finding in the opposite direction.

We thus find a high degree of convergence between individually oriented data and neighborhood data, suggesting a substantial amount of homogenity within census tracts. While cities smaller than Pueblo (see Clausen and Kohn, 1959) may not be characterized by identifiable neighborhood social stratification, Pueblo is clearly large enough so that it can be geographically subdivided into small, quite homogenous areas. The phenomenon of stratifiability along economic, demographic, and social deviance lines has been found repeatedly in American cities, and striking relationships between such characteristics and various measures of psychopathology have been found. It is not unreasonable to expect, however, that the kind of social stratification found in large American cities may not exist in European cities, for example, and thus that the spatial distribution of identified psychopathology may have a differing pattern of correlations with neighborhood characteristics.

A preliminary report of a study similar to the original Faris and Dunham project in Chicago (1939) conducted in Mannheim, Germany in 1965 (see Hafner and Rei-

Table 6–17.

NUMBERS OF AUTOMOBILES IN PATIENT GROUP CONTRASTED WITH
TOTAL COUNTY POPULATION: 1970 STUDY PERIOD

| | Number of Automobiles | | |
Frequency	None	One or More	Total
Observed	149	626	775[1]
Expected	104.6	670.4	
Cell Chi-Square	18.85	2.94	

$\chi^2 = 21.79; df = 1; P = <.001$
[1]Information not available for 344 patients

mann, 1970) suggests that that city is stratified along economic and social dimensions and that some of the relationships found by Faris and Dunham appear to hold true in Mannheim. But the relationships between census tract measures of social disorganization and annual incidence rates do not appear to be as close as those reported by Faris and Dunham, nor does Mannheim appear to be as stratified as Chicago, and the authors are continuing to search for reasons for high rates of admission in certain areas of the city. It would add greatly to our understanding of demographic and ecological correlates of psychiatric disability if one or two cities stratified along differing lines or substantially less stratified could be found where collaborative studies analagous to the current project could be instituted. Depending upon the outcome of such studies, it might be possible to separate out demographic from ecological factors in psychiatric disability.

Many European cities appear, impressionistically at least, to be far less economically stratified than American cities of comparable size. The poor and the affluent often live side by side, sharing the same shopping facilities, transportation systems, and neighborhood services. In those European cities where social welfare programs are well developed, certain forms of social disorganization seem substantially less prevalent. And certain other kinds of stratification, for example ghettos of immigrants, seem to be present in ways qualitatively different from those found in typical American cities. Yet the incidence of identified psychopathology, at least where services are well developed, appears to be roughly of the same order of magnitude as found throughout the United States. If these impressionistic differences can in fact be documented, there is the basis for potentially useful comparative study. For in spite of these presumed ecological differences, marital disruption, social isolation, undereducation, minority status, overcrowding, and mobility all exist as individual attributes, and their relationship to diagnosed psychopathology might be examined in vastly different ecological settings.

7

The Spanish
Surnamed Patient

Persons of Spanish surname constitute the largest separately identifiable ethnic minority group in Pueblo, comprising more than one-quarter of the total population. By contrast, less than two percent of the Pueblo population is Black. The Spanish surnamed group has been referred to on three separate occasions thus far. First, it has been indicated that the official count of Spanish surnamed people in Pueblo cannot be directly compared between the 1960 and 1970 study periods because of a change made by the Bureau of the Census in the criteria used to identify them. Second, the cluster analysis has shown that the proportion of Spanish surnamed or Spanish language background persons in each census tract is a stable component of the index of socioeconomic affluence. Third, it has been shown that while census tracts low on the index of socioeconomic affluence have excess numbers of psychiatric patients and tend to have disproportionately large numbers of Spanish surnamed persons living within them, such persons are in fact not consistently overrepresented among the patient population.

In 1960, when the definition was actually "persons of Spanish surname," 25,437 persons out of the total population of 118,707 (21.5 percent) met this criterion yet only 140 out of the total of 919 patients (15.2 percent) met the same criterion. In 1970, 37,088 out of the total population of 118,238 persons in Pueblo (31.4 percent) were identified as "persons of Spanish language or other persons of Spanish surname," while 298 out of 1119 (26.6 percent) first admission patients had Spanish surnames. In 1960, then, Spanish surnamed persons were clearly underrepresented amony psychiatric inpatients. In 1970, assuming no real change in the population at risk, Spanish surnamed persons were overrepresented among psychiatric inpatients.

Because we have been able to identify Spanish surnamed persons among first-admission inpatients in both the 1960 and 1970 study periods, our data allows us to divide the patient population into Spanish surnamed and non-Spanish surnamed, identify certain characteristics which significantly differentiate these two groups, and examine the stability of these differences across the decade. From the previous paragraph one fact is already apparent. A very large increase has taken place in the number of Spanish surnamed patients. Between 1960 and 1970 the number of Spanish surnamed patients admitted per year increased from less than 50 to nearly 150 —a 300 percent increase. By way of contrast, the number of non-Spanish patients admitted annually increased by only 60 percent—from 260 per year to 410 per year.

Because denominator data, furnished by the Bureau of the Census, cannot be directly compared between the two study periods, admission rates based on this denominator data are also not comparable. But the same list of Spanish surnames has been used in categorizing patients in both study periods, and we already know that there has been very little change in the total population of Pueblo across the decade. Accordingly we can examine numerator data in making initial comparisons between Spanish surnamed and non-Spanish surnamed persons. Let us first contrast age, sex, facility where treatment was obtained, and diagnostic differences between Spanish surnamed and non-Spanish patients and, where appropriate, with total county data, and determine what changes, if any, have taken place in these differences between the two study periods. These comparisons are shown in Table 7-1.

ETHNIC DIFFERENCES WITHIN THE COUNTY AND PATIENT POPULATION

In the general county population, there was no substantial difference in sex distribution between Spanish surnamed and non-Spanish surnamed persons either in 1960 or in 1970. The sexes divided equally in both ethnic groups. But as can be seen, there were clear and stable differences in age distribution in the total population. In 1960, while 39 percent of non-Spanish surnamed persons were under 21, 55 percent of Spanish surnamed persons were under 21. Slightly more Spanish surnamed were between ages 21 and 34 than among non-Spanish surnamed, and a substantially larger proportion of non-Spanish surnamed than Spanish surnamed persons were found in the two older age categories. The same differences in age distribution between Spanish surnamed and non-Spanish surnamed persons were found in 1970. Thus, in interpreting age and sex differences among Spanish surnamed and non-Spanish surnamed psychiatric patients, it is important to keep in mind that the Spanish surnamed patients come from a significantly younger population pool than do the non-Spanish surnamed patients.

Turning now to the patient population, it can be seen that both in 1960 and 1970, males were overrepresented among Spanish surnamed patients. In the case of non-Spanish surnamed patients, sex distribution was compa-

Table 7-1

COMPARISONS BETWEEN SPANISH SURNAMED AND NON-SPANISH SURNAMED ANNUAL FIRST INPATIENT ADMISSIONS WITH COUNTY POPULATION DISTRIBUTION: 1960 AND 1970 STUDY PERIODS

Demographic and Psychiatric Variables	1960 Patient and County Data						1970 Patient and County Data					
	Spanish Surnamed			Non-Spanish Surnamed			Spanish Surnamed			Non-Spanish Surnamed		
	Patients		County	Patients		County	Patients		County	Patients		County
	N	%	%	N	%	%	N	%	%	N	%	%
Sex:												
Male	25.7	55.0	50.5	131.0	50.4	49.2	84.0	56.4	50.1	185.0	45.1	48.7
Female	21.0	45.0	49.5	128.7	49.6	50.8	65.0	43.6	49.9	225.5	54.9	51.3
Age:												
Under 21	10.0	21.4	55	19.3	7.4	39	41.0	27.5	52	91.0	22.2	36
21-34	12.3	26.4	19	50.3	19.4	16	44.0	29.5	17	96.5	23.5	17
35-64	19.0	40.7	22	114.7	44.2	34	57.0	38.3	26	174.0	42.4	35
65+	5.3	11.4	4	75.3	29.0	11	7.0	4.7	5	49.0	11.9	12
Diagnosis:												
Psychoneuroses	14.3	30.7		86.0	33.1		66.0	44.3		224.0	54.6	
Personality Disorders	17.7	37.9		69.7	26.8		66.5	44.6		108.5	26.4	
Functional Psychoses	8.3	17.9		28.0	10.8		9.5	6.4		31.0	7.6	
Brain Syndromes	6.3	13.6		76.0	29.3		7.0	4.7		47.0	11.4	
Facility:												
Public	19.3	41.4		86.3	33.2		56.5	37.9		109.5	26.7	
Private	27.3	58.6		173.3	66.8		92.5	62.1		301.0	73.3	

rable to that of the total county in 1960, but females appeared to be overrepresented in 1970. Admission rate for females increased more for non-Spanish than for Spanish surnamed persons between 1960 and 1970. Age distribution was significantly different between the two ethnic patient groups in both 1960 and 1970, with more younger patients among the Spanish and more older patients among the non-Spanish. This difference in age distribution is what one would expect, however, given the differences in age distribution of Spanish surnamed and non-Spanish surnamed persons in the total county. To develop a greater understanding of age differences in the two ethnically different patient populations, age-specific admission rates need to be obtained.

ETHNIC DIFFERENCES IN ADMISSION RATES

It is possible to estimate age-specific admission rates in the entire county by assuming no appreciable change in the total number of Spanish surnamed and non-Spanish surnamed persons in the county between 1960 and 1970 (there was, it will be remembered, a change of less than one-half of one percent in the total population between 1960 and 1970). Applying the percentage figures in each age category to the total Spanish surnamed and non-Spanish surnamed population yields an estimated base population for each ethnic group in each age category; from these estimated populations at risk, one can calculate age-specific admission rates. The results of this analysis are presented in Table 7-2. Changes in age-specific admission rates between the two study periods in the two ethnic groups are readily apparent.

First, the general increase in total admission rate between 1960 and 1970 can be seen in both ethnic groups, with the amount of increase greater in the case of the

Table 7-2

ESTIMATED AGE-SPECIFIC FIRST INPATIENT ADMISSION RATES FOR SPANISH SURNAMED AND NON-SPANISH SURNAMED PATIENTS: 1960 AND 1970 STUDY PERIODS

| | 1960 Study Period | | | | | | 1970 Study Period | | | | | |
| | Spanish Surnamed | | | Non-Spanish Surnamed | | | Spanish Surnamed | | | Non-Spanish Surnamed | | |
Age Group	Estimated Population[1]	Annual Admissions	Adm. Rate (per 1,000)	Estimated Population[1]	Annual Admissions	Adm. Rate (per 1,000)	Estimated Population[1]	Annual Admissions	Adm. Rate (per 1,000)	Estimated Population[1]	Annual Admissions	Adm. Rate (per 1,000)
Under 21	13647	10.0	0.73	34161	19.3	0.57	12902	41.0	3.18	31533	91.0	2.89
21-34	4714	12.3	2.61	14015	50.3	3.59	4218	44.0	10.43	14891	96.5	6.48
35-64	5459	19.0	3.48	29781	114.7	3.85	6451	57.0	8.84	30657	174.0	5.68
65+	992	5.3	5.34	9635	75.3	7.82	1241	7.0	5.64	10511	49.0	4.66
Total	24812	46.6	1.88	87592	259.6	2.96	24812	149.0	6.01	87592	410.5	4.69

[1] Total county less census tract 3

190

Spanish surnamed. The decreased admission rate for patients age 65 and above, noted in earlier analyses of the total patient population, is now seen as a non-Spanish surnamed phenomenon. In fact, there was a slight increase in Spanish surnamed admission rates in the age 65 and above age category.

Second, in 1960 total first inpatient admission rates were substantially higher for non-Spanish surnamed patients than for Spanish surnamed patients, due particularly to the higher admission rates in the 21-34 and 65 and above age categories. In contrast, in 1970, the total first inpatient admission rates were higher for the Spanish surnamed and were higher in every age category. The biggest differences in the increased admission rates for Spanish surnamed patients in contrast to non-Spanish surnamed patients occurred in the adult years, that is, between ages 21 and 64. Admission rates increased three times as much in the case of Spanish surnamed than non-Spanish surnamed patients in these age groups.

Returning to Table 7-1, it can be seen that in both 1960 and 1970 there were a higher proportion of neurotics and brain syndromes among the non-Spanish and a higher proportion of personality disorders among the Spanish. Contrasting changes in diagnosis in the two ethnic groups reveals that nearly four times as many Spanish surnamed patients were given a personality disorder diagnosis in 1970 as in 1960, while in the case of non-Spanish surnamed the increase was only about 50 percent. A similar difference in admission rates by diagnosis in the two ethnic groups is seen in the case of the psychoneuroses. Thus the increased number of admissions of Spanish surnamed patients between 1960 and 1970 is attributable to persons in the adult years of life, particularly those persons given diagnoses of personality disorders or psychoneuroses.

Finally, in both 1960 and 1970, a larger proportion of Spanish surnamed than non-Spanish surnamed patients made use of public facilities, and a comparably smaller proportion were admitted into private facilities. There is every reason to believe that economic considerations play a role in this difference.

There are surprisingly few other significant differences between Spanish and non-Spanish patients. Contrasting questionnaire replies obtained in the 1970 study reveals only significant differences related to the generally lower socioeconomic status of the Spanish surnamed. Thus, Spanish patients less often own their homes than do non-Spanish; they tend to live in older homes, have less education, are more commonly employed in agricultural and unskilled jobs and, if they worked at all during the previous year, tended to work a smaller proportion of the year than did the non-Spanish surnamed patients. Since all of these differences are equally true of the total county population as of the patient population, it seems clear that for most of the characteristics we have assessed, both Spanish surnamed and non-Spanish surnamed patients are reasonably representative samples of the total county population of similar ethnic background.

In contrasting Spanish surnamed and non-Spanish surnamed first admission psychiatric inpatients over a decade, we have seen a major increase in the number and admission rate of Spanish surnamed patients. In 1960, Spanish surnamed persons were underrepresented among psychiatric patients. Constituting more than 21 percent of the total population, they made up only 15 percent of the patients. By 1970, Spanish surnamed patients were overrepresented, comprising nearly 27 percent of all patients. While admission rates were higher in 1970 than in 1960 for all patients, the increase was five times greater in the case of the Spanish surnamed than the non-Spanish surnamed patient. This increase was seen most dramatically in the productive adult years of life (ages 21-64) and among persons given diagnoses of psychoneuroses and personality disorders.

CENSUS TRACT CHARACTERISTICS AND ETHNIC-SPECIFIC ADMISSION RATES

This remarkable increase in Spanish surnamed admission rate could be a generalized phenomenon characterizing the entire county, or alternatively, might be specific to certain sections of the city and perhaps related to certain attributes of these neighborhoods. Thus, we turn to an analysis of census tract characteristics and their relationships to ethnic group-specific admission rates for the two study periods. One initial observation should be made. Both total census tract population and proportion of Spanish surnamed persons in each census tract remained very stable across the decade. Total population in each census tract in 1960 correlated +0.86 with the same figure in 1970, and proportion of Spanish surnamed (1960) and Spanish language (1970) correlated +0.85. That is to say, should large differences be found in numbers or admission rates of Spanish surnamed patients in each census tract when data from the two study periods are compared, these differences could not be attributable to changes in the ethnic composition or base population of the individual census tracts.

Because age distribution of Spanish surnamed persons is provided only for census tracts having 400 or more such people in residence, and because only two-thirds of the census tracts meet this criterion, age-adjusted admission rates cannot be calculated. Accordingly, we are limited to calculating crude ethnic group-specific rates. Since there is a high degree of census tract population stability across the decade, however, and since it is ethnic group-specific rates at two different points in time that are being contrasted, there is no great disadvantage in using these crude rates. It has already been reported (see Chapter 4) that total census tract age-adjusted first inpatient admission rates correlated +0.65 across the two study periods. When the patients are subdivided by ethnic group and ethnic group-specific admission rates are calculated, it is seen that for non-Spanish surnamed persons correlation of census tract admission rates across the two study periods is +0.62, while for Spanish surnamed persons, the similar correlation is not significantly different from zero ($r = +0.08$). Of course it is true that admission rates for Spanish surnamed persons are calculated on a smaller population base and are thus less reliable than rates calculated for non-Spanish surnamed persons, but in spite of the lower reliability of such rates, it is possible that meaningful changes took place during the decade in factors associated with the identification and hospitalization of Spanish surnamed psychiatric patients. The correlations just presented clearly suggest that the increase in Spanish surnamed admission rates is not a generalized countywide phenomenon.

Correlations of ethnic group-specific inpatient first admission rates with census tract cluster scores are shown in Table 7-3. Socioeconomic affluence, unrelated to total age-adjusted admission rate in 1960, is unrelated either to Spanish surnamed or non-Spanish surnamed crude admission rate. In 1970, the index of socioeconomic affluence was significantly negatively related to total age-adjusted admission rate. When ethnic group-specific rates are calculated, the index is significantly related only to non-Spanish surnamed admissions ($r = -0.51$). Census tracts low in socioeconomic affluence tend to yield disproportionately large numbers of non-Spanish sur-

Table 7-3
SIGNIFICANT CORRELATIONS OF CENSUS TRACT CLUSTER SCORES WITH ETHNIC GROUP-SPECIFIC CRUDE INPATIENT FIRST ADMISSION RATES: 1960 AND 1970

Ethnic Group and Study Period		Census Tract Cluster Score		
		Socioeconomic Affluence	*Social Disequilibrium*	*Young Marrieds*
Spanish Surnamed	1960			-0.35
	1970		+0.57	
Non-Spanish	1960		+0.80	-0.57
Surnamed	1970	-0.51	+0.73	

named patients, but admission rate for Spanish surnamed patients appears to be independent of the socioeconomic status of the census tract.

The young marrieds cluster score bears the same relationship to ethnic group-specific admission rates as it does to total age-adjusted admission rates for both 1960 and 1970, that is, a significant negative relationship in 1960 and a nonsignificant relationship in 1970. In 1960 those census tracts in which there were large numbers of young married persons tended to yield relatively few patients, regardless of ethnic group. In 1970, however, the association of young married families as a census tract characteristic with first inpatient admission rate had disappeared, again regardless of ethnic group.

Ethnic group-specific admission rates bear a most unusual relationship to the index of social disequilibrium. It will be remembered that this index was very closely related to total age-adjusted admission rates both in 1960 and in 1970. Yet in examining ethnic group-specific rates, it is found that in 1960 the non-Spanish surnamed rate is correlated –0.80 with the index of social disequilibrium, while there is no significant relationship between the index and Spanish surnamed crude admission rate. Census tracts characterized by high social disequilibrium did not produce disproportionately large numbers of Spanish surnamed patients, although these same tracts yielded large numbers of non-Spanish surnamed patients. In 1970, however, the index was significantly associated with both Spanish surnamed admission rate ($r = +0.57$) and non-Spanish surnamed admission rate ($r = +0.73$). In examining individual census tract characteristics it is found that not one of the ten variables comprising the social disequilibrium cluster was significantly related to Spanish surnamed crude admission rate in 1960 and, in contrast, every one was significantly related to admission rate in 1970. The extent of this change can be seen in Table 7-4. Factors were operating in 1960 to keep social disorder as a census tract characteristic, independent of admission rate for Spanish surnamed persons, and these factors were apparently inoperative in 1970.

Table 7–4

CORRELATION OF CENSUS TRACT VARIABLES IN SOCIAL
DISEQUILIBRIUM CLUSTER SCORE WITH SPANISH SURNAMED
INPATIENT FIRST ADMISSION RATES: 1960 AND 1970

Census Tract Variable	Correlation with Spanish Surnamed Admission Rate	
	1960	1970
1. Rooms Per Housing Unit	−0.07	−0.46
2. Marital Disruption	+0.20	+0.48
3. People Living Alone	+0.25	+0.53
4. Owner-Occupied Housing	−0.07	−0.44
5. Delinquency	+0.09	+0.53
6. Single Homes	−0.29	−0.56
7. Vacant Housing	+0.09	+0.40
8. Children Living with Both Parents	−0.20	−0.46
9. Household Fires	+0.28	+0.45
10. School Dropouts	+0.24	+0.58

ETHNIC ISSUES AND CHANGES ACROSS THE DECADE

Published reports of identified psychopathology among persons of Spanish surname have characteristically noted their underrepresentation. Karno and Edgerton (1969), for example, point out that in California, where Mexican-Americans constitute about 10 percent of the total population, they account for only two percent of state hospital admissions, three percent of state mental hygiene clinic admissions, and less than one percent of neuropsychiatric institute admissions. As of June 30, 1966, Mexican-Americans comprised less than four percent of the resident population of California's state hospitals for the mentally ill. In studying patients admitted to Texas psychiatric hospitals, Jaco (1960) similarly found Mexican-Americans to be underrepresented. Thus, the 1960 findings in Pueblo regarding the Spanish surnamed patients are similar to what has been reported in other settings, and the dramatic increase found between 1960 and 1970 is a phenomenon worthy of exploration and replication in other geographic areas.

There have been numerous explanations for the general finding that Spanish surnamed persons are traditionally underrepresented among psychiatric patients. Among these explanations have been the following: Spanish surnamed persons, in fact, suffer from less mental illness than Anglos because of a pattern of strong, warm, and accepting extended family relationships; Spanish surnamed persons express their psychopathology by criminal behavior, narcotics addiction, or alcoholism (and are thus seen in far larger numbers than would be expected in the criminal justice system); Spanish surnamed persons are more tolerant or less knowledgeable of deviant behavior; the stigma or shame often associated with mental illnesses is greater among Spanish surnamed than non-Spanish surnamed persons; current mental health programs are not organized or staffed to meet the language, financial, or ethnic-specific realities of Spanish surnamed individuals; Spanish surnamed persons make greater use of indigenous resources, priests, or family physicians in dealing with emotional disorders; and Spanish surnamed patients of recent Mexican origin may return to Mexico for psychiatric care (see Karno and Edgerton, 1969, pp 234–235). Karno and Edgerton (1969) have been able to show that the underutilization of psychiatric facilities by Mexican-Americans in the east Los Angeles area cannot be accounted for by the fact that they "share a cultural tradition which causes them to perceive and define mental illness in significantly different ways than do Anglos" [p. 237]. Their research has led them to conclude that the major reasons for this underrepresentation (in order of importance) are "a formidable language barrier; the significant mental health role of the very active family physician; the self-esteem reducing nature of agency-client contacts experienced by Mexican-Americans; the marked lack of mental health faculties in the Mexican-American community itself; . . . the open border across which return or significant numbers of Mexican-Americans . . . and the threat of 'repatriation' attached to a variety of perceived-as-threatening institutions and agencies of the dominant society" [p. 237]. These authors feel that relatively less important are such considerations as the use of folk medicine, folk psychotherapy, and other characteristics of the Mexican culture.

There are actually two major phenomena worthy of interpretation in the Pueblo data. First, the striking increase in the numbers of identified Spanish surnamed patients between 1960 and 1970; and second, the emergence of a significant relationship between census tract Spanish surnamed admission rate and measure of census tract social disequilibrium. In discussing these findings with groups of mental health professionals and their colleagues in Pueblo (both Chicano and Anglo), the increased utilization of inpatient facilities by Spanish surnamed persons is generally viewed in very positive terms. First, it is their impression that this increased utilization is a consequence of the improved image of the mental health service delivery system, and specifically of the fact that length of hospitalization is now so short (see Chapter 9). Second, it is their impression that increased utilization is the result of the employment of larger numbers of Chicano staff throughout the service delivery system and the employment of larger numbers of competent staff regardless of ethnic group. Finally, the availability of a variety of financial assistance programs has had a significant impact throughout the lower socioeconomic groups where, as has already been indicated, Spanish surnamed persons are overrepresented. This increased availability of financial aid has been instrumental in making it possible for persons to receive private sector inpatient care.

Regarding the emerging relationship of Spanish surnamed admission rate and ecological measures of social disequilibrium, the most persuasive explanations proposed by Pueblo residents lie in the changed relationships between the mental health and the criminal justice systems. These two systems existed quite independently of each other in 1960 but are substantially more interactive at present. In 1960 it was rare that a referral would ever be made from the criminal justice system to mental health agencies. Such referrals are now quite common. Thus, Spanish surnamed persons living in areas with high social disequilibrium might have been overrepresented in the courts and jails in 1960 but were by 1970 being seen in larger numbers in mental health facilities. It is the impression of many Chicano community representatives that, were adequate statistics available, it could be shown that as the number of Chicano patients increased in the mental health system, a parallel decrease took place in the criminal justice system. This interpretation is consistent with the findings from other communities that Spanish surnamed persons, while underrepresented among psychiatric patients, are overrepresented in correctional facilities. This interpretation suggests, furthermore, that it is only the locus of care that has changed for Spanish surnamed persons between 1960 and 1970, and not the number of persons in care, and thus that the new relationship of admission rate with social disequilibrium is an artifact of a change in where Spanish surnamed persons are treated.

Associated with the increased number of referrals to mental health services, and perhaps causally related to them, has been the emergence of Chicano civil rights issues, court decisions regarding equal rights to treatment, and vigorous case finding, all resulting in greater awareness on the part of the community and its human services systems of mental health needs of Chicano citizens.

At the same time, it is thought by some Chicano and Anglo mental health professionals that significant changes are taking place in Chicano family structure and that the role of the extended and often large family in caring for its psychiatric casualties is diminishing. It is this family role, when functioning, which could have partially accounted for the "immunity" of Spanish surnamed persons to neighborhood social disequilibrium in 1960 and a weakening of this role which could help account for the relationships found in 1970. Community members point out that there has been a loosening of family controls (for Chicanos and Anglos alike), a decreased birth rate and consequent reduction in family size, and that there is less cultural isolation of Chicanos.

Thus, some argue, Chicanos are now part of the community and subject to the same set of ecological stresses as have affected Anglos for many years.

These interpretations are entirely speculative in nature, of course, and while there is a certain logic, consistency, and parsimony about them, there is little data which can be gathered in support of these explanations, which thus have the status of hypotheses to be tested.

Part III

PSYCHIATRIC CARE IN 1970

8

The Spectrum of
Psychiatric Care: 1970

Until now, our presentation has dealt exclusively with first admission inpatients, the one group for whom substantial data is available for two different points in time. We have examined this group in considerable detail in order to identify their characteristics as well as the relationships between rates of admission and the social setting in which they live.

Data collected for the two year period of the 1970 study provides us a more complete appreciation of the whole spectrum of treated psychiatric disorder since not only was data available on first admission inpatients, but also regarding inpatients who had had histories of psychiatric hospitalization prior to the start of the study period, first admission outpatients, and finally, outpatients who had had psychiatric outpatient histories prior to the start of data collection. This four-way classification of patients is largely unduplicated. An inpatient is either a first admission or a readmission—never both. An outpatient is either a first admission or a readmission—never both. But in those instances when a patient had been both an inpatient and an outpatient during the data collection period, he was counted twice. In practice, this occured relatively infrequently. Of the 1119 first admission inpatients, 81 (7.2 percent) were at some subsequent time outpatients and are included in the appropriate outpatient tabulations. Of the 790 readmitted inpatients, 48 (6.1 percent) were at some subsequent time outpatients. Of the 1572 first admission outpatients, 73 (4.6 percent) became inpatients at some subsequent time, and of the 280 readmitted outpatients, 41 (14.6 percent) were admitted into inpatient facilities at some time after their initial outpatient admission during the study period. Thus a total of 3518 separate individuals were identified as receiving psychiatric care during the 1970 study period representing an annual treated rate of about 15 cases per 1000 population at risk, and of these persons, 243 (6.9 percent) were both inpatients and outpatients at some time during the period of data collection. For someone interested in the mental health service delivery system, the fact that so few patients receive both inpatient and outpatient care is itself remarkable. We will return to this finding when we discuss pathways in the service delivery system.

CONTRAST BETWEEN PATIENT GROUPS

We now have the opportunity to examine these four groups of patients in terms of their similarities and differences and in order to learn more about how the two inpatient groups differ from the total population. In addition we can determine whether similar environmental factors are associated with each of the four admission rates. By combining the information obtained from all four groups we can develop an understanding about the entire demand for psychiatric care in a community during a period of time when all forms of care were readily available. As was previously mentioned, our data on private outpatients is incomplete because of our failure to obtain information from one psychiatrist who was in private practice during a portion of the period. period. With

that one exception we have reason to believe that virtually all Pueblo residents obtaining mental health services
during the two year study period have been identified.

Tables 8-1 through 8-8 indicate the numbers of patients admitted and the annual admission rates for repeat
inpatients, first admission outpatients, repeat outpatients, and for all admissions combined (including first
admission inpatients for whom data has already been
presented in Chapter 4). It should be noted that there is
an approximately seven percent duplication in the count
due to the fact that that proportion of patients was reported by both inpatient and outpatient facilities. The
eight tables may be examined in pairs; the first of each
pair presents data analyzed by type of facility, age, and
sex, while the second of each pair presents data by type
of facility, diagnosis, and sex.

The pattern of repeat inpatient admissions by age (see
Table 8-1) is similar to that found in the case of first
inpatient admissions—less than one case per 1000 in the
youngest group, between five and six cases per thousand
in the middle years, with a smaller rate (approximately
four cases per 1000) in the oldest age group. The repeat
inpatient admission rates are consistently lower than first
inpatient admission rates with the greatest difference
found in the youngest age group. In this group the first
inpatient admission rate is more than five times the size
of the repeat inpatient admission rate. While in general,
first admission rate is higher than repeat admission rate
(see Tables 4-3 and 4-4), this difference is heavily in-
fluenced by type of facility. In the case of first inpatient
admissions, private facilities are utilized by nearly 70
percent of the patients. In the case of admission rates for
patients with histories of inpatient care prior to the start
of the 1970 study period, private facilities are utilized by
only 40 percent of the cases. There is a further interaction with the sex of the patient. Females, whether first or

Table 8-1

Inpatient Repeat Admissions and Repeat Admission Rates By Type of Facility, Age, and Sex: 1970 Study Period

Age[1]		Type of Facility and Sex								
		Public			Private			Total		
		Male	Female	Total	Male	Female	Total	Male	Female	Total
Under 21	N[2]	10	9	19	11	20	31	21	29	50
	R[3]	0.20	0.19	0.19	0.22	0.41	0.32	0.42	0.60	0.51
21–34	N	92	40	132	34	41	75	126	81	207
	R	4.99	2.00	3.43	1.84	2.05	1.95	6.83	4.04	5.38
35–64	N	216	55	271	76	101	177	292	156	448
	R	6.02	1.44	3.66	2.12	2.64	2.39	8.13	4.09	6.05
65+	N	31	23	54	13	18	31	44	41	85
	R	3.29	1.90	2.51	1.38	1.49	1.44	4.67	3.39	3.95
Total	N	349	127	476	134	180	314	483	307	790
	R	3.07	1.07	2.05	1.18	1.51	1.35	4.25	2.58	3.40

[1] For populations at risk, see Table 4-3
[2] Two-year total
[3] Annual admission rate per 1000 population at risk

repeat admissions, make greater use of private than of public facilities. In contrast, male first admission patients make greater use of private facilities but male repeat admission patients make greater use of public facilities.

Clear diagnostic differences are seen when first inpatient admissions are contrasted with repeat inpatient admissions (see Tables 8-2 and 4-4). In the case of first inpatient admissions, more than half of such patients were diagnosed as psychoneurotics, psychosomatic disorders, or other relatively mild more or less transient conditions. In contrast, psychoneurotics constitute only 28 percent of repeat admissions. In the case of functional psychotics, the situation is just the opposite. While they constitute only seven percent of first admissions, they represent 22 percent of repeat admissions. The repeat admission rate for functional psychotics is actually twice as high as the first admission rate.

Turning next to first outpatient admissions, it can be seen (Tables 8-3 and 8-4) that this rate is about 50 percent higher than first inpatient admission rate. Services are primarily in the public sector, and admission rate is substantially higher in the two youngest age groups in outpatient settings than is the case in inpatient settings. Almost no persons age 65 or above are seen in outpatient settings and in the 35-64 age group there is a very close agreement between first inpatient and first outpatient admission rates. The difference in first admission rates between inpatient and outpatient settings is almost entirely accounted for by psychoneurotics. Almost twice as many are admitted into outpatient settings as into inpatient settings. In the other diagnostic categories, admission rates are more comparable between inpatient and outpatient facilities.

Repeat outpatient admissions are relatively infrequent, representing only one case per thousand population per year (see Tables 8-5 and 8-6). Admissions seem

Table 8-2

INPATIENT REPEAT ADMISSIONS AND REPEAT ADMISSION RATES BY TYPE OF FACILITY, DIAGNOSIS, AND SEX: 1970 STUDY PERIOD

Diagnosis[1]		Type of Facility and Sex								
		Public			Private			Total		
		Male	Female	Total	Male	Female	Total	Male	Female	Total
Psychoneuroses	N[2]	22	17	39	62	120	182	84	137	221
	R[3]	0.19	0.14	0.17	0.55	1.01	0.78	0.74	1.15	0.95
Personality Disorders	N	225	47	272	42	23	65	267	70	337
	R	1.98	0.40	1.17	0.37	0.19	0.28	2.35	0.59	1.45
Functional Psychoses	N	82	46	128	17	30	47	99	76	175
	R	0.72	0.39	0.55	0.15	0.25	0.20	0.87	0.64	0.75
Brain Syndromes	N	20	17	37	13	7	20	33	24	57
	R	0.18	0.14	0.16	0.11	0.06	0.09	0.29	0.20	0.25
Total	N	349	127	476	134	180	314	483	307	790
	R	3.07	1.07	2.05	1.18	1.51	1.35	4.25	2.58	3.40

[1] For populations at risk, see Table 4–4
[2] Two-year total
[3] Annual admission rate per 1000 population at risk

Table 8-3

OUTPATIENT FIRST ADMISSIONS AND FIRST ADMISSION RATES BY TYPE OF FACILITY, AGE, AND SEX: 1970 STUDY PERIOD

Age[1]		Type of Facility and Sex									
		Public			Private			Total		
		Male	Female	Total	Male	Female	Total	Male	Female	Total
Under 21	N[2]	310	250	560	48	45	93	358	295	653
	R[3]	6.22	5.15	5.69	0.96	0.93	0.95	7.18	6.07	6.64
21–34	N	165	220	385	52	85	137	217	305	522
	R	8.95	10.98	10.01	2.82	4.24	3.56	11.77	15.22	13.57
35–64	N	87	127	214	77	93	170	164	220	384
	R	2.42	3.33	2.89	2.14	2.44	2.29	4.57	5.76	5.18
65+	N	3	3	6	3	4	7	6	7	13
	R	0.32	0.25	0.28	0.32	0.33	0.33	0.64	0.58	0.60
Total	N	565	600	1165	180	227	407	745	827	1572
	R	4.97	5.05	5.01	1.58	1.91	1.71	6.56	6.96	6.76

[1] For populations at risk, see Table 4–3
[2] Two-year total
[3] Annual admission rate per 1000 population at risk

Table 8-4

OUTPATIENT FIRST ADMISSIONS AND FIRST ADMISSION RATES BY TYPE OF FACILITY, DIAGNOSIS, AND SEX: 1970 STUDY PERIOD

Diagnosis[1]		Type of Facility and Sex								
		Public			Private			Total		
		Male	Female	Total	Male	Female	Total	Male	Female	Total
Psychoneuroses	N[2]	343	427	770	123	192	315	466	619	1085
	R[3]	3.02	3.59	3.31	1.08	1.61	1.35	4.10	5.21	4.67
Personality Disorders	N	172	127	299	45	21	66	217	148	365
	R	1.51	1.07	1.29	0.40	0.18	0.28	1.91	1.24	1.57
Functional Psychoses	N	32	30	62	9	10	19	41	40	81
	R	0.28	0.25	0.27	0.08	0.08	0.08	0.36	0.34	0.35
Brain Syndromes	N	16	10	26	3	4	7	19	14	33
	R	0.14	0.08	0.11	0.03	0.03 —	0.03	0.17	0.12	0.14
Total	N	563[4]	594[5]	1157	180	227	407	743	821	1564
	R	4.96	5.00	4.98	1.58	1.91	1.75	6.54	6.91	6.73

[1] For populations at risk, see Table 4-4
[2] Two-year total
[3] Annual admission rate per 1000 population at risk
[4] Two cases undiagnosed
[5] Six cases undiagnosed

Table 8-5

OUTPATIENT REPEAT ADMISSIONS AND REPEAT ADMISSION RATES BY TYPE OF FACILITY, AGE, AND SEX: 1970 STUDY PERIOD

Age[1]		Type of Facility and Sex								
		Public			Private			Total		
		Male	Female	Total	Male	Female	Total	Male	Female	Total
Under 21	N[2]	16	15	31	9	9	18	25	24	49
	R[3]	0.32	0.31	0.32	0.18	0.19	0.18	0.50	0.49	0.50
21–34	N	34	17	51	25	34	59	59	51	110
	R	1.84	0.85	1.33	1.36	1.70	1.53	3.20	2.54	2.86
35–64	N	23	34	57	31	26	57	54	60	114
	R	0.64	0.89	0.77	0.86	0.68	0.77	1.50	1.57	1.54
65+	N	3	1	4	1	2	3	4	3	7
	R	0.32	0.08	0.19	0.11	0.17	0.14	0.42	0.25	0.33
Total	N	76	67	143	66	71	137	142	138	280
	R	0.67	0.56	0.62	0.58	0.60	0.59	1.25	1.16	1.20

[1] For populations at risk, see Table 4–3
[2] Two-year total
[3] Annual admission rate per 1000 population at risk

213

Table 8-6

OUTPATIENT REPEAT ADMISSIONS AND REPEAT ADMISSION RATES BY TYPE OF FACILITY, DIAGNOSIS, AND SEX: 1970 STUDY PERIOD

Diagnosis[1]		Public			Private			Total		
		Male	Female	Total	Male	Female	Total	Male	Female	Total
Psychoneuroses	N[2]	18	30	48	25	50	75	43	80	123
	R[3]	0.16	0.25	0.21	0.22	0.42	0.32	0.38	0.67	0.53
Personality Disorders	N	38	18	56	22	9	31	60	27	87
	R	0.33	0.15	0.24	0.19	0.08	0.13	0.53	0.23	0.37
Functional Psychoses	N	10	15	25	19	12	31	29	27	56
	R	0.09	0.13	0.11	0.17	0.10	0.13	0.26	0.23	0.24
Brain Syndromes	N	10	4	14	0	0	0	10	4	14
	R	0.09	0.03	0.06	0.00	0.00	0.00	0.09	0.03	0.06
Total	N	76	67	143	66	71	137	142	138	280
	R	0.67	0.56	0.62	0.58	0.60	0.59	1.25	1.16	1.20

[1] For populations at risk, see Table 4–4
[2] Two-year total
[3] Annual admission rate per 1000 population at risk

equally divided between public and private facilities and between men and women. Admissions are highest in the middle years and, just as in the case of first outpatient admissions, they are restricted mainly to psychoneurotics.

Combining all patient categories (see Tables 8-7 and 8-8) it is now possible to analyze the entire identified demand for mental health services. This demand exhibits a clear interaction with sex and type of facility. While in general it is equally distributed by sex and slightly more visible in public facilities, male patients are treated predominantly in public settings and female patients are treated slightly more often in private settings. In the youngest and oldest age groups the total annual admission rate is approximately 10 cases per 1000. In the 21-34 age group it is nearly 30 cases per 1000 and in the 35-64 age group it approaches 20 cases per 1000. In all, the duplicated admission rate is about 16 cases per 1000 while, as already indicated, the unduplicated annual total admission rate is 15 cases per 1000. More than half of all patients are in the psychoneurotic diagnostic category; about 30 percent of all patients are considered personality disorders.

Basic demographic and psychiatric characteristics of the four groups of patients are shown in Table 8-9. Except for the overrepresentation of males among readmitted inpatients, sex differences among the four patient groups are not remarkable. Spanish surnamed persons make up a slightly smaller proportion of outpatients than they do of inpatients. Outpatients are substantially younger than readmissions. Less severe diagnoses (psychoneuroses and transient reactions) are substantially more common among outpatients than among inpatients and are more common among first admissions than among patients who have had prior psychiatric histories.

Table 8-7

TOTAL ADMISSIONS AND ADMISSION RATES BY TYPE OF FACILITY, AGE, AND SEX: 1970 STUDY PERIOD

Age[1]		Type of Facility and Sex								
		Public			Private			Total		
		Male	Female	Total	Male	Female	Total	Male	Female	Total
Under 21	N[2]	375	295	670	142	204	346	517	499	1016
	R[3]	7.52	6.07	6.81	2.85	4.20	3.52	10.37	10.27	10.32
21–34	N	368	297	665	183	272	455	551	569	1120
	R	19.96	14.82	17.28	9.93	13.57	11.83	29.89	28.39	29.11
35–64	N	424	249	673	315	420	735	739	669	1408
	R	11.81	6.52	9.08	8.77	11.00	9.92	20.58	17.52	19.00
65+	N	62	46	108	39	70	109	101	116	217
	R	6.58	3.80	5.02	4.14	5.79	5.07	10.72	9.59	10.08
Total	N	1229	887	2116	679	966	1645	1908	1853	3761
	R	10.82	7.46	9.10	5.98	8.13	7.08	16.80	15.59	16.18

[1] For populations at risk, see Table 4–3
[2] Two-year total
[3] Annual admission rate per 1000 population at risk

Table 8-8

TOTAL ADMISSIONS AND ADMISSION RATES BY TYPE OF FACILITY, DIAGNOSIS, AND SEX: 1970 STUDY PERIOD

Diagnosis[1]		Public			Private			Total		
		Male	Female	Total	Male	Female	Total	Male	Female	Total
Psychoneuroses	N[2]	416	498	914	367	728	1095	783	1226	2009
	R[3]	3.66	4.19	3.93	3.23	6.12	4.71	6.89	10.31	8.64
Personality Disorders	N	604	229	833	210	96	306	814	325	1139
	R	5.32	1.93	3.58	1.85	0.81	1.32	7.17	2.73	4.90
Functional Psychoses	N	141	100	241	64	88	152	205	188	393
	R	1.24	0.84	1.04	0.56	0.74	0.65	1.80	1.58	1.69
Brain Syndromes	N	66	54	120	38	54	92	104	108	212
	R	0.58	0.45	0.52	0.33	0.45	0.40	0.92	0.91	0.91
Total	N	1227[4]	881[5]	2108	679	966	1645	1906	1847	3753
	R	10.80	7.41	9.07	5.98	8.13	7.08	16.78	15.54	16.14

[1] For populations at risk, see Table 4-4
[2] Two-year total
[3] Annual admission rate per 1000 population at risk
[4] Two cases undiagnosed
[5] Six cases undiagnosed

217

Table 8-9

BASIC DEMOGRAPHIC AND PSYCHIATRIC CHARACTERISTICS OF FOUR PATIENT GROUPS: 1970 STUDY PERIOD

Characteristics	First Adm. IP		Readmitted IP		First Adm. OP*		Readmitted OP	
	N	%	N	%	N	%	N	%
Total	1119		790		1572		280	
Male	538	48.1	483	61.1	745	47.4	142	50.7
Female	581	51.9	307	38.9	827	52.6	138	49.2
Spanish Surname	298	26.6	222	28.1	362	23.0	60	21.4
Under 21	264	23.6	50	6.3	653	41.6	49	17.5
21–34	281	25.1	207	26.2	522	33.2	110	39.3
35–64	462	41.3	448	56.7	384	24.4	114	40.7
65+	112	10.0	85	10.8	13	0.8	7	2.5
Psychoneuroses	577	51.6	214	27.1	1091	69.8	128	45.7
Personality Disorders	352	31.5	345	43.7	353	22.6	81	28.9
Functional Psychoses	85	7.6	172	21.8	81	5.2	58	20.7
Brain Syndromes	105	9.4	59	7.5	39	2.5	13	4.6
Public	332	29.7	476	60.3	1165	74.1	143	51.1
Private	787	70.3	314	39.7	407	25.9	137	48.9

*8 patients undiagnosed

The data presented in Table 8-9 is cross-sectional rather than longitudinal in nature and will later be compared with longitudinal data based upon an analysis of single versus multiple episode cases (see Chapter 10). But the four patient groups are strikingly different from each other. Inpatients (whether first or repeat admissions) are very different from outpatients in age, diagnosis, type of treatment facility and, to a lesser extent, sex and ethnic group. First admissions (whether in- or outpatients) differ substantially from repeat admissions in age distribution and diagnosis. In each case, as might be expected, these differences suggest that problems are more serious and probably more long-standing among inpatients than among outpatients and among readmissions than first admissions.

Intercorrelations of age-adjustment admission rates are shown in Table 8-10. The results of this analysis indicate that census tracts which yield large numbers of first admission inpatients yield large numbers of all other kinds of patients as well. These intercorrelations are especially impressive when one considers that the four patient groups are almost entirely unduplicated counts. Those census tracts from which large numbers of inpatients come also yield large numbers of outpatients, and those census tracts from which large numbers of new patients come are also where large numbers of former patients live at the time they are readmitted for care.

Further examination of Table 8-10 indicates that this tendency for a census tract to yield similar numbers of all types of psychiatric patients is much more marked in the case of public facility admissions than in the case of private facility admissions. In fact, the only correlation which is clearly significant in the case of private facility admission rates is the one between first admission inpatients and repeat admission inpatients. In the case of public facilities, intercorrelations of the four patient

Table 8-10
INTERCORRELATIONS OF 1970 AGE-ADJUSTED ADMISSION RATES AMONG FOUR PATIENT GROUPS

Patient Group	First Inpt. Admission			Repeat Inpt. Admission			First Outpt. Admission		
	Public	Private	Total	Public	Private	Total	Public	Private	Total
First Inpatient Admission									
Repeat Inpatient Admission	+0.91	+0.62	+0.83						
First Outpatient Admission	+0.56		+0.78	+0.61		+0.64			
Repeat Outpatient Admission	+0.59		+0.64	+0.67	+0.36	+0.69	+0.73		+0.62

group admission rates are powerful indeed, and it should not prove difficult to identify those variables which characterize the census tracts from which these patients come. It can be seen that total age-adjusted admission rate intercorrelations remain high even though the private admission rate intercorrelations are often not significantly different from zero. Part of the reason for this phenomenon might lie in the fact that relatively few patients are admitted into private outpatient facilities either as first admissions or repeat admissions. With relatively few cases, census tract admission rates can be quite unstable with the result that admission rate intercorrelations can be quite low.

Census tract diagnosis-specific admission rates within the four patient groups are highest for personality disorders (averaging +0.81), lower for the psychoneuroses (averaging +0.50), and hardly significantly different from zero in the case of functional psychoses and brain syndromes. Age-specific admission rate intercorrelations are highest in the 35-64 age group (averaging +0.58) and somewhat lower in all other age groups (averaging between +0.34 and +0.40). Clearly in the case of diagnosis-specific rates and almost as clear in the case of age-specific rates, intercorrelations are lowest where numbers of cases are fewest and thus where census tract rates can be expected to be most unreliable.

First Inpatients Versus Repeat Inpatients

Except for data already presented, no other information is available often enough for outpatients to allow us to continue to differentiate the four patient groups. But considerable additional information is available for inpatients and it can be productive to develop a greater understanding of how new inpatients differ from those with prior treatment histories. We have already seen that new inpatients, when contrasted with repeat inpatients, tend to be more often female, younger, less severely disordered, and more often treated in private settings. As will be seen shortly (Chapter 9) they are also discharged more quickly and return less often for subsequent episodes of care. In examining the other data available from questionnaires completed by inpatients, it is possible to identify other differences between first admission and repeat admission inpatients. These two inpatient groups are not different in education, occupation, employment history, length of marriage, number of children, or length of time living in the country. But on variables associated with housing and family life, the two inpatient groups are found to be repeatedly and significantly different from each other.

Regarding family life characteristics, repeat inpatients live alone more than twice as often as first admission inpatients, and are characterized substantially more often by disrupted marriages. The marital histories of cohorts of ever-married first and repeat admission inpatients are contrasted in Table 8-11 on the basis of available data. In comparing these two inpatient groups, the excess divorce rate and excess pattern of multiple marriages in the case of repeat inpatients can be seen as well as the lower proportion of cases in which there has been only one marriage without any separations. As to housing characteristics, repeat inpatient admissions, in contrast to first admission inpatients, have lived for a significantly shorter time at their present addresses, and their homes are smaller, older, and significantly more often without adequate kitchen and toilet facilities. They live in single rooms three times as commonly as do first admission inpatients. Furthermore, repeat inpatients more often live in apartments and rooming houses and less

Table 8-11

MARITAL HISTORIES OF EVER-MARRIED FIRST AND REPEAT
ADMISSION INPATIENTS: 1970 STUDY PERIOD

Marital History	First Adm. IP		Rpt. Adm. IP	
	N	%	N	%
Married Once, never separated	217	39.5	156	29.3
Married Once, sep. 1+ times	57	10.4	70	13.1
Married Once, now divorced	75	13.7	97	18.2
Married Once, now widowed	42	7.7	37	6.9
Remarried following divorce	112	20.4	103	19.3
Remarried following widowhood	27	4.9	16	3.0
Other	19	3.5	54	10.1
Total	549[1]	100.1	533[2]	99.9

$\chi^2 = 34.38; df = 6; P = <.001$
[1]Information not available for 310 patients
[2]Information not available for 115 patients

often live in single homes than do first admission inpatients and, associated with this fact, more commonly are renters rather than home owners. Inpatients with psychiatric hospitalizations prior to the start of the 1970 study period give clear evidence of substantially greater interpersonal deterioration at the start of the study period than do inpatients who are first admissions into psychiatric facilities. When one adds to this fact the additional observation (to be presented shortly) that patients with hospitalization histories prior to the start of the study period are more vulnerable to repeated episodes of care during the study period, the spiraling character of psychiatric and interpersonal disability becomes clear.

It will be remembered that many of the differences found between first admission inpatients and repeat admission inpatients were also found when first admission inpatients were contrasted with the general population (see Chapter 6). We now see that in virtually every case where a significant difference between first admission inpatients and the general population was found, the same difference in more exaggerated form characterizes repeat inpatients. The marriages of first admission inpatients, for example, are more disrupted than in the total population. The marriages of repeat inpatients are even more disrupted. First admission inpatients were found to be more socially isolated than the general population. Repeat inpatients are even more isolated. This same sequence of relationships holds in the case of housing characteristics. Inpatients with prior psychiatric episodes of care are significantly more mobile (from house to house) than are first admission inpatients, who in turn are more mobile than the general population. First admission inpatients live more often in substandard, older, and smaller homes than is true of the general population. Housing conditions of repeat inpatients are even more limited.

CENSUS TRACT CHARACTERISTICS AND ADMISSION RATES OF FOUR PATIENT GROUPS

We turn now to an analysis of census tract characteristics associated with admission rates for the four differentiated patient groups. This data has already been presented for 1970 first inpatient admissions. It will be remembered that total age-adjusted admission rate for first inpatient admissions was significantly negatively related to the census tract index of socioeconomic affluence (due largely to the strong negative relationship in the case of public facility admissions), very strongly and positively associated with the census tract index of social disequilibrium, and unrelated to the census tract young marrieds cluster score. Admission rates with the personality disorder diagnosis were negatively associated with socioeconomic affluence, strongly positively associated with the social disequilibrium cluster score, and negatively related to the young marrieds index. The same relationships, although weaker, characterized admission rates for persons with all other diagnoses and for admission rates for persons under 65 years of age. We are now concerned with whether these census tract characteristics are related solely to first inpatient rates or whether the same general relationships hold in the case of census tract admission rates for inpatients with prior psychiatric histories and for outpatients as well.

The data responsive to this question will be found in Table 8-12. First, with respect to census tract characteristics associated with high admission rates of patients with psychiatric inpatient histories prior to the start of the 1970 study period, relationships with the socioeconomic affluence and social disequilibrium cluster scores found in the case of first inpatient admissions hold equally strongly and in some cases more strongly. Census tracts low in socioeconomic affluence and high in social disequilibrium yield the largest numbers of repeat inpatients. In the case of socioeconomic affluence, this fact holds true for total age-adjusted admission rates and more specifically for personality disorders and for patients in the productive adult years—between 21 and 64. Again, as in the case of first admissions, it is the public facility admission rate that accounts for this relationship. Census tract measures of socioeconomic affluence are neither useful predictors of private facility first inpatient nor repeat inpatient admission rate. In the case of the index of social disequilibrium, the significant relationships with repeat inpatient admission rate hold not only for age-adjusted figures in general, but specifically for each of the four diagnostic categories and for all but the oldest age group. Although the relationships tend to be stronger for public facility than for private facility admis-

Table 8-12

Significant Correlations of Census Tract Cluster Scores With Admission Rates in Four Patient Groups: 1970 Study Period

Patient Group and Admission Rate	Census Tract Cluster Score								
	Socioeconomic Affluence			Social Disequilibrium			Young Marrieds		
	Public	Private	Total	Public	Private	Total	Public	Private	Total
Age Adjusted									
First IP Admission	−0.56		−0.40	+0.78	+0.49	+0.76			
Repeat IP Admission	−0.44		−0.43	+0.84	+0.45	+0.87	−0.40		−0.45
First OP Admission		+0.54		+0.79		+0.66	−0.43	−0.34	−0.44
Repeat OP Admission				+0.75		+0.63			−0.36
Psychoneuroses									
First IP Admission									
Repeat IP Admission				+0.65		+0.44	−0.41		−0.40
First OP Admission		+0.58		+0.57		+0.34			
Repeat OP Admission		+0.37							
Personality Disorder									
First IP Admission	−0.50		−0.51	+0.77	+0.57	+0.83	−0.42		−0.38
Repeat IP Admission	−0.40		−0.40	+0.79	+0.46	+0.81			−0.44
First OP Admission				+0.84		+0.82	−0.37	−0.34	−0.41
Repeat OP Admission				+0.65		+0.65			

Functional Psychoses									
First IP Admission	-0.37			+0.53					
Repeat IP Admission				+0.66		+0.68	-0.34	-0.48	-0.44
First OP Admission				+0.42		+0.37	-0.38	-0.41	-0.41
Repeat OP Admission				+0.63		+0.56	-0.35		-0.43
Brain Syndromes									
First IP Admission	-0.34			+0.42	+0.41	+0.49	-0.41	-0.43	-0.49
Repeat IP Admission				+0.56	+0.54	+0.64	-0.38		-0.42
First OP Admission		+0.38							-0.34
Repeat OP Admission				+0.56		+0.56			
Under Age 21									
First IP Admission					+0.49	+0.48		-0.45	-0.48
Repeat IP Admission				+0.56		+0.40			
First OP Admission		+0.61		+0.73		+0.68	-0.47		-0.52
Repeat OP Admission				+0.42		+0.39			
Age 21-34									
First IP Admission	-0.58		-0.40	+0.50	+0.37	+0.80			-0.47
Repeat IP Admission	-0.43		-0.44	+0.73		+0.39	-0.42		
First OP Admission		+0.39		+0.57		+0.54			
Repeat OP Admission				+0.56					

227

Table 8-12 (cont'd)

SIGNIFICANT CORRELATIONS OF CENSUS TRACT CLUSTER SCORES WITH ADMISSION RATES IN FOUR PATIENT GROUPS: 1970 STUDY PERIOD

Patient Group and Admission Rate	Census Tract Cluster Score								
	Socioeconomic Affluence			Social Disequilibrium			Young Marrieds		
	Public	Private	Total	Public	Private	Total	Public	Private	Total
Age 35-64									
First IP Admission	-0.41			+0.76	+0.43	+0.70			
Repeat IP Admission	-0.41		-0.39	+0.82	+0.49	+0.85	-0.40		-0.43
First OP Admission				+0.61		+0.50	-0.34		-0.35
Repeat OP Admission				+0.62		+0.47			
Age 65 and above									
First IP Admission									
Repeat IP Admission		+0.39							
First OP Admission									
Repeat OP Admission									

sions, areas of high social disequilibrium produce excess numbers of both first and repeat inpatient admissions into private facilities.

The young marrieds index, which was not significantly related to first inpatient admission rate is, however, significantly negatively related to repeat inpatient admission rate. Inpatients with prior psychiatric hospitalizations do not live in census tracts characterized by large numbers of young families. That this finding is not due to the generally younger age level in these tracts can be seen from the fact that the relationship holds true in the case of age-specific rates in the middle years as well as diagnosis-specific rates. We have already noted, however, that repeat admission inpatients tend much more than first admission inpatients to live by themselves in those kinds of housing accomodations which would be unsuitable for young families—old single rooms or very small rental apartments sometimes without complete kitchen and toilet facilities. Just as in the case of the other two census tract cluster scores, the relationships of the young marrieds cluster score with repeat inpatient admission rates tend to be somewhat stronger in the case of public facilities than private facilities. In part this may be due to the relatively small number of repeat inpatients admitted into private facilities with the resulting unreliability of the calculated rates.

Turning next to first admission outpatients, it can be seen that census tracts high on the index of socioeconomic affluence yield the largest number of private patients, most particularly in the psychoneurosis diagnostic category and in the under-21 age group, and census tracts high on the index of social disequilibrium produce the highest rates of public patients, not only in general, but in every diagnostic category except brain syndromes and in every age group except the oldest. Affluent census tracts are not overrepresented in public outpatient facility caseloads, and socially disorganized census tracts are not overrepresented in private outpatient facility caseloads. There is a tendency for census tracts high on the young marrieds cluster score to yield relatively few first admission outpatients, particularly into public settings. This tendency is specifically evident in the case of personality disorders and functional psychotics and in the under-21 age group.

Finally, where correlation coefficients are significant between census tract characteristics and admission rates for outpatients with psychiatric histories prior to the start of the study period, they tend to be similar in direction and magnitude to those found in the case of first admission outpatients. Just as affluent census tracts tend to yield high rates of private sector first outpatient admission psychoneurotics, so do they with respect to repeat admission outpatient psychoneurotics. The relationships described above linking the census tract index of social disequilibrium and the young marrieds cluster score with first admission outpatient rates holds reasonably well for repeat admission outpatient rates. In general, however, relationships, even when significantly different from zero, are not very close.

This pattern of relationships should suggest that correlations between public and private admission rates are quite low and such is in fact the case. Only in the case of first admission inpatients does one find that those census tracts yielding large numbers of public patients also yield large numbers of private patients, and even in this case the relationship is not a powerful one. As for the other three patient categories public and private admission rates are virtually completely unrelated to each other.

Given that inpatient and outpatient, first and repeat admission rates are all generally highly intercorrelated, it is, of course, not surprising that all of these admission rates bear the same general relationship to neighborhood characteristics. The significant finding is that these various admission rates are so highly correlated. When one considers the variety of routes which must be taken by potential patients in petitioning for psychiatric care, and the fact that as individuals there are major age and diagnostic differences between persons who ultimately become inpatients when contrasted with those who become outpatients, it is actually quite impressive that these admission rate intercorrelations are so high. Clearly one explanation consistent with our data is that ecological characteristics play a significant role in the production of psychopathology. This social causation hypothesis would be much more difficult to sustain if it had been shown that inpatient and outpatient admission rates or first and repeat admission rates were in fact independent of each other.

On the other hand we cannot escape the traditional dilemmas in interpreting these findings. It is possible that psychopathology or the potential for psychopathology predates the arrival into the residential setting. It is possible that there is a kind of readiness for help-seeking which can be shown to characterize those census tracts from which large numbers of patients come, and that factors in determining the site of treatment distribute themselves more or less randomly within such help-seekers.

At the same time we should not underestimate those differences in patterns of correlations between census tract cluster scores and admission rates. In the specific case of socioeconomic affluence, inspection of Table 8-4 indicates that affluent census tracts yield large numbers of private outpatients and poor tracts yield large numbers of public inpatients. This is a complex interaction with affluence, involving as it does both mode of payment and type of facility. Assuming, as we now can (see Chapter 6) that patients living in census tracts character-

ized by high socioeconomic affluence are generally affluent, one can see that outpatient care tends to be offered
to patients able to pay for services, and inpatient care
tends to be made available for persons unable to pay.
While there is probably some relationship between economic status and the nature and severity of psychopathology, it is surely not persuasive enough to suggest
that if one is poor he should be treated in a public inpatient setting rather than a public outpatient setting, or if
he is well off he should be treated as a private outpatient
rather than a private inpatient. A simple association between affluence and mode of payment for psychiatric
care would be easier to account for. Public facilities are
usually mandated not to treat patients who can afford
private care, and patients in sound economic conditions
may very well prefer to be treated in private rather than
public settings. But our results suggest that the issue of
inpatient versus outpatient treatment figures into the
decision-making process as a function of affluence, and
this additional element may be less appropriate.

Two explanations of this complex relationship have
been advanced by mental health professionals in Pueblo.
First, a very large number of patients admitted into public inpatient facilities are in fact delivered there by the
police. There is apparently little choice for those persons
deemed in need of psychiatric care but unable to pay for
it other than being taken to the state hospital. Public
outpatient facilities in Pueblo (mainly the community
mental health center) are either unable to accept such
unanticipated emergency admissions or have not worked
out any procedure with the police for developing alternatives to using the state hospital. A second reason for
the apparent overutilization of inpatient facilities in the
case of the poor is the absence of a public general (nonpsychiatric) hospital in the area. There is a strong effort

being made at the state hospital to convert part of it into a general medical facility to serve not only Pueblo but much of south-central Colorado. This new proposed program emphasis has raised a number of complex issues within the local medical community and in the legislature, and as of 1970 hospitalizations for nonpsychiatric reasons were undertaken without fanfare and with a certain amount of circumspection. But on certain occasions patients are admitted to the state hospital primarily for medical reasons. A former patient, now in a nursing home for example, who needs dentures or other medical repair is often readmitted to the state hospital for such care. But because of administrative policy, his primary diagnosis is psychiatric.

This cross-sectional view of psychiatric patients served during the 1970 study period raises a number of provocative issues. On the one hand, many findings seem to have a high level of rationality. Thus, as might be expected, patients with prior treatment histories, when contrasted with new psychiatric patients, are more severely incapacitated and have life styles that give evidence of substantially more personal disruption. On the other hand, other characteristics of the service delivery system seem more difficult to account for on the basis of clinical considerations. First, nearly all patients who are admitted into inpatient facilities become inpatients without an initial effort being made to treat them as outpatients. Second, outpatient facilities seem to play an insignificant role in the management of patients above age 65. Third, private inpatient facilities which play such an important role in the treatment of new patients are far less involved in the care of patients with prior psychiatric histories. Fourth, there is a strong tendency for males to be treated in the public sector while females are treated in the private sector. Fifth, patients who are relatively affluent have a far greater likelihood of being treated as outpatients, while poorer patients are much more often treated in inpatient settings.

One of the important consequences of the fact that inpatients with histories of prior psychiatric care lead more disrupted lives than do first admission inpatients is that those sections of the city characterized by low socio-economic affluence and high social disequilibrium yield a very large proportion of repeat admission inpatients into both public and private facilities. Financial consider-ations are undoubtedly playing a very important role in these clinically rational findings, but perhaps almost as important is the need for a broad spectrum of rehabilita-tive services for discharged psychiatric patients, particu-larly those who live or move into the more socially disorganized portions of the city. Such activities, if effec-tively carried out, and if they include a full range of health, welfare, employment, housing, and homemaking services, would have the potential of breaking the circle of psychiatric and personal disruption.

The findings reported in this chapter are cross-sec-tional in nature; patients were characterized in terms of the presence or absence of previous psychiatric care at the time of their initial entry into the 1970 study period. Because all episodes of care were reported during the two year period of time of the 1970 study, supplemen-tary longitudinal information is also available on those patients with multiple episodes of care. These data will be reported in Chapter 10 and will allow us to develop another view of the problems associated with chronicity.

9

Length of Episodes
of Care

Recent literature regarding psychiatric treatment (particularly in inpatient settings) has been virtually unanimous in noting the striking reduction in length of episodes of care during the past decade. The National Institute of Mental Health has noted this trend on a nationwide basis but has been hesitant to attribute it to improved methods of care. Rather, they suggest that improved treatment effectiveness may be one among many reasons for shortened inpatient stays, and indicate that, in addition, some patients who might require long-term hospitalization are now cared for elsewhere, that the increasing availability of community aftercare facilities may make it possible to discharge patients sooner than might otherwise have been the case, and that aside from these factors, mental hospital administrators may be making a deliberate effort to reduce the number of patients in residence (see Bethel and Redick, 1972).

The efforts being made by outpatient facilities to reduce length of episodes of care are equally well known, although precise information is not as readily available. The development of crisis intervention services and open intake policies during the past decade has been undertaken in part because of the promise such services hold for shortening length of treatment and reducing waiting lists, although concentration on short-term care has not escaped criticism (see, e.g̃., Kubie, 1968).

FACTORS ASSOCIATED WITH LENGTH OF EPISODES OF CARE

Yet not all patients are discharged quickly and certain types of patients require relatively large allocations of institutional resources before a discharge can be accomplished (see Bloom, 1970a). Data from the 1970 study period permits us to identify some of the factors associated with long episodes of care. The concept of length of an episode of care, meaning the time between admission and discharge, is not really comparable between inpatient and outpatients, because in the case of outpatients there is no clear relationship between length of a care episode and amount of treatment. Table 9-1, analyzing length of first episode of care in the four patient groups, presents some useful information regarding the 1970 study period in Pueblo. First, in the case of inpatients, about 35 percent are discharged within a week of admission and 80 percent are discharged within one month. Only eight percent of first admission inpatients and only 14 percent of repeat admission inpatients are hospitalized for longer than two months. Initial episodes of care tend to be longer in the case of repeat admission inpatients than first admission inpatients but for all inpatients treatment is remarkably short.

The same relative episode length holds true in the case of outpatients, that is, first admission outpatients tend to be discharged more quickly than outpatients who have had prior outpatient histories. There is an accumulation of cases whose initial episodes of care as outpatients exceeds three months; first admission patients tend to be underrepresented in this group. Of course, it is well known that outpatient settings discharge large numbers

Table 9-1
LENGTH OF FIRST EPISODE OF CARE IN FOUR PATIENT GROUPS: 1970 STUDY PERIOD

Patient Group	Length of First Episode of Care										Total
	One Week or Less		One Week to One Month		One to Two Months		Two to Three Months		Over Three Months		
	N	%	N	%	N	%	N	%	N	%	N
First Inpatient Admission	442	39.5	498	44.5	92	8.2	23	2.1	64	5.7	1119
Repeat Inpatient Admission	217	27.5	365	46.2	95	12.0	35	4.4	78	9.9	790
First Outpatient Admission	505	32.1	270	17.2	223	14.2	128	8.1	446	28.4	1572
Repeat Outpatient Admission	55	19.6	39	13.9	36	12.9	18	6.4	132	47.1	280

of patients because they cease keeping appointments or "drop out" of treatment, and it would be foolhardy to equate a short episode of care with rapid and significant improvement. But whatever the reasons for discharging patients, episodes of care while longer for repeat patients than for new patients are remarkably short for most patients, whether admitted into inpatient or outpatient settings.

Our data permit us to make a somewhat more detailed analysis of factors associated with length of first episode of care. For both inpatients as well as outpatients we can determine to what extent length of care is related not only to type of admission (first or repeat) but type of facility, sex, age, diagnosis, and ethnic group membership. Data for inpatients is shown in Tables 9-2 and 9-3, and for outpatients in Tables 9-4 and 9-5. The descriptive information is presented in the first of each pair of Tables, and results of tests of significance are presented in the second of each pair.

In the case of inpatients, every comparison with the exception of ethnic group yields significant findings. Female patients are hospitalized for significantly shorter periods of time than are male patients. There is a general age progression in length of hospitalization with each age group hospitalized for a longer period of time than all younger groups. Nearly half of all inpatients less than 21 years old are discharged within one week, and there is a large accumulation of patients in the age 65 and above group who are hospitalized for longer than three months. A similar progression by diagnosis is noted, with the mildest conditions requiring the shortest periods of hospitalization. Very great differences in length of hospitalization are noted when public and private facilities are contrasted, with private facilities discharging patients much more quickly than public facilities. In fact, less than seven percent of private patients are hospital-

Table 9-2

VARIABLES ASSOCIATED WITH LENGTH OF FIRST EPISODE OF INPATIENT CARE: 1970 STUDY PERIOD

Variables		Total	Length of First Episode of Inpatient Care (in days)									
			7 or less		8–14		15–30		31–90		91+	
			N	%	N	%	N	%	N	%	N	%
Total Inpatients		1909	659	34.5	421	22.1	442	23.2	245	12.8	142	7.4
Sex:	Male	1021	321	31.4	213	20.9	243	23.8	150	14.7	94	9.2
	Female	888	338	38.1	208	23.4	199	22.4	95	10.7	48	5.4
Age:	Under 21	314	154	49.0	48	15.3	51	16.2	31	9.9	30	9.6
	21–34	488	192	39.3	116	23.8	104	21.3	64	13.1	12	2.5
	35–64	910	289	31.8	210	23.1	258	28.4	118	13.0	35	3.8
	65+	197	24	12.2	47	23.9	29	14.7	32	16.2	65	33.0
Diagnosis:												
Psychoneuroses		801	347	43.3	196	24.5	180	22.5	59	7.4	19	2.4
Personality Disorders		687	245	35.7	135	19.7	165	24.0	103	15.0	39	5.7
Functional Psychoses		256	41	16.0	54	21.1	74	28.9	54	21.1	33	12.9
Brain Syndromes		165	26	15.8	36	21.8	23	13.9	29	17.6	51	30.9
Spanish Surname:	Yes	520	169	32.5	129	24.8	109	21.0	78	15.0	35	6.7
	No	1389	490	35.3	292	21.0	333	24.0	167	12.0	107	7.7
Type of Facility:	Public	808	162	20.0	143	17.7	191	23.6	173	21.4	139	17.2
	Private	1101	497	45.1	278	25.2	251	22.8	72	6.5	3	0.3
Type of Admission:	First	1119	442	39.5	243	21.7	255	22.8	115	10.3	64	5.7
	Repeat	790	217	27.5	178	22.5	187	23.7	130	16.5	78	9.9

Table 9-3

CHI-SQUARED ANALYSIS OF VARIABLES ASSOCIATED WITH LENGTH
OF FIRST EPISODE OF INPATIENT CARE: 1970 STUDY PERIOD

Comparison	χ^2	df	P
Male versus Female	23.1	4	<.001
Under 21 vs. 21–34	33.5	4	<.001
Under 21 vs. 35–64	55.8	4	<.001
Under 21 vs. 65+	92.0	4	<.001
21–34 vs. 35–64	13.4	4	<.01
21–34 vs. 65+	153.4	4	<.001
35–64 vs. 65+	187.4	4	<.001
Psychoneurosis vs. Personality Disorder	39.8	4	<.001
Psychoneurosis vs. Functional Psychosis	121.5	4	<.001
Psychoneurosis vs. Brain Syndrome	201.9	4	<.001
Personality Disorder vs. Functional Psychosis	42.7	4	<.001
Personality Disorder vs. Brain Syndrome	103.9	4	<.001
Functional Psychosis vs. Brain Syndrome	26.8	4	<.001
Spanish Surname vs. Non-Spanish Surname	8.1	4	n.s.
Public vs. Private Facility	357.3	4	<.001
First vs. Repeat Admission	44.6	4	<.001

ized for longer than one month while nearly 40 percent of public patients are hospitalized for longer than one month. The generally longer period of hospitalization for patients with prior histories of inpatient care than for first admissions has already been noted.

Of all the comparisons, the one between public and private facilities is most striking. Supplementary analyses indicate that shorter hospitalizations in private than in public facilities hold true for every diagnostic group and for every age group as well as for each sex and for each ethnic group and regardless of whether the analysis is made for first admissions or for patients with prior inpatient histories.

Table 9-4
VARIABLES ASSOCIATED WITH LENGTH OF FIRST EPISODE OF OUTPATIENT CARE: 1970 STUDY PERIOD

Variables	Total	Length of First Episode of Outpatient Care (in days)									
		7 or less		8-14		15-30		31-90		91+	
		N	%	N	%	N	%	N	%	N	%
Total Outpatients	1852	560	30.2	112	6.0	197	10.6	405	21.9	578	31.2
Sex:											
Male	887	275	31.0	54	6.1	96	10.8	173	19.5	289	32.6
Female	965	285	29.5	58	6.0	101	10.5	232	24.0	289	29.9
Age:											
Under 21	702	217	30.9	45	6.4	82	11.7	169	24.1	189	26.9
21-34	632	195	30.9	44	7.0	69	10.9	135	21.4	189	29.9
35-64	498	142	28.5	22	4.4	44	8.8	94	18.9	196	39.4
65+	20	6	30.0	1	5.0	2	10.0	7	35.0	4	20.0
Diagnosis:											
Psychoneuroses	1208	408	33.8	85	7.0	130	10.8	268	22.2	317	26.2
Personality Disorders	452	111	24.6	21	4.6	50	11.1	104	23.0	166	36.7
Functional Psychoses	137	31	22.6	4	2.9	14	10.2	26	19.0	62	45.3
Brain Syndromes	47	10	21.3	1	2.1	2	4.3	6	12.8	28	59.6
Spanish Surname:											
Yes	422	140	33.2	26	6.2	44	10.4	91	21.6	121	28.7
No	1430	420	29.4	86	6.0	153	10.7	314	22.0	457	32.0
Type of Facility:											
Public	1300	403	31.0	74	5.7	139	10.7	286	22.0	398	30.6
Private	544	157	28.9	37	6.8	57	10.5	118	21.7	175	32.2
Type of Admission:											
First	1564	505	32.3	98	6.3	170	10.9	350	22.4	441	28.2
Repeat	280	55	19.6	13	4.6	26	9.3	54	19.3	132	47.1

In this connection it is good to remember that private inpatients are not readamitted any more often than public inpatients, although our data does not permit us to assert that private facilities are just as effective as public facilities. We already know that private and public patients are quite different from each other. It is entirely possible that upon further study public inpatients of whatever sex, age, or diagnosis would be found to be more seriously or chronically ill than comparable private inpatients. But on the basis of the data we have, we can assert that the shorter periods of hospitalization which characterize private facilities do not result in any obvious negative consequences.

Table 9-5

CHI-SQUARED ANALYSIS OF VARIABLES ASSOCIATED WITH LENGTH OF FIRST EPISODE OF OUTPATIENT CARE: 1970 STUDY PERIOD

Comparison	χ^2	df	P
Male versus Female	5.9	4	n.s.
Under 21 vs. 21-34	2.5	4	n.s.
Under 21 vs. 35-64	22.5	4	<.001
Under 21 vs. 65+	4.0	4	n.s.
21-34 vs. 35-64	13.2	4	<.02
21-34 vs. 65+	3.0	4	n.s.
35-64 vs. 65+	5.7	4	n.s.
Psychoneurosis vs. Personality Disorder	24.5	4	<.001
Psychoneurosis vs. Functional Psychosis	24.8	4	<.001
Psychoneurosis vs. Brain Syndrome	27.3	4	<.001
Personality Disorder vs. Functional Psychosis	3.7	4	n.s.
Personality Disorder vs. Brain Syndrome	10.5	4	<.05
Functional Psychosis vs. Brain Syndrome	3.8	4	n.s.
Spanish Surname vs. Non-Spanish Surname	2.9	4	n.s.
Public vs. Private Facility	2.2	4	n.s.
First vs. Repeat Admission	43.2	4	<.001

Factors associated with length of first outpatient episode are dramatically different from those found in the case of inpatients. The general pattern for all outpatients is for a large number (over 30 percent) to be discharged within one week, most probably after one contact. Some proportion of these patients were undoubtedly helped in this single contact. With other patients it may not have been possible to arrange acceptable conditions for continued treatment, and for still others appointments might not have been kept. The proportion of patients discharged between one and two weeks after their initial contact drops substantially, and then there is a gradual increase in proportion of patients with longer and longer episodes of care. About as many patients are discharged after three months of care as are discharged after one contact.

Length of first outpatient episode has fewer significant associations with the demographic variables under consideration than was the case with length of first inpatient episodes. There is no significant difference between public and private agencies in length of outpatient episode of care. No significant sex difference is seen, nor is there a difference as a function of ethnic group. There is no systematic difference by age, although patients in the 35-64 age group have significantly longer episodes of outpatient care than do patients under age 21. The only striking difference by diagnosis is that those patients with the mildest conditions (psychoneuroses, psychosomatic disorders, and transient situational reactions) have consistently shorter episodes of care than all of the other diagnostic groups.

The one outstanding finding is the longer period of care in the case of patients with prior outpatient histories than newly admitted outpatients, although patients who might tend to drop out of treatment after a single interview would surely be underrepresented among those who petition for care after having had a prior episode of outpatient care. The programatic significance of this finding is furthermore reduced by the fact that such a small proportion of outpatients have had prior episodes of outpatient care. Thus, while scattered significant associations between length of first episode of outpatient care and the demographic variables under consideration have been found, it would be prudent to conclude that if variables importantly related to length of outpatient care exist, we have not identified them in this analysis.

Of all inpatients, more than one-third are discharged within one week and 80 percent are discharged within one month. This rapidity of discharge is different enough from the situation characterizing inpatient facilities a decade or more ago as to constitute a most remarkable phenomenon. Regarding public inpatient facilities (where more than 60 percent of patients are discharged within one month) it seems likely that the administrative changes which took place at the state hospital are primarily responsible for the difference. The state hospital, organized to retain patients in 1960, was by 1970 organized to discharge patients. The whole thrust of the geographic decentralization was to create an easily accessible pathway from the hospital back to the community, and there seems little question but that this effort has been extraordinarily successful.

PUBLIC AND PRIVATE INPATIENT EPISODE LENGTHS

While private inpatient facilities discharge patients even more quickly than do public inpatient facilities (93 percent of patients admitted to private facilities are discharged within one month), one might think that this difference could be accounted for by the differing age, sex, and diagnostic characteristics of patients admitted to public versus private facilities. Those types of patients discharged most quickly (females, the young, and the mildly disabled) are the very ones admitted most commonly into private facilities. But as has already been noted, this explanation is not correct. In the case of the under-21 age group, for example, 20 percent of such patients are discharged within one week from public facilities, while 60 percent of such patients are discharged within one week from private inpatient facilities. To take another example, more than twice the proportion of admitted females are discharged within one week from private facilities as from public facilities. Or, in the case of psychoneurotics, to cite one final example, 32 percent of such patients are discharged within one week from public facilities, but 49 percent of such patients are discharged within one week from private facilities. It is clear, then, that private facilities discharge all types of patients more quickly than do public facilities. This persistent trend is undoubtedly due, in large measure, to factors having to do with modes of payment for care. With limited out-of-pocket or third party funds available for private care, rapid discharge from private facilities is a virtual necessity. But since readmission rate is no higher in private facilities than in public facilities, clinical considerations may play a large part in the discharge process. Two possibilities suggest themselves as worthy of further exploration. First, as has already been mentioned, patients of the same sex, age, and diagnostic group admitted into public versus private facilities may differ from each other in factors such as chronicity or severity, with those patients admitted into public facilities the more seriously disturbed. Second, it is entirely possible that clinical treatment goals differ substantially between public and private facilities, necessitating longer periods of hospitalization in public facilities.

It is possible to make a preliminary assessment of the first possibility by contrasting public and private first admission inpatients in a single age-sex-diagnosis group. Male patients between ages 35-64 with the diagnosis of personality disorder were selected, of whom 52 were first admissions into private inpatient facilities and 82 were first admissions into public facilities. When length of hospitalization was compared in these two groups, the private patients had significantly shorter stays (X^2 =32.37; df=3; P=<.001). While 31 of the 52 private patients (60 percent) were discharged within one week, only 13 out of the 82 public patients (16 percent) were discharged that quickly. Similarily, while only two out of the 52 patients (four percent) were hospitalized for longer than one month, 19 out of the 82 public patients (23 percent) were hospitalized for that long. Thus, the general finding of significantly shorter hospitalizations in private facilities has been found for this specific patient group.

In then examining to see whether other differences between public and private patients in this specific age-sex-diagnosis group could be found, several significant differences appear. In contrast to public facility inpatients, pr vate patients, for example, have lived in Pueblo longer (P=<.02), more commonly own rather than rent their homes (P=<.01), live in larger homes (P =<.05), more frequently live in homes with complete kitchen facilities (P=<.02), less frequently have disrupted marriages (P=<.02), have higher level occupations (P=<.10), and have more successful recent employment histories (P=<.01). Thus, when private patients are contrasted with public patients in the same age, sex, and diagnostic group, private patients are found to be economically and socially less disordered.

Under the best of circumstances, it might be possible in a community such as Pueblo to assign patients matched for a small set of appropriate variables randomly to public and private facilities. A controlled study of this type should rather quickly determine whether the more rapid discharge from private facilities continues, and if so, should identify what factors, clinical, financial, or otherwise, are likely to be responsible for this persistent trend.

It has been noted that patients with histories of psychiatric hospitalization prior to the start of the 1970 study period have significantly longer episodes of care than do patients who are new to the psychiatric service delivery system. But when this phenomenon is examined in greater detail, contrasting public and private facilities and contrasting patients in varying age, sex, ethnic, and diagnostic groups, the general finding is by no means uniform. First, longer episodes of care in repeat admission patients are not accounted for either by age or sex. Within each sex group separately considered and within each age group separately considered, length of initial episode of care is no greater in repeat inpatients than in new inpatients. Second, differences in length of episodes of care, where they occur, are attributable only to private facilities. In no case does a comparison of length of episodes of care of public facility new inpatients with repeat inpatients yield significant findings. Our analysis reveals that the greater length of episodes of care in the case of inpatients with prior hospitalization histories is attributable to private facilities, and specifically to psychoneurotics and to non-Spanish surnamed.

In the case of psychoneurotics, which comprise a very large proportion of private inpatient admissions, those patients with prior hospital histories have significantly longer episodes of care ($X^2=20.9$; $df=4$; $P=<.001$). While 49 percent of newly admitted psychoneurotics are discharged from private facilities within one week, only 36 percent of repeat admission psychoneurotics are discharged within one week. In all the longer time categories, repeat admission patients are discharged in larger proportions than new inpatients. In the case of non-Spanish surnamed, who likewise comprise the bulk of admitted private patients, the facts are almost identical. Again a significantly larger proportion of new patients than of repeat patients are discharged within one week, and smaller proportions are discharged in all other time periods ($X^2=16.9$; $df=4$; $P=<.01$).

Finally, in the case of inpatients, it is important to make some observations about diagnosis and length of episodes of care. We have noted that there is a regular progression in episode length by diagnosis, in which the mildest category has the shortest length of care. Not only is the progression a regular one, but each diagnostic category is significantly different in episode length from all other diagnostic categories. While the diagnostic system in psychiatry is subject to a wide variety of criticisms, there is clearly some validity to the four category grouping used in this research. Whatever is meant by the four terms, they have clear significance for at least one important aspect of clinical course, namely length of an episode of inpatient treatment. While the diagnostic terms may not be used with extreme precision, it is equally clear that they are not used capriciously.

The relationship between age and diagnosis has already been noted, with milder diagnoses generally associated with younger patients and the brain syndrome diagnosis restricted almost completely to those patients aged 65 or above at the time of admission. Thus, the progression of episode length with increasingly severe diagnosis is paralleled by a similar progression with age. Again in each case the difference in episode length between age groups is a statistically significant one. One would like to think that the relationship between length of inpatient treatment episode on the one hand, and age and diagnosis on the other hand, makes a strong case for early case-finding, that is, for secondary prevention. But while such a conclusion is consistent with these findings, it probably does not necessarily follow. Long-term studies would need to be undertaken before the preventive power of early case-finding could be appropriately demonstrated.

In the case of length of episodes of care in outpatient facilities, the most striking finding was that those patients with outpatient histories prior to the start of the 1970 study period had significantly longer episodes of care than those patients new to outpatient care. Upon closer examination, it is seen that this finding is attributable almost entirely to public outpatient services and to the larger number of repeat admission public sector outpatients with episodes of care in excess of three months. On the average, about twice as many repeat public outpatients have episodes of care longer than three months as do new public outpatients (60 percent versus 27 percent). This difference is particularly marked in the case of persons between ages 21 and 64 and in the case of patients diagnosed as personality disorders or functional psychotics. In the case of private sector outpatient services no such relationship is noted, and length of episodes of care are approximately the same in new as contrasted with repeat outpatients. Furthermore, first admission public sector outpatients do not have significantly longer or shorter care episodes than do first admission private sector outpatients. Thus the difference is a function of the long episodes of public sector care in the case of patients with prior outpatient histories.

Large numbers of patients, having had prior outpatient care, apparently settle in for relatively extensive continuing psychotherapy in public settings. Long-term outpatient care is more economical in public settings, of course, and the diagnostic groups where this phenomenon is most marked are the ones where long-term care is most often required. Outpatient facilities stand ready to treat patients who petition for help. A substantial proportion of new outpatients leave treatment after a single interview. This phenomenon is much less common in the case of outpatients with prior outpatient histories. But we do not know how the earlier outpatient experience relates to the seeking of additional treatment. Likewise we know little of the reasons why nearly one-third of new outpatients do not continue in treatment beyond their initial interview, or the consequences of continuing or not continuing. These are important clinical and administrative questions which can be studied by the allocation of resources to follow-up efforts. In the absence of such studies, it would be difficult for outpatient facilities to do much more than simply continue to be willing to treat those patients who are willing to be treated. Adequate follow-up studies could very well identify those kinds of patients on whose behalf special efforts should be expended in order to keep them in some kind of therapeutic liaison, and other kinds of patients for whom a rapid termination from treatment seems to have no negative consequences. Such studies might help mental health agencies allocate their resources more wisely.

Lengths of Consecutive Episodes of Care

In the case of those 851 patients with two or more episodes of care, it is possible to study the interrelationships of the length of the first and second episodes of care as a function of the setting in which the two episodes took place. For this analysis patients are divided into four groups according to whether each episode took place in an inpatient or outpatient setting. Results of this analysis are presented in Tables 9-6 through 9-9.

Table 9-6

LENGTH OF FIRST TWO EPISODES OF CARE, BOTH EPISODES AS
INPATIENT: 1970 STUDY PERIOD

First Episode	Second Episode				
	Less Than One Week	One—Two Weeks	Two Weeks— One Month	More Than One Month	Total
Less than one week	65	25	34	19	143
One—two weeks	46	23	22	22	113
Two Weeks—One month	40	27	36	25	128
More than one month	26	17	28	34	105
Total	177	92	120	100	489

χ^2 (2 x 2) = 11.20; df = 1; P = <.001

In the case of the 489 patients whose two initial episodes of care took place in inpatient settings (Table 9-6), it can be seen that first episodes tend to be somewhat longer than second episodes with the biggest difference being in the frequency of episodes of care of less than one week in duration. While 29 percent of first episodes of care are less than one week in length, the similar figure for second episodes is 36 percent. While the relationship of length of care during the first two episodes is far from perfect, it is a significant one. There is a tendency for those patients with short initial episodes to have short second episodes, and for those patients with longer first episodes to have longer second episodes.

A total of 87 patients with two or more episodes of care during the 1970 study period were admitted to inpatient facilities for their first episode of care and to outpatient facilities for their second episode (see Table 9-7). As can be seen, in most cases the first (inpatient) episode was less than two weeks in length, and the second (outpatient) episode was most commonly either less than one week or more than a month in length. The length of the inpatient episode is not predictive of the length of the subsequent outpatient episode. The multiple episode histories of another 114 patients was the reverse of the above group, that is, following an initial episode in an outpatient setting, a second episode in an inpatient setting was reported. Again (see Table 9-8) it can be seen that while outpatients, these patients had episodes of either very short or very long duration. Episode length as subsequent inpatients was more evenly distributed. In moving from outpatient to inpatient status, a significant and programatically important relationship of lengths of episodes of care is found. Those patients with shortest outpatient episodes tended to have longest subsequent inpatient episodes, while those patients with longest outpatient episodes tended to have relatively short subse-

Table 9-7

LENGTH OF FIRST TWO EPISODES OF CARE—FIRST EPISODE AS
INPATIENT, SECOND EPISODE AS OUTPATIENT: 1970 STUDY PERIOD

First Episode	Second Episode				
	Less Than One Week	One–Two Weeks	Two Weeks– One Month	More Than One Month	Total
Less Than One Week	14	4	5	18	41
One–Two Weeks	5	0	4	10	19
Two Weeks–One Month	1	2	0	11	14
More Than One Month	3	0	2	8	13
Total	23	6	11	47	87

χ^2 (2 x) = 2.56; df = 1; P = not significant

253

Table 9-8

Length of First Two Episodes of Care—First Episode as Outpatient, Second Episode as Inpatient: 1970 Study Period

First Episode	Second Episode				
	Less Than One Week	One–Two Weeks	Two Weeks– One Month	More Than One Month	Total
Less Than One Week	5	7	9	9	30
One–Two Weeks	0	0	1	1	2
Two Weeks–One Month	9	2	3	1	15
More Than One Month	24	12	20	11	67
Total	38	21	33	22	114

χ^2 (2 x 2) = 3.88; $df = 1$; $P = <.05$

Table 9-9

LENGTH OF FIRST TWO EPISODES OF CARE, BOTH EPISODES AS
OUTPATIENT: 1970 STUDY PERIOD

First Episode	Second Episode				
	Less Than One Week	One–Two Weeks	Two Weeks– One Month	More Than One Month	Total
Less Than One Week	11	4	7	24	46
One–Two Weeks	1	1	4	6	12
Two Weeks–One Month	3	0	3	9	15
More Than One Month	15	4	9	60	88
Total	30	9	23	99	161

χ^2 (2 x 2) = 1.23; df = 1; P = not significant

quent inpatient episodes. There is some indication, then, that outpatients who terminate care quickly, usually after one interview, require disproportionately long episodes of subsequent inpatient care if such care is required at all.

The final comparison examines length of episodes of care in the case of the 161 patients for whom two consecutive outpatient episodes were reported (see Table 9-9). In this case the two episode lengths are independent. The same episode length appears as was found earlier regarding outpatient treatment—about a quarter of the patients are discharged in less than one week, and more than half of the patients are seen for longer than one month. By far the most common pattern for patients having two outpatient episodes is for both episodes to be more than a month in length. But more than half of those outpatients whose initial episodes terminated within one week also had second episodes of longer than a month, and half of those patients whose second episode lasted less than one week had initial outpatient episodes of longer than one month.

Thus in contrasting episode lengths in the case of those patients with two or more episodes, it is seen that neither the length of inpatient nor outpatient initial episodes is predictive of subsequent outpatient episodes. By contrast, both the length of initial inpatient and outpatient episodes is predictive of subsequent inpatient care. The longer the initial inpatient episode, the longer the subsequent inpatient episode; and the longer the initial outpatient episode, the shorter the subsequent inpatient episode.

10

Multiple Episodes and Multiple Pathways in the Service Delivery System

During the 1970 study period, which lasted two years, data was collected for all admissions from all agencies to which Pueblo residents might be expected to turn in their quest for mental health services. When the data collection had been completed, it became possible to identify those persons who had had multiple episodes of care. Matching of such cases was not difficult in view of the fact that name, address, sex, and date of birth were all known. With this grouping in hand, it became possible to engage in a retrospective tracking of all patients for whom more than one episode had been reported, and to identify those factors for which data was available which distinguished single episode from multiple episode cases.

Much has been written in recent years about the need for interagency collaboration in the provision of mental health services. It has been asserted that one of the reasons why public psychiatric inpatient facilities have been able to reduce their patient load is the increased availability and presumed utilization of community services, making it less necessary for discharged patients to be rehospitalized. Our data provided us the means to study interagency collaboration, that is, to identify the pathways taken by multiple episode cases in what had become by 1970 a fairly complex and multifaceted service delivery system.

Furthermore, our data allowed us to contrast those patients having only one known episode of care with those patients for whom two or more episodes had been reported. Such comparisons must be viewed fairly conservatively, however, since we must assume that the lack of a report about a second episode of care constitutes interpretable data. But while in many cases it can mean that the patient did not need additional treatment, the lack of a report can also signify that the patient was dead, that he no longer lived in Pueblo, that he was under the care of a nonreporting agency such as a prison or a social service facility, or that he needed care but chose not to obtain it. In this sense, our data suffers from the same defect as do all case registers. By stationing data collection centers solely in admitting rooms of participating agencies, we cannot learn what events relevant in the lives of psychiatric patients occur elsewhere. For this reason, case register studies can profitably be supplemented by data collection procedures which focus on a cohort of patients, following them as they traverse their self-selected care channels. These two study designs would be highly complementary, with each contributing significantly to a greater understanding of patient–agency interaction.

To the extent, however, that clearly significant differences emerge when single episode and multiple episode patients are contrasted, we can draw some tentative conclusions. Such conclusions have high potential clinical and administrative utility since patients newly admitted to psychiatric facilities will include those who have characteristics associated with multiple episode care and who thus represent a special high-risk group for whom special programs or special attention could be directed.

The first finding of importance in examining pathways in the service delivery system is that the vast majority of patients who were admitted into inpatient facilities came into them directly without ever having been outpatients. Of the 1119 patients admitted to inpatient facilities with no prior psychiatric inpatient history, 1038 (93 percent) came directly into inpatient facilities. Of the 790 patients admitted to inpatient facilities with some psychiatric hospitalization history prior to the start of the data collection period, 742 (94 percent) came directly into inpatient facilities. It is true that early in the data collection period there would have been no opportunity to have had a prior outpatient episode reported, but even during the last three months of the study period, when nearly two years of data collection had taken place, admissions into inpatient units were overwhelmingly first episodes of care. Of the 52 patients admitted into public inpatient facilities during the last three months of data collection, only 10 (19 percent) had had a prior outpatient episode reported. Similarly, of the 94 patients admitted into private inpatient facilities during the last three months of the study period, only nine (10 percent) had had a previous episode of outpatient care.

This situation is similar and, of course, less surprising in the case of outpatients. More than 95 percent of first admission outpatients came directly into outpatient facilities, and more than 85 percent of outpatients with psychiatric histories prior to the start of the study period were admitted directly into outpatient facilities without first having been inpatients.

It is thus clear that inpatient facilities are adept at attracting a clientele directly from the public and that outpatient clinics do not serve a triage function. It is not uncommon, for example, for private psychiatrists to admit patients into the hospital upon referral from other physicians and have their initial face-to-face encounter with these patients at the hospital. Yet throughout the data collection period large numbers of patients had multiple episodes of care. Pathways clearly exist within the caretaking system even though these pathways might not have been planned in advance to meet specific patient needs. As can be seen in Table 10-1, while the majority of patients identified during the study period had only one episode of care, a total of 851 had two or more episodes, 292 had three or more episodes, and 117 had four or more individual episodes of care. For want of a better method, the pathways can be *induced* by examining the flow of those patients for whom multiple episodes were reported. The critical questions regarding this flow are (1), its prevailing directionality and (2), whether its character bears some interpretable relationship to patient characteristics.

PREVALENCE AND AGENCY PARTICIPATION IN MULTIPLE EPISODE CASES

As can be seen in Table 10-1, nearly a quarter of the patients had a second episode, more than seven percent had three episodes or more, and about three percent had four or more episodes during the study period. Since the average length of observation of each patient is approximately one year, these figures can be interpreted as annual risk rates. These results compare quite favorably with similarly collected data in other sections of the United States. In a recent study based upon patients discharged from a public mental hospital in Maryland between February 1963 and July 1964, for example, about 31 percent were rehospitalized once during the year following discharge and 6.5 percent had two or more episodes of care after the initial discharge (see

Table 10–1
Total Episodes of Care During the 1970 Study Period as a Function of First Episode Setting and Previous Psychiatric History

First Episode Setting and Previous Psychiatric History	Total Episodes of Care								Total
	One		Two or More		Three or More		Four or More		
	N	%	N	%	N	%	N	%	N
First Inpatient Admission									
Total	866	77.4	253	22.6	80	7.1	35	3.1	1119
Public	250	75.3	82	24.6	30	9.0	14	4.2	332
Private	616	78.3	171	21.8	50	6.4	21	2.7	787
Repeat Inpatient Admission									
Total	467	59.1	323	40.9	146	18.5	64	8.1	790
Public	276	58.0	200	42.0	95	19.9	41	8.6	476
Private	191	60.8	123	39.2	51	16.2	23	7.3	314
First Outpatient Admission									
Total	1348	85.8	224	14.3	55	3.5	17	1.1	1572
Public	983	84.4	182	15.7	51	4.4	15	1.3	1165
Private	365	89.7	42	10.3	4	1.0	2	0.5	407
Repeat Outpatient Admission									
Total	229	81.8	51	18.2	11	3.9	1	0.4	280
Public	119	83.2	24	16.8	5	3.5	1	0.7	143
Private	110	80.3	27	19.7	6	4.4	0	0.0	137
Total Sample									
Total	2910	77.4	851	22.6	292	7.8	117	3.1	3761
Public	1628	76.9	488	23.0	181	8.6	71	3.4	2116
Private	1282	77.9	363	22.0	111	6.8	46	2.8	1645

Michaus *et al.*, 1969). The likelihood of multiple episodes of care is substantially higher if the initial episode takes place in an inpatient rather than outpatient setting; it is also substantially increased for those patients who have had prior psychiatric treatment histories. Even though there is a sharply differentiated use of private in contrast to public facilities as a function of prior psychiatric history, whether we are looking at inpatients or outpatients, multiple episodes of care occur with striking similarity in those patients seen in public as contrasted with private settings. If the frequency of repeated admission is an index of treatment failure, public facilities are neither less nor more effective than private facilities for any group of patients.

Information regarding agency involvement in the transition from first to second episode of care as a function of patient type can be found in Table 10-2. First, there is a striking tendency for repetitive involvement by the same agency, particularly in the case of public agencies. Of the 282 patients with two or more episodes of care whose first episode took place in a public inpatient facility, 238 (84 percent) had their second episode in a public inpatient setting as well. Of the 206 patients with multiple episodes whose first episode was in a public outpatient facility, 107 (52 percent) returned to public outpatient settings for their second episode of care. Repetitive involvement of private agencies is less common. Of the 294 patients with two or more episodes of care whose initial episode took place in a private inpatient facility, 157 (53 percent) returned to a private inpatient facility for their second episode of care. Of the 69 patients with two or more episodes of care whose first episode was in a private outpatient facility, 24 (35 percent) returned to a private outpatient facility for that second episode.

Second, the predominant trend in the case of changes of agency from first to second episode is from private to

Table 10-2
Pathways From First to Second Episodes of Care: 1970 Study Period

Nature of Pathway	Type of Patient							
	First IP Adm.		Rpt IP Adm.		First OP Adm.		Rpt OP Adm.	
	N	%	N	%	N	%	N	%
Public to Public	74	29.2	185	57.3	130	58.0	19	37.3
Public to Private	8	3.2	15	4.6	52	23.2	5	9.8
Private to Public	66	26.1	42	13.0	13	5.8	11	21.6
Private to Private	105	41.5	81	25.1	29	12.9	16	31.4
IP to IP	196	77.5	293	90.7				
IP to OP	57	22.5	30	9.3				
OP to IP					92	41.1	22	43.1
OP to OP					132	58.9	29	56.9
Total	253		323		224		51	

public with respect to inpatient care and from public to private with respect to outpatient care. In the latter case, however, the differences are not great and as will be seen are interactive with the chronicity of the condition for which the patient is being treated. This finding, obtained from a longitudinal approach, is identical to that identified earlier in the cross-sectional data—first admission inpatients are treated primarily in the private sector, while patients with histories of prior inpatient care are more often treated in the public sector. The opposite trend for outpatients is noted both in the cross-sectional and longitudinal data. In the case of those patients whose initial episode of care was in an inpatient setting, a total of 131 changed either from public to private agencies or private to public agencies between their first and second episodes of care. Of these 131 patients, the direction of change was from public to private in 23 (18 percent) and from private to public in 108 (82 percent). In contrast, of the 81 patients whose initial episode of care took place in an outpatient setting and who changed either from public to private or from private to public agencies between their first and second episode of care, in the case of 57 patients (70 percent) the change was from public to private and in only 24 cases (30 percent) was the change from private to public.

In the case of patients whose initial episode of care took place in an inpatient setting, there is no interaction of direction of agency change and prior psychiatric history. Whether or not there was a history of inpatient care prior to the start of the 1970 data collection period, the predominant trend in agency shifts between first and second episode of care was from private to public settings. Of the 74 patients with no prior inpatient psychiatric history, 66 (89 percent) transferred from private to public settings. Of the 57 patients who had a prior inpatient history, 42 (74 percent) transferred from private to public settings for their second episode of care. In the case of patients whose initial episode of care was in an outpatient setting, there is a fairly strong interaction factor in evidence. First, with respect to those patients with no prior outpatient histories, of the 65 who transferred agency types between the first and second episode of care, in the case of 52 (80 percent) the transfer was from public to private settings. In the case of the 16 patients with two or more episodes of care whose initial episode took place in an outpatient setting and who had had an outpatient history prior to the start of the study, only five (31 percent) transferred from public to private settings for their second episode of care.

With regard to the pathways between inpatient and outpatient care from the first to the second episode, the results indicate that first episode inpatients tend predominantly to become second episode inpatients and first episode outpatients remain outpatients (although not as predominantly) during their second episode of care. Of the 253 first episode inpatients with no inpatient history prior to the start of the study period, 196 (77 percent) are inpatients during their second episode of care, although there is, as has already been noted, a shift from private to public settings. Of the 323 first episode inpatients with inpatient psychiatric histories prior to the start of the study, 293 (91 percent) remain inpatients. In the case of first episode outpatients, prior psychiatric history appears to be unrelated to the setting for the second episode. Just under 60 percent remain outpatients for their second episode of care, regardless of prior history.

In the case of inpatients, a financial factor is undoubtedly operating in causing the shift from private to public agencies. Most prepaid insurance programs (the predominant source of payment for private care) have built-in limitations on the amount and duration of coverage available to their subscribers. As this coverage limit is reached, patients requiring additional care have little recourse other than to seek or be referred to services in the public sector. It is certainly difficult to make a case that public sector services are more appropriate than private sector services for those patients requiring additional episodes of inpatient care, and the financial constraints which are surely operative thus bear little relationship to those factors which might best determine the setting within which treatment should take place.

In the case of outpatients, a financial factor may also be operating, but in a more complex manner. Assuming that outpatients with no prior outpatient psychiatric history are better risks for psychotherapy than those more chronic outpatients who have prior treatment histories, they might make unusually attractive referrals to mental health professionals working in private settings, particularly if their own financial resources make such referrals realistic. Chronic outpatients, among whom the less affluent are overrepresented, would clearly make less desirable referrals to private sector services.

THREE OR MORE EPISODES OF CARE

Analysis of the pathways taken by the 292 patients requiring three or more episodes of care and of the 117 patients for whom four or more episodes of care were reported can be presented without additional tables. Most of these instances occurred to patients whose initial episode of care was in an inpatient setting. The predominant pattern in the case of inpatients whose initial hospitalization took place in a public setting is for them to remain in the public inpatient setting for all subsequent episodes of care. Two-thirds of public inpatients with no prior hospitalization history exhibited this pattern, and

an even larger proportion—more than three-quarters—
of public inpatients for whom a psychiatric hospitalization had taken place prior to the start of the study returned to public inpatient settings for all subsequent
episodes of care. For patients whose initial episode of
care occurred in a private inpatient setting, public sector
inpatient services play an increasingly important role
with each succeeding episode of care. Of the 292 patients with three or more episodes of care, 226 (77 percent) began as inpatients and only 66 (23 percent) began
as outpatients. Of the 226 inpatients, 125 began as public inpatients and of these 92 (74 percent) returned consistently to the same setting where they started. Only 20
of these 125 patients (16 percent) were ever private inpatients, and only 15 (12 percent) were ever outpatients.
Of the 101 patients with three or more episodes who
began as private inpatients, only 37 (37 percent) consistently returned to private inpatient settings, 39 (39 percent) were at some time public inpatients, and only 29
(29 percent) were ever outpatients.

Of the 66 patients whose initial episode of care took
place in an outpatient setting and who had three or more
episodes of care, 56 began as public outpatients. Ten (18
percent) consistently remained public outpatients
through all subsequent episodes of care. Eight patients
(14 percent) were at one or more subsequent episodes
private outpatients, and 41 (73 percent) were inpatients
at one or more subsequent episodes. In addition to the
increasingly important role played by public sector services as the number of episodes increases, one cannot
help but be struck by the unusually small role played by
outpatient settings (either public or private) in the management of multiple episode cases, particularly for those
patients whose psychiatric care begins in public inpatient
settings. Inpatient facilities not only serve as the initial
locus of treatment for large numbers of psychiatric pa-

tients, but they retain these cases for all subsequent episodes of care.

While this tendency may speak well for the sense of security and confidence patients feel in the setting where they obtain their initial care, it does require each agency to develop programs or skills to meet a great variety of problems. If patients are to return to the same agency regardless of the specific character of the difficulty, each agency then must move toward broad generic competencies rather than specialized, more narrow ones. Our description of the changing character of mental health service programs between 1960 and 1970 has underlined this attribute. Most agencies have become generic and multipurpose in character.

These results indicate that there is, in fact, relatively little interagency collaboration in the provision of continuing psychiatric services. Pueblo is atypical, of course, in that it is the seat of the public psychiatric hospital. Pueblo residents discharged from the state hospital do not need to travel long distances to return to the hospital for additional care. Involvement of local agencies in the management of former state hospital patients in the case of communities distant from the state hospital would undoubtedly be greater than that found in Pueblo. One of the consequences of the easy access to the state hospital, however, appears to be a very high readiness to rehospitalize patients in need of additional psychiatric care. One reason advanced for this phenomenon is the consequence of the large number of public inpatients recently discharged into nursing homes and other community-based protected settings. Some of these patients have had to be rehospitalized and that so many are in this category is a result of the fact that so many were discharged during the late 1960s. Thus, mental health professionals in Pueblo feel that this apparent overutilization of the major public inpatient facility is transitory and should diminish in time.

One of the basic axioms of the community mental health orientation is to avoid hospitalization and rehospitalization wherever possible. In many cases, of course, hospitalization is the treatment of choice (see Mendel, 1967), but the data from the 1970 study suggests that rehospitalization may take place with unusually high frequency. Even though hospitalized Pueblo residents are geographically in the community, this is the only sense in which it is true. By being hospitalized they are removed from their families, their friends, their neighborhood, and their work, and following discharge a period of reintegration must take place. Neither the necessity for such reintegration nor the initial separation would occur if patients requiring additional episodes of care could be seen as outpatients.

Furthermore, it is difficult to make a case that when more than one agency is involved in the treatment of a patient, clinical considerations prevail in this decision. The transfer of patients from private to public inpatient facilities seems to be due in greatest measure to financial considerations, and there is some likelihood that these considerations hold true in the transfer of some outpatients from public to private settings.

DIAGNOSTIC STABILITY IN MULTIPLE EPISODE CASES

We have an unusual opportunity, in the case of the 851 patients with two or more episodes of care, to examine the stability (and perhaps the reliability) of assigned diagnoses, since with the second episode of care there was the opportunity to review and revise the diagnosis which had been established at the time of the initial episode. Within the four-category system employed in these studies, one would not expect a large number of changes to have taken place, although changes would not be clinically impossible. But the diagnostic groupings are broad enough and the time between episodes short enough that it would be surprising if there were a large number of changes. This is especially so in view of the fact that so many second episodes take place at the same facility where the first episode occurred.

It is possible, however, to identify separately those clear changes in facility by examining diagnoses in those instances where one episode takes place in an inpatient setting and the other in an outpatient setting. Of the 851 patients with two or more episodes of care, 87 cases involved an initial episode in an inpatient setting and a second episode in an outpatient setting; in the case of an additional 114 cases, the shift between the first two episodes was from outpatient to inpatient setting. The largest number of multiple episode cases (489) involved two consecutive inpatient episodes. As for the remaining 161 cases, both episodes were in outpatient settings. One might expect a predictable directionality in the case of shifts between inpatient and outpatient settings—an increase in milder diagnoses when the move is from inpatient to outpatient facility, and a decrease in milder diagnoses when the shift takes place in the opposite direction. One might also anticipate greater diagnostic consistency when both episodes take place in the same facility type than when there is a change. Finally, simply by virtue of the fact that a second episode is required, one might anticipate more changes in the direction of severe diagnoses than in the direction of the milder diagnoses. We are, of course, using a very imperfect scale of severity, with psychoneuroses considered the least severe, personality disorders somewhat more severe, functional psychoses still more severe, and brain syndromes the most severe. There is some justification for this scale, however, since we have already found that length of hospitalization increases linearly with this ordering.

The foregoing hypotheses, however, serve primarily to organize the examination of the data and many, but not all, are supported. Data regarding cross-episode diagnostic stability are shown in Tables 10-3 through 10-6. First, in every case, diagnostic stability exceeds diagnostic change. Second, stability of diagnoses is substantially more common in the case when both episodes take place in the same facility type than when there is a change. In the case when both admissions are in inpatient units or when both admissions are in outpatient settings, 82 percent of the diagnoses are unchanged between first and second episode. In contrast, when there is a shift be-

Table 10-3

DIAGNOSTIC STABILITY AMONG PATIENTS WITH TWO EPISODES OF CARE, BOTH IN INPATIENT SETTINGS: 1970 STUDY PERIOD

Diagnosis: First Admission	Diagnosis: Second Admission				
	PN	PD	FP	BS	Total
Psychoneuroses	108	17	12	2	139
Personality Disorders	20	220	4	5	249
Functional Psychoses	10	5	56	2	73
Brain Syndromes	2	1	5	20	28
Total	140	243	77	29	489

Table 10-4

DIAGNOSTIC STABILITY AMONG PATIENTS WITH TWO EPISODES OF CARE—FIRST ADMISSION IN INPATIENT SETTING, SECOND ADMISSION IN OUTPATIENT SETTING: 1970 STUDY PERIOD

Diagnosis: First Admission	Diagnosis: Second Admission				
	PN	PD	FP	BS	Total
Psychoneuroses	38	17	2	1	58
Personality Disorders	7	5	0	0	12
Functional Psychoses	0	4	6	1	11
Brain Syndromes	2	3	0	1	6
Total	47	29	8	3	87

tween inpatient and outpatient setting (in either direction), the diagnoses are unchanged in only 60 percent of cases.

The directionality shift hypothesis in the case when there is a change from inpatient to outpatient or outpatient to inpatient setting is not supported. In fact, the results are just opposite to what was anticipated, that is, second diagnoses are more severe when the shift is from inpatient to outpatient setting and less severe when the shift is from outpatient to inpatient setting. Closer examination of the two tables in question indicates that this result is the consequence of the psychoneurosis–personality disorder diagnostic change. In the case of the trans-

Table 10-5

DIAGNOSTIC STABILITY AMONG PATIENTS WITH TWO EPISODES OF CARE—FIRST ADMISSION IN OUTPATIENT SETTING, SECOND ADMISSION IN INPATIENT SETTING: 1970 STUDY PERIOD

Diagnosis: First Admission	Diagnosis: Second Admission				
	PN	PD	FP	BS	Total
Psychoneuroses	33	8	5	2	48
Personality Disorders	18	25	1	0	44
Functional Psychoses	4	4	12	1	21
Brain Syndromes	1	0	0	0	1
Total	56	37	18	3	114

Table 10-6

DIAGNOSTIC STABILITY AMONG PATIENTS WITH TWO EPISODES OF CARE, BOTH IN OUTPATIENT SETTINGS: 1970 STUDY PERIOD

Diagnosis: First Admission	Diagnosis: Second Admission				
	PN	PD	FP	BS	Total
Psychoneuroses	86	11	1	0	98
Personality Disorders	11	34	3	0	48
Functional Psychoses	2	0	5	0	7
Brain Syndromes	0	1	0	7	8
Total	99	46	9	7	161

fer from inpatient to outpatient settings, 17 patients whose initial diagnosis was psychoneurosis are given a diagnosis of personality disorder at the time of their second episode of care. In the case of only seven patients is the change in diagnosis in the other direction. The figures are virtually the opposite in the case of patients whose initial episode was in an outpatient setting and whose second episode was in an inpatient setting. Eighteen patients initially considered personality disorders are subsequently diagnosed as psychoneurotics, and only eight patients initially psychoneurotics are given personality disorder diagnoses at the time of their second episode of care.

Finally, there is no evidence that second diagnoses are generally more severe than initial diagnoses, at least by the criteria employed in this analysis. Among patients with two inpatient care episodes, there are just as many diagnostic changes in one direction as the other. The same finding holds true in the case of patients with two outpatient episodes. Shifts among each of the four diagnostic groups are as common one way as the other between the first and second episodes of care. Thus, there is a reasonably satisfactory degree of diagnostic stability between episodes, but none of the hypotheses relating to the rationale for shifts in diagnosis is supported. Inpatient settings tend to use the psychoneurosis label with a relatively greater frequency than do outpatient settings, and this practice is not limited to private facilities alone, nor just to first episodes. Psychoneuroses and personality disorders are, at least theoretically, easily distinguishable, and although differences in symptomatology could account for changes in diagnosis, it is not impossible that diagnostic practices at inpatient and outpatient settings differ. Additional study would be needed to identify the factors involved in this pattern of diagnostic shifts.

SINGLE CONTRASTED WITH MULTIPLE EPISODE PATIENTS

We turn now to the question of whether, at the time of their first admission, inpatients who have only that one admission during the study period differ in any significant ways from those patients for whom two or more episodes of care are reported. Since we will be contrasting these two groups of patients on the basis of data collected at the time of their first admission, we are in effect trying to determine whether patients at risk of multiple admissions can be identified at the time of their first admission. Of the 27 variables on which the two patient groups could be compared, four comparisons yield significant differences ($P = <.01$).

First, single episode cases are found in the oldest age group (65+) more than twice as often as multiple episode cases and proportionately less often in all other age groups. Second, single episode cases are more commonly given diagnoses of psychoneuroses and brain syndrome and less commonly given diagnoses of personality disorders and functional psychoses than are multiple episode cases. Third, single episode cases have substantially shorter lengths of hospitalization than patients for whom subsequent episodes of care are reported. And finally, single episode cases have lived for significantly longer periods of time in their current residence than patients who subsequent to their discharge have additional episodes of care.

Thus, the patient most likely to have repeated episodes of care is a person below age 65 with a diagnosis of personality disorder or functional psychosis who has lived in his current residence a relatively short period of time and who has an unusually long initial period of hospitalization. Of the four significant variables, the most powerful predictors are diagnosis and length of hospitalization, although it should be noted that using these four variables in any combination in order to identify patients with high risk of readmission would result in a large number of false positives. In fact, predictions of repeat episodes based upon these variables would yield more overall errors than if one predicted but a single episode for every case. It is perhaps enough to have indicated these significant differences between single and multiple episode cases and to note that, in spite of the fact that each of these differences is a statistically significant one, our data do not include any variables upon which a programmatically feasible control program could be launched.

Part IV

**SERVICE STATISTICS
AND EPIDEMIOLOGY**

11

Psychiatric Care Data and the Epidemiology of Mental Disorder

The primary findings of the Pueblo studies have now been presented. Before leaving the data, we have the opportunity to determine whether there are any implications relevant to the control of mental disorders. Yet, one must exercise considerable care in making the transition from the unequivocal facts of hospital and clinic admission to the more risky assertions about mental disorders in the community and their possible causes.

Social scientists have for many years been interested in identifying factors which might be etiologically related to mental disorders, not only to develop a more complete understanding of psychiatric disability, but also to institute programs which might hold the hope of preventing such disorders from occurring. Thus we arrive at our concern with epidemiology. Epidemiology, according to MacMahon, is "the study of the distribution of disease in human populations and of the factors that determine that distribution. Its predominant, though not exclusive, purpose is the understanding of disease etiology and the identification of preventive measures" [1967, p. 81]. For these purposes, medical care statistics, useful in their own right, may alone be inadequate.

SERVICE STATISTICS VERSUS HOUSEHOLD SURVEYS

The initial dilemma in viewing this project from an epidemiological perspective is to evaluate the extent to which the distribution of the phenomenon under investigation, in this case psychiatric disorders, has been identified. The two general strategies which have been traditionally used have been (1) to develop indices based on identified psychiatric patients, that is, to use treated rates as a measure of psychiatric disability in a population, and (2) to identify psychiatric disability by means of household surveys, whether or not persons so identified have ever been officially designated "patients."

In an examination of these alternative strategies, Blum has carefully reviewed the issues involved. Regarding the utilization of treated rates as an index of the extent of psychiatric disorder in a community or in subpopulations within a community as in the present study, Blum writes, "In the past, becoming a patient has been the primary case-finding method for psychiatry; it must not be overlooked in planning future community studies" [1962, p. 272]. Yet the defects of this method of case identification are readily apparent. From the large pool of potential patients, an unknown proportion elect to become or are selected to become actual patients. Not only is the proportion unknown, but it is likely that identified patients are not a random sample of the larger potential patient pool. Becoming a patient is the end result of a complex chain of events dependent upon the nature of the symptomatology, alternative forms of available support, social class, community value systems, availability of treatment facilities, economics, and willingness to accept the patient role.

One final objection that has commonly been raised to the utilization of treated rates in epidemiologic investigations is that the act of hospitalization for a psychiatric disorder is less an indication of psychopathology on the part of the patient, and more an indication of society's reaction to what it labels as deviant behavior. While this hypothesis has been a popular one, it has, until recently, received little systematic attention. But in two papers by Gove (1970a, 1970b) substantial empirical evidence has been gathered to document that the primary determinant of hospitalization as well as of the consequences of hospitalization is the patient's psychiatric status.

While it is conceivable that a person may be denied the patient role having petitioned for it, this is a relatively rare phenomenon. It is reasonably safe to assume that identified psychiatric patients have some form of disability. The difficulty in using patient care data as a measure of psychiatric disability in a population, however, is not only the danger of systematic underestimation, but the assumption that one is forced to make, namely, that while rates based upon identified patients may be lower than rates based on population surveys, patient rates are sufficiently highly correlated with rates calculated on the basis of population surveys to serve as a valid criterion of "true" psychiatric disability rates. Dohrenwend and Dohrenwend note, for example, that relations between treated rates and social class are "strongly affected by such factors as the greater availability of private psychiatrists to high-income groups . . . and the relatively favorable orientation to psychiatric treatment" in one community compared to another, and thus conclude that they cannot assume that "an empirical relation between social status and rate of psychological disorder based on treated rates necessarily reflects the true relationship" [1969, p. 7].

To put this assumption into the context of the present study, in order to have confidence in derived implications of the sociocultural correlates of treatment rates across the Pueblo census tracts, or in identified differences between patients and the total population, one needs to assume that census tract treatment rates are significantly correlated with rates which would have been obtained from a population survey in the same tracts. And if it had been possible to conduct such a population survey with adequately reliable and valid results, why, then, bother with rates calculated on the basis of treated cases? The answer, regrettably, is not hard to find. Identifying the extent of psychiatric disability in a community by means of population surveys is perhaps even more complex and even more fraught with methodological problems than those involved in basing one's conclusions on medical care statistics. This is not to suggest that efforts to improve household survey case identification methods should be abandoned—quite to the contrary. For until such time as persons in need of mental health services freely and generally avail themselves of these services, medical care statistics will always bear an imperfect relationship to the actual amount of psychiatric disability in a community.

Whatever method is employed in identifying psychiatric disability by means of population surveys, the validity of the method depends on its results agreeing with some type of criterion. Blum suggests that the psychiatric interview, the means by which the psychiatrist arrives at a diagnosis, is the "ultimate criterion against which other means for identifying psychiatric disorder are validated" [1962, p. 254]. But his review of studies attempting to document reliability of diagnoses based on psychiatric interviews indicates that interpsychiatrist agreement on diagnosis is disturbingly low, that the rate of neuropsychiatric rejections from military service vary geographically by such an extraordinary amount (rejection rates are 100 times higher in certain military induction centers than in others, for example) as to throw considerable doubt on the entire diagnostic process, and finally, that assertions as to diagnosis as well as to the broader question of presence or absence of psychiatric disability are so unstable that "the psychiatric interview can prove to be a very unreliable and inadequate tool for epidemiological use" [1962, p. 259].

Apart from the fact that the criterion measure is itself far from satisfactory, and thus that other techniques for identifying psychiatric disability in a population have no satisfactory criterion against which to judge their validity, population surveys using structured or unstructured interviews, rating scales, questionnaires, or psychological tests each have their own difficulties in achieving acceptable scientific credibility.

An overview of the more than 40 population surveys in nearly that many different communities conducted in the past 30 years is presented by Dohrenwend and Dohrenwend (1969), and the range in the reported prevalence rates of identifiable mental disorder extends from less than one percent to over 60 percent—a range that defies credibility. Furthermore, except for social class, which has generally been found to vary inversely with obtained rates, and recency of the survey, which has been found to vary directly with obtained rates, no variables on which the communities can be differentiated have been shown to be consistently related to these rate variations. And neither social class nor recency of the survey is so strongly associated with obtained rates as to account for the extraordinary variation in findings. The Dohrenwends have concluded that "there is no way to account for this great variability on substantive grounds. Rather, the differences are found to be related to differences in thoroughness of data collection procedures and, even more, to contrasting conceptions of what constitutes a 'case'" [1969, p. 170]. Manis and his colleagues, in their discussion of the problems in arriving at a valid measure of the prevalence of mental illness, come to a similar conclusion. They suggest that "our interpretation is that the differences in the reported rates of untreated illness arise *primarily* from lack of agreement, stated or implicit, in the criteria used to establish the cutting-point between the sick and the well" [1964, p. 89]. This variation in obtained rates led Pasamanick to note, "It is the borderlines between the psychoses, on the one hand, and the neuroses, personality disorders and psychosomatic psychophysiologic disorders, on the other, and between them, that we encounter major difficulties. It is between the latter three and no illness, or with social maladjustment without psychiatric disorder, that we encounter our greatest unreliability. Since these are our most common disorders, surveyors, of course, have, as a consequence, arrived at the fantastically varying rates which create such hilarity in the literature" [1968, p. 38]. And in a related observation, the Expert Committee on Mental Health of the World Health Organization concluded that "in epidemiological studies, the definition of a 'case' is of crucial importance. The Committee has come to the conclusion, however, that there seems to be little prospect of producing a definition which would cover all the major and minor aberrations in social behavior or manifestations of disordered thought and would be applicable to all communities throughout the world, irrespective of their cultural background and social customs" [1960, p. 15]. This is the issue of content validity, of course, and Dohrenwend and Dohrenwend comment that "it is doubtful whether content validity, in the strictest sense, can be achieved in the measurement of untreated psychological disorder, since there appears to be no universe of items which experts agree on as defining the variable" [1965, p. 56].

Even with a less equivocally defined disorder, household surveys have been shown to be inadequate. Let us take the case of developing a survey instrument by which it might be possible to identify alcoholics. In an imaginative effort to assess the validity of such an instrument, Mulford and Wilson (1966) selected a sample of urban housing units "loaded" with addresses of households containing known alcoholics and concealed this fact from their otherwise carefully trained interviewers. Records of several community agencies and such other persons as police, AA leaders, company personnel managers, clergymen, and judges were consulted to obtain the names of a group of known alcoholics. This list of names was submitted to resource persons in the community who might be expected to be most knowledgeable about the local community and its alcoholics and only persons whose name was submitted or confirmed by two or more sources were considered as known alcoholics for the purposes of this study. The questionnaire employed by the interviewers was derived from a substantial body of previous research in the community, research which had already shown that the questionnaire appeared to have acceptable reliability and validity, yet using this instrument the interviewers missed half of the known alcoholics. Failure to identify known alcoholics was not random. The interview instrument was about twice as successful in identifying lower socioeconomic status alcoholics as it was in identifying alcoholics who had higher incomes and education.

There is no reason to believe that the problem of false negatives (failure to identify known cases) by means of household surveys is unique to alcoholics. In the Midtown Manhattan Study (see Srole *et al.* 1962) nearly half (19 out of 40) of current outpatients were judged not to have impaired states of mental health.

Even if the problem of false negatives did not exist, there remains the distinct possibility that cases (particularly of persons never in psychiatric treatment) identified by means of community surveys might differ in such significant ways from patients known to caretaking agencies as to constitute false positives. Major studies of psychiatric disability based on community surveys (see Srole *et al.* 1962 and Leighton *et al.*, 1963, for example) have concluded that substantial proportions of the general population are psychiatric cases and that the large majority of these cases have never been in treatment. Unfortunately, no studies to date have determined whether such persons are at higher risk of becoming patients at some future time than individuals found reasonably free of psychiatric disability in the same surveys (see Dohrenwend and Dohrenwend, 1965, p. 57). The assumption is that the psychiatric conditions of such untreated "cases" are similar to those of typical psychiatric patients. In an effort to test this assumption, Dohrenwend employed two rating scales with samples of community leaders, heads of households, outpatients, and inpatients in northern Manhattan. In contrasting, for example, those heads of households judged to be almost certainly psychiatric cases with clinic outpatients judged similarly, a significant difference was found in degree of impairment. The outpatients were significantly more impaired. On the basis of this and other findings, Dohrenwend concludes, "typical 'cases' in the community, according to the Midtown Study and the Stirling County Study psychiatric ratings, are simply not the same as typical cases in either outpatient clinics or mental hospitals" [1970, p. 1061].

There are still other problems in assessing mental health in a general population, particularly if one is interested in evaluating social class or other sociocultural variables as possible etiological factors. It has been found that there are significant differences in symptom expression between members of different ethnic groups, in the case of medical conditions (see Zola, 1966) as well as psychiatric conditions (see Dohrenwend, 1969).

Questionnaire replies are difficult to interpret across social classes and ethnic groups because of systematic differences in modes of symptom expression (see Crandell and Dohrenwend, 1967), in acquiescence (see Dohrenwend, 1969 and Phillips and Clancy, 1970) and in perceived social desirability (see Phillips and Clancy, 1970 and Dohrenwend and Chin-Shong, 1967). Clear sex differences in symptom expression have been found (see Phillips and Segal, 1969). It has been shown that respondents from the general population are less likely to be rated as cases on the basis of interviews conducted by psychiatrists than on the basis of their interpretations of protocols of interviews conducted by others (see Dohrenwend, Egri, and Mendelsohn, 1971) and in a recent study the question of the reliability of self-reports of stressful events has been raised (see Hudgens, Robins, and Delong, 1970).

We are thus drawn to conclude that the best available population survey instruments designed to assess psychiatric disability not only fail to identify known patients but succeed in designating as "cases" such a high proportion of people (the vast majority of whom have never sought treatment) that their validity has yet to be convincingly established. Given this state of affairs, it would be foolhardy to ignore studies based on treated rates, particularly when the studies are undertaken in communities where the major and obvious objections to relying on such rates do not hold.

Incidence Versus Prevalence Measures

Given that the potential legitimacy of using treated rates as indices of psychiatric disability has been increased by the foregoing discussion, the question then becomes, what should be the basis for the calculation of such a set of rates? If one is to judge by the existing literature, the choice seems to be between some measure of incidence and some measure of prevalence. Incidence is defined as the number of new cases of a disease occurring within a specified period of time and is reported as so many new cases per unit population per specified time period. Thus the incidence of acute leukemia for the time period 1948–1952 based on data collected for the white population in Brooklyn, New York, is 32.4 per million population per year, based on the identification of 410 new cases in a five year period in a population of 2,525,000 (see MacMahon, Pugh, and Ipsen, pp. 59-60). Prevalence is defined as the number of cases of a disease present in a specified population group as of a specified moment or period of time. From the same study, on January 1, 1952, there were 21 cases of acute leukemia known to be alive. Thus the prevalence at that point of time (usually referred to as point prevalence) was 8.3 cases per million population. During 1952 an additional 68 cases were identified. Thus a total of 89 cases were known to have existed at some time during the year and the prevalence of acute leukemia for the entire year (usually referred to as period prevalence) can be calculated as 35.2 cases per million.

At first glance, it would appear that one could either utilize measures of treated prevalence (total number of known psychiatric patients at some specified time interval) or treated incidence (total number of persons entering into psychiatric treatment status during some specified time interval). Both types of rates have been employed in investigations of psychiatric disability. But consider the following two statements. First, Stokes and Dawber (1956), referring to their epidemiologic studies of rheumatic heart disease (a chronic disorder), state "The cardinal statistic in the epidemiology of rheumatic heart disease is the overall prevalence" [p. 1228]. By direct contrast, Kramer (1957) has written "Usually the prevalence rate can be determined more easily than the incidence rate since it can be estimated by a single case-finding survey of a population group. This particularly is true for the chronic diseases, but this should not obscure the fact that the incidence rate is the fundamental epidemiologic ratio" [p. 827].

From these two statements, it would seem that the choice of measuring incidence or prevalence is more a matter of principle than caprice and that each investigator selects which measure to use on the basis of what he considers most correct. The issue will have to be examined in greater detail. Srole and his colleagues have presented a vigorous defense of their use of prevalence figures as the fundamental treatment data for identifying potential etiologic factors in the development of psychiatric disorders and refer to the Stokes and Dawber statement as part of their justification. Their argument rests less on the virtues of measures of prevalence, however, than on the presumed defects of measures of incidence, and it is important to note their objections to using an incidence rate in defining psychiatric status of a given population. While acknowledging the appropriateness of incidence rates for studies of acute disorders, they insist that prevalence rates are superior for studies of chronic disorders. Regarding the deficiencies of incidence rates, they suggest (1) that the point of onset of a mental disorder is at best highly equivocal; (2) that treated rates are very imperfectly related to true community rates; (3) that institutional records rarely report whether or not a patient is a first admission; (4) that treated rates are typically calculated from a limited and incomplete network of service delivery agencies; and (5) that because of population mobility which can vary among communities and within communities over time, the actual denominator (that is, the population at risk) is never known. Thus, they argue that "use of the incidence rates produced by the Midtown Treatment Census would be indefensible" [1962, pp. 381–382].

Kramer's position on the relative merits of measures of incidence and prevalence stands in sharp contradiction. He writes:

> ... incidence measures the rate at which new cases are added to the population of sick persons and— in conjunction with the decrement rate, *i.e.*, the rate at which the disease is 'arrested,' 'cured,' or at which affected individuals are removed from the population by death—determines the size and composition of the sick population. Thus, the prevalence rate of a disease is a function of the incidence rate and the duration of the disease. ... although the prevalence of a disease differs among communities, the inference cannot be drawn that the community with the highest prevalence also has the highest incidence. ... Since the prevalence rate is a function of the annual incidence and the duration of the illness, it should be clear that interpretation of differences in prevalence between communities is dependent on knowledge of these two factors. ...

> The purpose of epidemiologic investigations of the mental disorders is to discover associations that may lead to the determination of factors—biologic, psychologic, familial, socioenvironmental—that cause these disorders, and which are responsible for the disability they produce. These associations are determined by studies of the rate at which disease develops in various population groups and in various segments of these populations, and the differential duration of disease and mortality in affected individuals. The proof of etiologic relationships must then be sought through more extensive clinical or experimental investigations. If we are to learn more about the role played by socioen-

vironmental variables in the production of mental disorder then we must extend our knowledge of the incidence of these disorders in various population groups. Similarly, if we are to understand the influence of these variables on the course of specific mental disorders, then we must also study variations in remission, relapse, and mortality rates. Studies of prevalences alone leave these basic questions unanswered. . . .

Although the first admission rate (*i.e.,* the rate of coming under hospital treatment) for one disorder is high, if the separation rate is also high (*i.e.,* average duration of stay in the hospital is short) patients with this disorder may constitute a relatively small proportion of the population under treatment on any one day. On the other hand, a disorder with a relatively low admission rate may constitute a high proportion of patients under treatment because of a relatively long duration of stay. Thus, the fact that an inverse relationship exists between social class and prevalence of treated mental disorder does not mean necessarily that a similar relationship exists between the rate at which people enter into treatment and social class. Nor does it mean necessarily that a similar relationship exists between social class and the rate at which the mental disorder develops (incidence). The number of people with a particular mental disorder who are under a specific type of treatment on a given day is a resultant not only of the incidence of that disorder but also of the availability of various types of psychiatric treatment facilities and a series of medical, social, economic, environmental, personal, familial, educational, legal and administrative factors which determine who receive treatment in the various facilities and how long they stay under such treatment. Thus, much additional research is needed to determine how much of the observed difference in prevalence of treated mental disorder between various classes of the population is due to differences in (a) incidence (the rate at which the disorder occurs), (b) the rate at which individuals come under treatment, and (c) how long they stay under the care of these treatment facilities [1957, pp. 827, 829, 835–836, 837].

Perhaps we had better turn to a standard reference work on epidemiologic methods. MacMahon, Pugh, and Ipsen have written as follows:

A variety of rates . . . are related to the frequency of a disease in a population. The use of one rather than another is dependent on the relevance of the one selected to the particular problem in mind. Where the problem is epidemiologic the rate of choice obviously is incidence. . . . In practice it is often impossible to measure incidence directly, since definite timing of an onset of illness is commonly uncertain. Usually certain arbitrary points in the disease process are used as approximations. Thus, measurements such as onset of symptoms, time of diagnosis, and date of notification or of hospitalization are judged to be events related to how many cases arise within a specified period of time. . . . For epidemiologic purposes point prevalence measurements are inferior to incidence measurements, since two sets of factors determine point prevalence: those connected with the occurrence of cases, and those connected with course and duration (prognosis) of the cases once they are established. Although the same factors may at times be operative in both mechanisms, there would appear to be a much greater chance of correctly assigning the role of individual factors if the two processes were studied separately by investigation of incidence rates on the one hand, and of prognosis on the other. . . . On the other hand, many administrative situations require knowledge of how many patients with a given disease exist in the community. Clearly the answer to such a question rests in point prevalence [pp. 62, 54–55, 63].

In another view of the incidence versus prevalence issue in epidemiological studies, Mishler and Scotch (1963) write: "It is worth noting that the distinction between incidence and prevalence has received considerably more attention in studies of mental illness than in studies of physical illness, where prevalence measures tend to be the rule and have provided much of the basic data in the field. The main reason for this is that the durations of physical illnesses do not seem to be associated differentially with the basic sociodemographic variables. In the mental illnesses, while definitive data are lacking, there is enough evidence to suggest that duration is associated with such variables as social class and marital status to argue against a casual use of prevalence as if it were equivalent to incidence" [pp. 323–324].

With this background information, it seems possible to arrive at a summary statement. The kind of measure used to index the extent of psychiatric disability depends on the objectives of the study. From the point of view of the administration or program planner, who is interested in such questions as facility planning, doctor–patient ratio, and certain aspects of medical care, prevalence is the more useful statistic, regardless of whether the disorder in question is acute or chronic. A competent medical administrator is as interested in the prevalence of appendicitis in his community as he is in the prevalence of diabetes. The Stokes and Dawber assertion about prevalence being the cardinal statistic in the epidemiology of rheumatic heart disease can be understood in this medical management context, since it is immediately preceded by the statement "Information about the entire clinical spectrum of rheumatic heart disease is of interest to the practicing physician since it will help him to manage the asymptomatic patient encountered in medical practice" [1956, p. 1228]. But if one is interested in identifying factors that might be etiologically related to a specific disease, incidence (however imperfectly measured) seems irresistibly the measure of choice. Srole and his colleagues have properly identified major difficulties in measuring incidence. But the solution is to attempt to surmount these difficulties rather than to abandon the attempt to assess incidence. Some difficulties are essentially insurmountable, notably the question of when a disease process starts. But this problem is in no sense unique to the psychiatric disorders and has been resolved, for better or for worse, by coming to some common agreement as to the point in time when, for purposes of epidemiologic research, a disease can be said to have started. For, ultimately, the answer to the question of when a disease actually starts, just as the answer to the question of what the actual cause of a disease might be, may lie in the realm of philosophy and not in the realm of science.

We have tried, in deriving our measures of treated incidence, to deal with the cogent critique of Srole and his colleagues. We have determined with the greatest feasible accuracy whether an admission to a psychiatric facility constitutes the first such admission for each particular patient. We have identified every psychiatric facility where a Pueblo resident might reasonably be expected to turn in his efforts to obtain help from a mental health professional. We have selected for study a community where there is extensive availability of a wide spectrum of mental health services (to such an extent that, to our knowledge, no waiting lists existed at any facility). And we have not only selected for study a single community with unusually low population mobility, but have studied that same community at two widely different points in time, between which relatively little change has taken place in that population stability.

In our judgment, epidemiological investigation of mental disorder based on treated rates (see Pugh and MacMahon, 1972; Faris and Dunham, 1939; and Hollingshead and Redlich, 1958) have yielded findings consistent with and no less useful than studies based on field surveys. Under the best of circumstances, such studies can have a high level of clinical as well as public health utility. Psychiatric hospitalization is rarely undertaken lightly. Psychiatric patients are virtually always psychiatrically impaired. In those communities where ample inpatient facilities are available and where there is a reasonable degree of confidence in the mental health service delivery system, analysis of the characteristics of psychiatric patients can play an especially useful role, not only in understanding the service delivery system but also in understanding some of the factors associated with the development of psychopathology. And psychiatric patients (particularly inpatients), of whatever diagnosis, are sufficiently incapacitated so that the notion of a transient stress reaction in an otherwise reasonably intact personality seems less relevant than in the case of persons identified as impaired in community field surveys. While there still remain problems of false negatives, the risk of identifying false positives seems minimal.

This is not to suggest that the problem of underestimation of psychiatric disability is not a serious one when one uses measures of treated incidence. Not only are large numbers of persons who ought to be receiving care not doing so, but it is generally agreed that a substantial proportion of the caseload of primary physicians have significant psychiatric pathology. The same phenomenon is probably the case with nonpsychiatric social service or social welfare agencies and, to a somewhat lesser degree, with persons who seek help from the clergy (see

Mechanic, 1970). In a recent survey of the metropolitan Boston area, Ryan (1969) found that more psychiatric patients were being treated by clergymen than by psychiatrists. Identifying these patients has never been successfully accomplished, and this study as well is deficient in this regard. But we believe that with its deficiencies, studies based on treated incidence have a significant place in psychiatric epidemiology.

The single assumption which must be made is that measures of treated incidence in a population bear *some* positive relationship to the "true" incidence of all disorders (treated and untreated) in the same population. In spite of the inadequacies of measures of treated incidence, given the difficulties in identifying mental disorder in the total population, it seems imprudent not to proceed on that assumption. In rejecting epidemiological investigations based on treated rates, one must make the alternative assumption, namely, that measures of incidence bear no relationship to "true" incidence, and that assumption seems substantially less defensible.

12

Toward the Control
of Mental Disorders

We have tried to argue that measures of treated incidence are useful for indicating the extent of newly developing psychopathology in the community we have studied, and that it is this measure which is most pertinent to the development of control programs. Stable relationships have been demonstrated between environmental characteristics and these treated rates at two points in time separated by ten years. For the 1970 study period, demographic differences between patients and the general population have also been shown. Two interrelated variables, marital disruption and social isolation, characteristic of both neighborhoods and of persons have been most clearly shown to be related to treated rates. Our final analysis of the data is designed to determine the relative contribution of person characteristics and place characteristics to this relationship.

The strategy for additional research studies which must precede the development of rational control programs depends on the outcome of this final analysis of our data. A sense of direction for next steps in studying social factors in the development of psychopathology can be determined to the extent that either environmental or personal characteristics can be shown to play a major role in explaining the association with treated rates.

Our sole intent is to attempt to provide greater definition of possible stressor variables. We do not propose to
outline specific intervention programs, since such a step
would go well beyond our data. We do believe, however,
that mental health professionals working with their colleagues in related areas could develop the details of trial
programs if encouraged to do so, particularly if a careful
review of existing literature evaluating programs which
have already been attempted is undertaken.

MARITAL DISRUPTION AS A STRESSOR VARIABLE

Our data have indicated that first admission inpatients
were overrepresented, both in 1960 and 1970, in those
census tracts characterized by a high level of marital
disruption. Furthermore, in 1970, when it was possible
to contrast patients with the general population, it was
found that first admission inpatients were significantly
more likely to have disrupted marriages than the population as a whole and that repeat admission inpatients were
significantly more likely than first admission inpatients to
have disrupted marriages. A recent study, interestingly,
has suggested that marital disruption (death of spouse,
divorce, or separation) may be the single most powerful
predictor of stress-related physical as well as emotional
illness (see APA, 1973, p. 8). We can now analyze the
interaction of these ecological and demographic findings
in order to develop a more refined perspective on marital disruption as a stressor variable.

In order to make this analysis, we will divide the 33
Pueblo census tracts into three groups, according to the
level of marital disruption within them. Within each
group we will tabulate the number of first and repeat
admission patients aged 14 and above who, at the time
of admission, had nondisrupted marriages (married and

living together with spouse) and disrupted marriages (divorced plus married and living apart from spouse) based on all data available to us. Then, within each group of census tracts, we will identify the population at risk, that is, the total number of persons aged 14 and above with disrupted and nondisrupted marriages. On the basis of these two sets of figures, it will be possible to calculate annual admission rates specific for marital status within each of the three groups of census tracts. The interpretation of the resulting admission rate calculations will depend on the patterning of these rates. If marital disruption is a stressor primarily at an individual or demographic level, we will expect to find that admission rates for maritally disrupted patients are substantially higher than rates for those patients with nondisrupted marriages, regardless of the level of marital disruption of the census tracts where they live. If marital disruption acts as a stressor at an environmental level, we should find admission rates substantially higher in those census tracts characterized by high marital disruption than in those tracts where marital disruption is less common regardless of the marital status of individual patients in the census tracts. Minority status as a special kind of stressor will receive support if it is found that admission rates for the maritally disrupted are unusually high in those census tracts where there is very little marital disruption and admission rates for the nonmaritally disrupted are unusually high in those census tracts where there is a great deal of marital disruption. No new data are introduced in the following analyses. Rather, data already presented are reexamined with the intent of estimating the relative contribution of personal and environmental factors in the relationships already found.

This analysis appears in Table 12-1, where it can be seen that marital disruption serves as a stressor primarily

Table 12-1

INTERACTION OF DEMOGRAPHIC AND ECOLOGICAL MEASURES OF MARITAL DISRUPTION WITH FIRST AND REPEAT INPATIENT ADMISSION RATES: 1970 STUDY PERIOD

Raw Data and Admission Rates	Census Tract Marital Disruption Ratio							
	Low: Range = 12.8–44.6		Med.: Range = 57.1–80.7		High: Range = 82.0–508.7		Total	
	First IP	Rpt IP	First IP	Rpt IP	First IP	Rpt IP	First IP	Rpt IP
No. of Census Tracts	11		11		11		33	
Population Age 14+:								
Disrupted Marriages	1301		1425		1771		4497	
Nondisrupted Marriages	25994		15501		10573		52068	
TOTAL	27295		16926		12344		56565	
Patients Age 14+:								
Disrupted Marriages	45	48	47	59	72	126	164	233
Nondisrupted Marriages	139	110	112	86	84	65	335	261
TOTAL	184	158	159	145	156	191	499	494
Annual Admission Rates per 1000—Patients with:								
Disrupted Marriages	17.3	18.4	16.5	20.7	20.3	35.6	18.2	25.9
Nondisrupted Marriages	2.7	2.1	3.6	2.8	4.0	3.1	3.2	2.5
TOTAL	3.4	2.9	4.7	4.3	6.3	7.7	4.4	4.4

at the individual level both for first admission and repeat admission inpatients. While the differentials are not consistent, first admission inpatients with disrupted marriages are nearly six times more likely to be admitted into psychiatric facilities than first admission patients with nondisrupted marriages, regardless of the character of the census tract. Repeat admission patients with disrupted marriages are ten times more likely to be admitted than those without disrupted marriages. Admission rates even for non-maritally disrupted generally increase as the census tract index of marital disruption increases, however, but this differential is substantially less striking than that found on the individual level of analysis.

The fact that admission rates for patients with disrupted marriages and prior psychiatric histories are consistently higher than rates for patients with disrupted marriages who have not had prior psychiatric inpatient treatment suggests that psychiatric disability may, in some cases, precede marital disruption, but the data to test this hypothesis are not available in the present study.

Two additional observations from Table 12-1 should be noted. First, the differential between first admission and repeat admission rates in the case of patients with disrupted marriages increases dramatically as the character of census tracts with respect to disrupted marriage ratio changes. In those census tracts where the disrupted marriage ratio is low, there is very little difference between first admission and repeat admission rates in the case of patients with disrupted marriages. In those census tracts characterized by high marital disruption, on the other hand, repeat admission rates are substantially higher than first admission rates for patients with disrupted marriages. Second, first admission rates for patients with nondisrupted marriages are consistently higher than repeat admission rates for patients with nondisrupted marriages, a difference which is fairly stable regardless of the character of the census tract.

It is possible to examine the interaction of demographic and ecological measures of marital disruption at a finer level of analysis by subdividing both patients and the population at risk by sex. The analysis of the resultant sex-specific rates is shown in Table 12-2 for males and in Table 12-3 for females. Comparing these two analyses reveals that males with disrupted marriages are at substantially higher risk of hospitalization than females, and that the differential holds consistently for all levels of census tract marital disruption and for first admissions as well as for patients with prior histories of psychiatric hospitalization. In fact, the total risk of hospitalization for psychiatric conditions for males with disrupted marriages is of epidemic proportions, averaging more than 75 cases per 1000 persons at risk per year.

The observation that risk of psychiatric hospitalization is so much higher in males with disrupted marriages than in females has been made elsewhere (see Gove, 1972). Marital disruption may be a greater stress in males than in females because males are generally separated from their children, they are generally the ones who must move, and are thus generally more socially isolated by the marital disruption than are females. Unfortunately, marital status information was not available for outpatients. It is entirely possible, for example, that females with disrupted marriages are overrepresented in outpatient settings.

This analysis suggests that intervention strategies designed to exercise a preventive or control function would need to be developed at an individual rather than a census tract level, or, to put it in another way, that it is persons rather than neighborhoods who should be the target of trial intervention programs. Admission rates are actually quite high for persons with disrupted marriages, averaging more than two percent per year, and thus it is feasible to develop appropriate programs and

Table 12-2.

INTERACTION OF DEMOGRAPHIC AND ECOLOGICAL MEASURES OF MARITAL DISRUPTION WITH FIRST AND REPEAT INPATIENT ADMISSION RATES, MALES ONLY: 1970 STUDY PERIOD

Raw Data and Admission Rates	Census Tract Marital Disruption Ratio							
	Low		Medium		High		Total	
	First IP	Rpt IP	First IP	Rpt IP	First IP	Rpt IP	First IP	Rpt IP
No. of Census Tracts	11		11		11		33	
Population Age 14+								
Disrupted Marriages	437		518		795		1750	
Nondisrupted Marriages	12936		7698		5262		25896	
TOTAL	13373		8216		6057		27646	
Male Patients Age 14+								
Disrupted Marriages	22	31	29	40	54	91	105	162
Nondisrupted Marriages	70	63	49	45	50	39	169	147
TOTAL	92	94	78	85	104	130	274	309
Annual Admission Rates per 1000—Patients with:								
Disrupted Marriages	25.2	35.5	28.0	38.6	34.0	57.2	30.0	46.3
Nondisrupted Marriages	2.7	2.4	3.2	2.9	4.8	3.7	3.3	2.8
TOTAL	3.4	3.5	4.7	5.2	8.6	10.7	5.0	5.6

Table 12-3

INTERACTION OF DEMOGRAPHIC AND ECOLOGICAL MEASURES OF MARITAL DISRUPTION WITH FIRST AND REPEAT INPATIENT ADMISSION RATES, FEMALES ONLY: 1970 STUDY PERIOD

Raw Data and Admission Rates	Census Tract Marital Disruption Ratio							
	Low		Medium		High		Total	
	First IP	Rpt IP	First IP	Rpt IP	First IP	Rpt IP	First IP	Rpt IP
No. of Census Tracts	11		11		11		33	
Population Age 14+:								
Disrupted Marriages	864		907		976		2747	
Nondisrupted Marriages	13058		7803		5311		26172	
TOTAL	13922		8710		6287		28919	
Female Patients Age 14+:								
Disrupted Marriages	23	17	18	19	18	35	59	71
Nondisrupted Marriages	69	47	63	41	34	26	166	114
TOTAL	92	64	81	60	52	61	225	185
Annual Admission Rates per 1000—Patients with:								
Disrupted Marriages	13.3	9.8	9.9	10.5	9.2	17.9	10.7	12.9
Nondisrupted Marriages	2.6	1.8	4.0	2.6	3.2	2.4	3.2	2.2
TOTAL	3.3	2.3	4.6	3.4	4.1	4.9	3.9	3.2

evaluate them within a reasonable length of time. But possible interactions between person and place characteristics have been noted, and it is likely that control programs, while being developed for persons at risk, may well keep in mind the special characteristics of neighborhoods where such persons live.

It is, of course, necessary to collect more data before proceeding with an intervention program designed to provide support at the time of marital disruption. Specifically, we are interested in learning more about the stresses associated with marital disruption and how these stresses are typically managed. Samples of both patients and nonpatients undergoing marital disruption can be located in collaboration with attorneys, clergyman, and the courts, as well as through welfare, mental health, and social service agencies, and interviews can reveal a good deal of information on issues related to marital disruption (see Meyers, 1972, for example). In no sense are we suggesting that the stresses associated with marital disruption are limited to those which are psychiatric in nature. Some stresses are economic. Others, particularly in the case of women, are associated with problems of employment and socialization. But data collected from a broad spectrum of persons who are undergoing marital disruption will help establish both the legitimacy and the specifics of an intervention program. Since admission rates are especially high in the case of patients with disrupted marriages who have prior histories of psychiatric hospitalization, it would be useful to include current and former psychiatric patients among those persons selected for interviewing.

SOCIAL ISOLATION AS A STRESSOR VARIABLE

Our data have shown that census tracts in which large numbers of persons live alone tended to produce excess numbers of first admission inpatients both in 1960 and 1970, and that somewhat more first admission inpatients live alone than would be expected on the basis of general population statistics for heads of households. Furthermore, living alone is twice as common for repeat inpatients as for first admission inpatients. The identical pattern of findings is associated with living in very small (often one- or two-room) housing units, and there is considerable evidence at the individual level of analysis that mobility (primarily from house to house rather than from outside to inside the county) is associated with excess hospitalization rate.

These findings taken together suggest that social isolation may be a stressor associated with psychiatric hospitalization. The social isolation hypothesis, first advanced by Faris and Dunham (1939) serves to link these diverse findings by suggesting that persons living alone, persons living in one-room housing units, and new arrivals in a residential area are all at high risk of being relatively isolated from their neighbors and that such isolation can have, as one of its consequences, the development of that kind of psychopathology which results in identification as a patient and subsequent hospitalization.

Since there is a high level of interdependence between living alone and living in small housing units (the correlation between the proportion of persons living alone and rooms per housing unit is –0.78 in 1960 and –0.87 in 1970), our analysis will be limited to a study of persons living alone and to mobility.

The analysis of persons living alone, shown in Table 12-4, must be restricted to heads of households in order to conform to census reports in which data are presented on housing units rather than persons. That is, from census reports it can only be ascertained how many housing units are occupied by only one person. From this analysis

Table 12-4

INTERACTION OF DEMOGRAPHIC AND ECOLOGICAL MEASURES OF SOCIAL ISOLATION WITH FIRST AND REPEAT INPATIENT ADMISSION RATES. I. PEOPLE LIVING ALONE: 1970 STUDY PERIOD

Raw Data and Admission Rates	Low: Range = 3.50–10.9%		Med.: Range = 11.3–18.8%		High: Range = 20.4–57.1%		Total	
	First IP	Rpt IP	First IP	Rpt IP	First IP	Rpt IP	First IP	Rpt IP
No. of Census Tracts	11		11		11		33	
Heads of Households:								
Living Alone	1118		1648		3288		6054	
Not Living Alone	12603		8957		7753		29313	
TOTAL	13721		10605		11041		35367	
Patient Heads of Households:								
Living Alone	15	17	18	22	50	106	83	145
Not Living Alone	83	69	82	46	66	68	231	183
TOTAL	98	86	100	68	116	174	314	328
Annual Admission Rates per 1000 Population at Risk:								
Living Alone	6.7	7.6	5.5	6.7	7.6	16.1	6.9	12.0
Not Living Alone	3.3	2.7	4.6	2.6	4.3	4.4	3.9	3.1
TOTAL	3.6	3.1	4.7	3.2	5.3	7.9	4.4	4.6

it can be seen that both first admission and repeat admission inpatients are overrepresented among persons living alone. This overrepresentation is more striking in the case of patients with histories of psychiatric hospitalization prior to the start of the 1970 study period than in the case of new inpatients, and the admission rate for prior patients who live alone is remarkably elevated in those census tracts where large numbers of persons live alone. At the same time it can be noted that for persons not living alone the risk of hospitalization tends to be highest in those census tracts in which large numbers of persons do live alone. In the case of first admission inpatients, the differential either by census tract or by personal characteristics is not great, however, with admission rates in the most socially isolated tracts or among most socially isolated individuals less than twice as high as those found among least socially isolated tracts or individuals. But in the case of patients with prior histories of psychiatric care there is evidence that they are not only at high risk of readmission if they live alone, but also that this risk is even greater if they live in socially isolated sections of the city. Here then is evidence that suggests that environmental intervention designed to increase opportunities for social interaction may be useful to explore.

The analysis of length of time in current residence, shown in Table 12-5, is again restricted to heads of households. In this case there is a rather steady increase in admission rates as length of time in current residence decreases, and as census tracts increase in the proportion of heads of households living there less than two years. In both of these analyses the group most vulnerable to hospitalization appears to be patients with histories of prior hospitalization living in the most socially isolated census tracts. These findings suggest that secondary and tertiary preventive intervention efforts, could well be directed to psychiatric inpatients at the time of discharge in an attempt to assist them in establishing less isolated life styles.

The interrelatedness of marital disruption and social isolation has already been mentioned. When inpatients with disrupted marriages are contrasted with those with nondisrupted marriages, separately by sex as well as by whether they are first admissions or readmissions, married patients have lived in their current place of residence consistently and significantly longer than patients who are divorced or separated. A substantial portion of maritally disrupted patients are new to their places of residence. In the case of male first admissions, 37 percent have lived at their present addresses less than six months. By way of contrast, only 17 percent of nonmaritally disrupted male first admissions have lived so short a time at their present addresses. In the case of female first admissions, the difference is even more striking. Of those female first admissions who marriages are disrupted, 40 percent have lived at their current addresses less than six months. Of married female first admissions, less than 15 percent have lived so short a time at their present addresses.

In the case of readmitted patients, that is, of patients with histories of psychiatric hospitalizations prior to the start of the study period, the differences are just as significant. Of male readmitted patients, 13 percent of married patients have lived at their current addresses for less than six months, while the same figure for male readmitted patients whose marriages are disrupted is 44 percent. In the case of female readmitted patients, the figures are similar—nine percent for patients with nondisrupted marriages and 47 percent for patients with disrupted marriages.

In this context it should also be mentioned that there are no meaningful differences between patients with dis-

Table 12-5

INTERACTION OF DEMOGRAPHIC AND CENSUS TRACT MEASURES OF SOCIAL ISOLATION WITH FIRST AND REPEAT INPATIENT ADMISSION RATES. II. LENGTH OF TIME IN CURRENT RESIDENCE, HEADS OF HOUSEHOLD: 1970 STUDY PERIOD

Raw Data and Admission Rates	Proportion of Housing Units Occupied Less Than Two Years			
	Low: Range = 16.0–22.0	Med.: Range = 22.8–31.8	High: Range = 31.9–53.1	Total
No. of Census Tracts	11	11	11	33
No. of Housing Units Occupied:				
Less Than Two Years	2316	3434	4301	10051
Two to Five Years	1751	2246	2129	6126
Five Years or More	7558	6584	5054	19196
TOTAL	11625	12264	11484	35373

	First IP	Rpt IP	First IP	Rpt IP	First IP	Rpt IP	First IP	Rpt IP
No. of Patients Living in Current Housing Unit:								
Less Than Two Years	26	25	38	37	57	101	121	163
Two to Five Years	9	13	22	19	22	17	53	49
Five Years or More	40	37	54	37	37	34	131	108
TOTAL	75	75	114	93	116	152	305	320
Annual Admission Rate per 1000 Persons at Risk Living in Current Housing Unit:								
Less Than Two Years	5.6	5.4	5.5	5.4	6.6	11.7	6.0	8.1
Two to Five Years	2.6	3.7	4.9	4.2	5.2	4.0	4.3	4.0
Five Years or More	2.6	2.4	4.2	2.8	3.7	3.4	3.4	2.8
TOTAL	3.2	3.2	4.6	3.9	5.1	6.6	4.3	4.5

rupted and nondisrupted marriages of either sex in age distribution or in diagnosis.

MINORITY STATUS AS A STRESSOR VARIABLE

One final analysis which bears on the issue of social isolation as a stressor relates to admission rates by ethnic group as a function of the proportion of persons of that ethnic group in the population. The social isolation hypothesis advanced by Faris and Dunham was strengthened by their finding that "rates for Negro, foreign-born, and native-born are all significantly higher in areas not primarily populated by their own members" (1939, p. 177). That is, for each group studied, admission rates were highest in those areas where the group constituted a minority and where, therefore, it could be presumed that they were socially isolated. This finding has been supported by at least two subsequent studies.

Wechsler and Pugh (1967) studying all first admission inpatients during a three-year period in Massachusetts were able to show that for nine of 15 tests, significant results supporting the minority status hypothesis were obtained, although racial or ethnic group was not among the nine. Klee, Spiro, Bahn, and Gorwitz (1967), studying diagnosed mental illness in the census tracts of Baltimore, were able to show that both White and non-White census tract admission rates were directly related to the extent to which each group constituted a minority.

It is possible to examine the minority status hypothesis for Pueblo data for first and repeat admission inpatients and for first admission outpatients in 1970 by following the same methodology already used, that is, by grouping census tracts according to the proportion of Spanish surnamed persons living within them and then studying admission rates specific for ethnicity within each of the combined groups of tracts. There were too few readmission outpatients to perform the analysis for this group. Analysis of the data for the 1960 study is shown in Table 12-6, where it can be seen that support for the minority status hypothesis is somewhat equivocal. Spanish surnamed admission rate is highest in those census tracts where they constitute the most notable minority, but differences across the groups of tracts either for Spanish surnamed or non-Spanish surnamed are small and not consistently related to minority status. The analysis for 1970 inpatients is shown in Table 12-7. Again the first admission rate for Spanish surnamed persons is highest in those tracts where they constitute the smallest minority. In addition, the first admission rate decreases for Spanish surnamed persons as their proportion in the population increases. Findings in the case of Spanish surnamed patients with prior histories of psychiatric hospitalization are far less regular, although the lowest admission rate does occur in those tracts where the largest proportion of Spanish surnamed live. If we treat the non-Spanish surnamed data in the same way, we find some additional support for the minority status hypothesis in that admission rates (both first admission and readmission) are highest in those census tracts where the proportion of non-Spanish surnamed is lowest. But again, while the results of these analyses are reasonably consistent with the minority status hypothesis, differences in admission rates across groups of census tracts are not great.

The analysis of first admission outpatient data is shown in Table 12-8. Here it can be seen that admission rates for both Spanish surnamed and non-Spanish surnamed decrease as the proportion of Spanish surnamed persons living in census tracts increases, that is, that outpatient first admission rates are highest in those census tracts where fewest Spanish surnamed persons live.

Table 12-6

INTERACTION OF DEMOGRAPHIC AND ECOLOGICAL MEASURES OF MINORITY STATUS WITH FIRST INPATIENT ADMISSION RATE: 1960 STUDY PERIOD

Raw Data and Admission Rates	Proportion of Spanish Surnamed Persons			
	Low: Range = 1.3–9.5	Medium: Range = 11.3–24.6	High: Range = 27.0–62.9	Total
No. of Census Tracts	11	11	11	33
No. of Persons:				
Spanish Surnamed	2075	6484	16253	24812
Non-Spanish Surnamed	35515	28830	23247	87592
TOTAL	37590	35314	39500	112404
No. of Patients:				
Spanish Surnamed	20	32	88	140
Non-Spanish Surnamed	283	291	205	779
TOTAL	303	323	293	919
Annual Admission Rate per 1000 Persons at Risk:				
Spanish Surnamed	3.2	1.6	1.8	1.9
Non-Spanish Surnamed	2.7	3.4	2.9	3.0
TOTAL	2.7	3.0	2.5	2.7

Table 12-7

Interaction of Demographic and Ecological Measures of Minority Status With First and Repeat Inpatient Admission Rates: 1970 Study Period

Raw Data and Admission Rates	Proportion of Spanish Surnamed Persons							
	Low: Range = 1.3–9.5		Med.: Range = 11.3–24.6		High: Range = 27.0–62.9		Total	
	First IP	Rpt IP	First IP	Rpt IP	First IP	Rpt IP	First IP	Rpt IP
No. of Census Tracts	11		11		11		33	
No. of Persons[1]:								
Spanish Surnamed	2075		6484		16253		24812	
Non-Spanish Surnamed	35515		28830		23247		87592	
TOTAL	37590		35314		39500		112404	
No. of Patients:								
Spanish Surnamed	45	21	92	78	161	123	298	222
Non-Spanish Surnamed	325	188	247	166	249	214	821	568
TOTAL	370	209	339	244	410	337	1119	790
Annual Admission Rate per 1000 Persons at Risk:								
Spanish Surnamed	10.8	5.1	7.1	6.0	5.0	3.8	6.0	4.5
Non-Spanish Surnamed	4.6	2.6	4.3	2.9	5.4	4.6	4.7	3.2
TOTAL	4.9	2.8	4.8	3.5	5.2	4.3	5.0	3.5

[1] 1960 Figures used for denominator.

But the differential in admission rates between those tracts with high as contrasted to low proportions of Spanish surnamed persons is much greater in the case of Spanish surnamed admission rates than in the case of non-Spanish surnamed admission rates. Again, by a substantial margin, admission rate for Spanish surnamed persons is highest in those tracts where they constitute the smallest minority.

There is thus some evidence, to be sure not as dramatic as one might like, implicating minority status, with its assumed association with social isolation as a stressor, for both Spanish surnamed and non-Spanish surnamed ethnic groups.

Preventive Intervention and Social Disequilibrium

Twelve years ago, the Program Area Committee on Mental Health of the American Public Health Association published its guide to control methods for mental disorders (APHA, 1962). The committee sought to gather together in one document whatever information was known about the prevention of mental disorders and about efforts which could be successfully undertaken toward reducing severity or duration or degree of disability. At that time, and today as well, there were far more disorders whose control was not known than disorders which could be controlled. Included among conditions of unknown etiology, not susceptible to effective prevention, were the functional psychoses, most childrens' disorders, the psychoneuroses, disorders of the senium, psychosomatic disorders, personality disorders, and sociopathic conditions including alcohol and drug addiction. Faced with this state of affairs, the authors of the control manual reviewed some general measures for prevention of mental disorders which might be employed

Table 12-8

INTERACTION OF. DEMOGRAPHIC AND ECOLOGICAL MEASURES OF MINORITY STATUS WITH FIRST ADMISSION
OUTPATIENT RATE: 1970 STUDY PERIOD

Raw Data and Admission Rate	Proportion of Spanish Surnamed Persons			
	Low: Range = 1.3–9.5	Medium: Range = 11.3–24.6	High: Range = 27.0–62.9	Total
No. of Census Tracts	11	11	11	33
No. of Persons[1]:				
Spanish Surnamed	2075	6484	16253	24812
Non-Spanish Surnamed	35515	28830	23247	87592
TOTAL	37590	35314	39500	112404
No. of Patients:				
Spanish Surnamed	65	139	158	362
Non-Spanish Surnamed	548	398	264	1210
TOTAL	613	537	422	1572
Annual Admission Rate per 1000 Persons at Risk:				
Spanish Surnamed	15.7	10.7	4.9	7.3
Non-Spanish Surnamed	7.7	6.9	5.7	6.9
TOTAL	8.2	7.6	5.3	7.0

[1] 1960 figures used for denominator.

and at the same time urged expanded and improved research programs which might increase our understanding of mental disorders, their etiology and their control.

In spite of the increase in research studies which has taken place since the report was issued, it is remarkable how short a distance has been traversed since the original Faris and Dunham studies more than 30 years ago. This phenomenon is, of course, a tribute to the thoughtfulness and brilliance of their work as well as an admission of the difficulties in going beyond it. The relationships between social class and social disorganization in urban areas and the incidence or prevalence of mental illness have been demonstrated again and again (see Kohn, 1968, pp. 156-158). In arguing whether this association comes about because certain characteristics inherent in lower socioeconomic groups or environments produce psychopathology (the social causation hypothesis) or because persons already psychiatrically disabled drift or move into lower socioeconomic or more socially disorganized areas (the social selection hypothesis), reviewers have been unable to arrive at an unequivocal conclusion.

Dunham, whose initial work led him to support a social causation hypothesis, has in recent years moved toward the belief that none of the social causation hypotheses is adequately supported by more recent research findings (see Dunham, 1968 and 1971, for example). With respect to schizophrenia at least, he believes that an interdisciplinary strategy, including biological and genetic research, will be needed before we will learn significantly more about its causes. In contrast, Kohn, writing about the relationship between social class and the incidence of schizophrenia, has concluded the following: "My assessment is that the weight of this evidence clearly indicates either that schizophrenics have been no more downwardly mobile (in fact, no less upwardly mobile) than other people from the same social backgrounds, or at minimum, that the degree of downward mobility is insufficient to explain the high concentration of schizophrenia in the lowest socioeconomic strata" [1968, p. 159].

The social selection and social causation hypotheses are not mutually exclusive, and to some extent, they can both be valid. To whatever extent social factors contribute to the development of psychopathology, these factors should be identified, and with the use of limited trial programs, where possible, efforts to reduce their consequences should be evaluated. The general concept of stress has served as the single organizing principle within which to examine social factors in the development of psychopathology. It is within this context that the first general measure for the prevention of mental disorders proposed by the APHA Program Area Committee on Mental Health was "support in times of stress" [APHA, 1962, pp. 57–58] or what Rogers, in another context, has called "general preventive measures directed at the determination and control of the underlying patterns of environmental relationships" which might "prove more efficient and effective in the long run than so-called specific measures" [1962, pp. 759–760]. And such research as that of Dohrenwend and his colleagues, already referred to, is designed to identify the more or less transitory stressors associated with lower social class status and to determine the extent to which such stressors can be held partially responsible for the observation of greater psychopathology in lower social classes.

It is, of course, true that not all persons living in areas of high social disorganization or in areas of low socioeconomic level develop demonstrable psychopathology. Ultimately it would be enormously useful to understand differential vulnerabilities. But at least the partial prevention of mental disorder need not wait for our ability to predict which persons in socially disorganized areas, for example, will break down and which persons will continue to function adequately. The fact that we cannot predict which persons exposed to the tubercle bacillus will develop tuberculosis does not make us hesitate to implicate that bacillus as an etiological agent. The role of the water supply in the production of cholera noted by British physician Snow (1936) and the subsequent removal of the offending water pump handle as a preventive device has never been questioned even though not everyone who drank the impure water developed cholera. Deaths among persons who drank impure water were on the order of 15 per 1000 during the fourteen weeks of the 1854 cholera epidemic in London, for example. While the question of why those particular 15 persons per 1000 died is an important and interesting one for the further understanding of the etiology of cholera, not knowing the answer did not inhibit the development of an effective preventive strategy. Similarly, the connection between diet and pellagra was convincingly established by Goldberger and his colleagues (see Terris, 1964) even though only a relatively small proportion of persons with defective dietary intake developed pellagra and which particular persons would develop this disease could not be predicted. We are, of course, suggesting that correlates of treated incidence rates give us clues as to possible etiologically related sources of stress—some at the personal level, others at the ecological level. Whether these presumed stressors are in fact associated with subsequent psychopathology can best be determined by mounting programs, limited in scope to be sure, designed to reduce these stresses and then determining if a convincing reduction in treated incidence takes place when contrasted with sections of the community where such programs have not been inaugurated.

This proposal is based upon a frank social causation hypothesis, and is in keeping with a prevalent point of view that social stress can precipitate as well as perpetuate psychiatric disorder. Illustrative of this point of view is the work of Porter, who interviewed representatives of mental health and related agencies in ten cities regarding the efficacy of mental health personnel in a community planning role in Model Cities areas. He found that "the majority in all groups also are in agreement that there *is* an appreciable relationship between the social problems of the urban ghetto and the incidence of mental illness; and that the planning of community programs aimed at the prevention of social stress is fundamentally the same task as the planning of programs for the prevention of mental illness" [quoted in Warren, 1971, p. 46].

The social causation hypothesis is more an ideology than an empirically supported assertion, however, and research to date has not convincingly demonstrated that reduction of stress results in a subsequent reduction in psychopathology. It is in recognition of this state of affairs that the need for improved research, particularly longitudinal research, as well as the need for soundly planned and evaluated trial intervention programs is being underlined. In a recent assessment of the empirical literature in primary prevention, Wagenfeld has suggested that the temporal sequence of stress and psychopathology needs to be documented, but that, "There is no reason, however, on either scientific or humanitarian grounds, why both intervention programs and scientific research cannot or should not be undertaken simultaneously" [1972, p. 198; see also Cumming, 1972].

There is some debate in the literature as to the place of ecological studies for analyses at the individual level. As was indicated in Chapter 6, individuals living in census tracts characterized by high social disequilibrium may not themselves be so characterized. More generally, it is argued, it is improper to draw any inferences at an individual level from data collected at an ecological level (see Dunham, 1964 or Dunham, 1965, for example). But in discussing the utility of ecological analyses for epidemiological purposes, Mishler and Scotch make the point that ". . . the criticism of the ecological studies on statistical grounds does not in itself suffice to dismiss these studies as spurious at the level of individual interpretation. Ecological variables have conceptual as well as operational meaning, and the problem is no different in principle from the problem of correlating occupation with schizophrenia and interpreting occupation as an index of a social-class life style. If, for example, the variable 'living in a high-rent census tract' is defined conceptually as an index of social aspirations, then a study of differential rates by rental value of census tracts may be interpreted in terms of psychological as well as ecological theory, and no change in statistical procedures is required to interpret it one way rather than the other. . . . the ecological approach has a valuable role to play in epidemiological research. Some combination of ecological and individual designs would seem to be particularly powerful . . ." [1963, p. 324; also see Levy and Rowitz, 1973, pp. 23–24].

With respect to ecological measures, we are clearly faced with the question of how the outside gets inside, that is, how characteristics of the environment come to be internalized with resulting symptoms of psychopathology. This important question is unanswered by ecological studies, or by individually-oriented studies for that matter, but preventive programming need not wait for such answers. It is enough if one can document that an ecological change results in a subsequent decrease in the incidence of psychopathology (see MacMahon, Pugh, and Ipsen, 1960, pp. 11–22). This issue is qualitatively no different from that faced by scientists interested in controlling infectious diseases. All disease processes can be viewed as the end result of an unhappy convergence of host, agent, and environmental factors, and most can be controlled by a significant intervention at any of these levels. It is the agent, the complex process or means by which environmental factors invade the host, that we understand so little of, but there is substantial evidence that control programs can be successfully mounted in the absence of this knowledge. This is certainly the case with infectious and nutritional diseases, and, hopefully, may be demonstrable in the case of psychiatric disability as well.

Social class *per se* has not been found, in this study, to be convincingly associated with treated rates. In a recent critical discussion of theories linking social class and schizophrenia, Mechanic has helped clarify this issue by noting that "the psychological impact of stress, of course, depends not alone on the occurrence of events but rather on the relationship between the demands an event makes and the individual's capacity to cope. . . . It has been too readily assumed by many writers in this field that the poor are always at a disadvantage, but it seems reasonable to anticipate that the poor are equally capable or superior to higher-status persons in dealing with some kinds of misfortunes. The development of coping capacities comes frequently through experience and practice, and in some areas of living, persons of lower economic status get greater opportunity to develop skills. Moreover, successful mastery builds confidence and a sense of effectiveness, and many persons of lower socioeconomic status, despite their low income, develop a strong sense of self. To talk of lower-status persons as a monolithic group on the basis of modest statistical differences among the social classes is conducive to asking the wrong research questions" [1972, p. 307].

We have attempted in the preceding analyses to examine the association of some personal and census tract measures of social disequilibrium with rates of treatment for identified psychopathology. Of all the measures available to us in this study, variables conceptualized as indices of social disequilibrium have stood out most strikingly as associated with psychiatric admission rates. Census tracts high in each of the measures we have been able to examine tend to yield excess numbers of patients, in some instances even in the case of patients not themselves characterized by the type of social disequilibrium under investigation. This is particularly true in the case of males with nondisrupted marriages living in census tracts in which large numbers of persons with disrupted marriages live, persons who have lived relatively long periods of time in their homes in census tracts characterized by large numbers of newcomers, and Spanish-surnamed persons living in census tracts in which there are found relatively few Spanish-surnamed.

But the most striking findings have linked persons experiencing a variety of types of social disequilibrium with excess psychiatric treatment rates regardless of the character of the neighborhoods in which they live. Thus throughout the city and county of Pueblo, persons with disrupted marriages are at high risk of psychiatric hospitalization, particularly if male; it is similarly the case with persons living alone and persons relatively new in their neighborhoods. The differences in admission rates tend to be more evident in the case of persons with histories of previous psychiatric hospitalization than in the case of new patients, and thus there is some indirect evidence that psychiatric disability may precede social maladjustment. But far too little information is available from this study to make firm assertions about the sequence of events linking social disequilibrium and psychopathology.

There is enough evidence in our data to suggest a twofold approach in our further efforts to control mental disorders, namely, the development of specific trial intervention programs, on the one hand, and the further study of suspected linkages on the other hand. These various measures of social disequilibrium are not independent of each other. Persons with disrupted marriages (particularly males) tend to live alone and tend to move more often. In the 1970 study period, there was a significant association between living alone and residential instability, particularly in the case of patients with prior histories of psychiatric hospitalization. We already know, from our analysis of the Pueblo census tracts, that social disequilibrium as an environmental characteristic has become more sharply concentrated in the past decade, in contrast to environmental measures of socioeconomic affluence or the set of variables we have referred to as the young marrieds cluster. In fact, the decrease in differences among census tracts in affluence and in proportion of young families during the past decade may help account for the fact that these two ecological measures are generally less closely associated with psychiatric admission rates in 1970 than they were in 1960.

Thus it should be those areas characterized by high social disequilibrium and those persons undergoing personal or social disruption who should be the primary target population for addition inquiry and for special trial programming. Additional inquiry must involve longitudinal cohort studies by which the long-term consequences of major types of social disequilibrium can be evaluated. Such longitudinal studies are overdue, even though they are difficult, time-consuming, and costly. But we are dealing with relatively proximal events and have found that in those persons subject to high social disequilibrium that psychiatric disability is infrequent but not rare. Accordingly, the time may be here for undertaking well-designed cohort studies, and particularly for exploring the possibilities of identifying and tracking retrospective cohorts, for example, persons who were divorced five or more years ago and contrasting them with a suitably selected nondivorced comparison group. Such cohort studies have the possibility for evaluating the social causation hypothesis and when accompanied by trial intervention programs with persons currently undergoing social stress, may result in a significant breakthrough in psychiatric epidemiology.

13

Community Mental Health:
The Hope and The Reality

The changes in mental health services between 1960 and 1970 witnessed in Pueblo and described earlier were paralleled by similar events throughout the United States. These changes had their ideological roots in the community mental health movement of the early 1960s, a movement which attempted to be responsive to the criticisms of existing mental health services, which had been heard increasingly over the preceding nearly twenty years. The community mental health movement, in turn, drew its conceptual base from the fields of public health, medical sociology, economics, psychology, and organizational management, among others, and was part of a larger movement toward generally increased interest in civil liberties and social responsibility.

In evaluating the consequences of the expanded availability of mental health services, it is well to keep in mind the criticisms which had been levied against traditional pre-1963 mental health systems. These services were thought of as being inappropriately institutional in character, divorced from the communities in which patients lived. They were viewed as being focused too much on those patients who were able to afford, or, in the case of public agencies, to find services rather than seeing themselves as proactively responsible for the mental health of a defined population group. Traditional mental health

327

services were seen as almost exclusively devoted to largely unevaluated direct therapeutic services with too few resources allocated to program evaluation, on the one hand, and to preventive interventions, on the other. Mental health practitioners, it was believed, needed to devote more time consulting with the staffs of other mediating caretaking agencies, that is, in the provision of indirect services. Too little attention was being paid to the provision of briefer forms of therapy which might make it possible to treat larger numbers of patients more promptly. There was thought to be generally poor coordination among mental health services and between mental health and related health and welfare agencies. Professionalism and professional training was thought to be so highly valued that too little effort was being made to identify and employ nontraditional, often less costly sources of manpower. Furthermore, limiting mental health staff to fully trained professionals inevitably meant that there were serious disjunctions between the socioeconomic and ethnic character of the staff and of their patients. It was believed that community residents had been insufficiently involved in mental health program development. Finally, it was believed that mental health agencies should allocate more of their resources toward the identification and reduction of sources of stress in the community. The community mental health center, such as the one established with federal support in Pueblo, was envisioned as the focal point for dealing with these criticisms (see Bloom, 1973).

With respect to the direct treatment activities of the mental health system, the community mental health center was to ensure their comprehensiveness. While the term "comprehensive" is variously defined, its major dimensions appear to include a commitment toward the restoration and maintenance of psychological well-being within the limits of existing knowledge; the prevention of all preventable psychiatric disorders in the sense both of their occurrence and their recurrence; the concept of continuity of care, in health as well as in sickness, and in all stages of illness; a recognition of the need to be person-centered rather than organ-centered, of the interdependence of health and environment and of mind and body; the need to make services available in sufficient supply to meet the requirements of the population at risk; and an emphasis upon services of demonstrated high quality.

We have seen that in this city there has been a clear responsiveness to some of these imperatives, but that many others have not yet received the attention that was envisioned when federal legislation establishing and supporting community mental health services was enacted. What was found in Pueblo is likely true throughout much of the country. Additional mental health services were created and existing services were expanded, but these services functioned in a relatively uncoordinated manner. While there appears to be a sufficient amount of mental health care available and accessible, numerous problems remain. Thus, the expansion of outpatient services did not result in decreased utilization of inpatient facilities. To the contrary, inpatient services were expanded, they developed a sharply increased case load, and they functioned surprisingly independently of the enlarged outpatient agencies. Nearly all inpatients, public as well as private, bypassed the outpatient service delivery system, and new inpatient programs were developed to meet needs which might have been more rationally met in outpatient settings. The greatest increase in admissions into inpatient facilities between 1960 and 1970 took place in that patient group which might be thought of as most suitable for outpatient care—the young and the mildly disturbed. There appeared to be very little planned collaboration, particularly between public and private agencies, and one might argue that most mental health agencies acted as if they were as concerned with expanding their own role in the service delivery system as with providing care which would be most appropriate and least disruptive to patient needs. There was surely no common agreement that outpatient facilities might serve a screening function and that patients might be hospitalized only after an effort to treat them as outpatients. Outpatient agencies developed no programs for providing emergency care, with the result that when psychiatric emergencies did arise, hospitalization was often the only alternative available. There was a profound change in the locus of care of elderly patients, but again outpatient facilities played a very minor role.

Economic considerations continued to have a pervasive influence on the provision of psychiatric care. With the advent of medicare and with the increase of third-party insurance programs, private facilities provided an increasing proportion of care for those who were previously unable to pay for such care. But when benefits were exhausted, there was little alternative other than to transfer patients into public facilities. Male patients, who would ordinarily be hardest hit by the economic consequences of psychiatric disorder, were treated in disproportionate numbers in public facilities. Perhaps of greatest importance, data were not available on the basis of which it might have been possible to outline a more rational approach to the question of choice of treatment facility. It is entirely possible that certain kinds of programs would have been more effective for certain kinds of patients. Public inpatient facilities might very well have been able to develop effective specialized treatment programs for certain types of problems, and by common consent those programs might have been made available independently of financial considerations. That is, there was little attention to the question as to what services outpatient facilities or private or public inpatient facilities might best be able to provide.

The mental health service delivery system acted as if all it could do was to try to keep up with the demand for care. Little if any attention was directed toward efforts to develop preventive services, in any of the ways that term is used. It is clear, from evidence already presented, that people at excess risk of being admitted into the psychiatric service delivery system can be identified. Neighborhoods that yield excess numbers of patients are equally identifiable. Personal and environmental characteristics associated with unusually high risk of rehospitalization have been found. While it would be inappropriate to suggest that the social etiologies of psychiatric disorder have been found, target populations for the development of primary prevention efforts, if only to test these etiological propositions, are readily distinguishable. Similarly, groups of former patients for whom rehabilitative services might well be provided can be distinguished. If there is reluctance to inaugurate preventive services on the basis of equivocal evidence such as presented in this report, there is no reason why continued efforts to identify factors potentially associated with the development of psychopathology should not be undertaken in the clinical setting. Surely there is a sense in which the patient is a valuable informant about how personal and environmental stressors play a role in the precipitation or perpetuation of his psychiatric disability.

Areas of the city characterized by high social disequilibrium are powerfully associated with excess admission rates. This relationship was very clear in 1960, was even stronger in 1970, and has been shown to apply not only to new inpatient admissions but to readmissions as well. Certain personal characteristics have been shown to be equally powerfully associated with excess risk of admission. Any hope for finding alternatives to continued and unremitting allocation of resources to the provision of treatment must rest on further exploration of these relationships. Thus, few aspects of the mental health system qualify it for the label "comprehensive," and much remains to be done in improving the "system," that is, that whole which achieves its objectives by virtue of the interdependence of its parts. And this raises more basic questions. What, indeed, are the purposes of a mental health service delivery system? What are the criteria by which optimal interdependence of its parts can be ascertained? Can it be shown that when a mental health system is created, it achieves its objectives more successfully or more economically than the more typical, uncoordinated services that exist in most communities?

There is considerable evidence that Pueblo's mental health services are still inappropriately institutional in character. There is certainly too little outreach, too little sense of wanting to know about mental health in the community. While the resources devoted to consultative services have been sharply increased, there is no evidence that such services have had an impact on the incidence or prevalence or severity of psychiatric disability. Brief therapy is being provided, but it is not clear to what extent this is planned and effective and to what extent it represents a failure to engage patients successfully. Coordination and collaboration among social agencies still seem far from adequate. The community may not yet be broadly enough involved in developing mental health services. And the challenging clues as to sources of community stress have yet to be adequately explored.

Mental health agencies can take considerable satisfaction, however, in their success in involving paraprofessionals, particularly those from Chicano backgrounds, in the provision of care. The evidence, although somewhat indirect, strongly suggests that these new sources of mental health manpower have been a major factor in the

greater acceptance of services by the Chicano population, a previously underserved group. There is also substantial evidence that treatment, particularly in public
inpatient settings, is significantly shorter in duration
than it was a decade ago. Length of treatment continues
to be still shorter in private inpatient facilities, however,
but the determinants of this difference are not yet clear.
There is evidence, for example, that patients who are
admitted into private facilities are less interpersonally
and economically disrupted than patients admitted into
public inpatient facilities, even when these two groups of
patients are equated for age, sex, and diagnosis. The
finding that readmission rate is no higher for inpatients
treated in private facilities than for those treated in public facilities in spite of the shorter length of treatment in
the private facilities may be related to this generally
lower level of personal disruption, but additional studies
should be undertaken to develop further understanding
of this phenomenon.

There is considerable evidence throughout the country that public funds are being shifted from hospital to
community settings. Public outpatient facilities, including community mental health centers, are competing
with state hospitals for scarce resources, and the astonishing ability of outpatient facilities to maintain patients
in the community without the need for large inpatient
facilities has not gone unnoticed. Publicly supported
inpatient facilities are consolidating their services and
beginning to recentralize as funds traditionally appropri-
ated to them are being diverted into community facilities. This phenomenon has already begun in Pueblo, and
the role of the state hospital in this era of community-
based services will undoubtedly be the subject of extensive debate during the next year or two.

But at the same time, the concept of the community
mental health center as it has been known for the past
decade is undergoing considerable challenge. Federal

support is being sharply reduced. Issues regarding the treatment of psychiatric patients are caught up in the more urgent concerns for modifying the organization and financing of general medical care. Psychiatric services, historically more in the public domain than other medical services, are likely to be significantly effected by the public sector–private sector debate and by proposals for the establishment of health maintenance organizations. There is a growing move on the part of both the federal and of many state governments to get out of the direct medical care business and to replace direct care by the provision of support for cost- and quality-conscious contractual private sector services. Thus there seems to be some likelihood that psychiatric services will gradually be integrated into a system of general comprehensive health care, and that agencies whose exclusive purpose is the provision of psychiatric care may find themselves increasingly unable to justify separate status.

We are living in an era of cost accountability. While the community mental health center is but a small part of a far larger problem of increasing competition for scarce resources and of very rapidly increasing medical care costs, it is nevertheless being called upon to defend its budgetary requests and expenditures as never before. As part of this process, it is being asked to document its effectiveness, and statistics as to the provision of direct services may no longer serve as acceptable documentation. Questions being asked by many funding sources are now far more sophisticated. How does a community mental health center know that its services are effective? Can it show that its treated patients are able to contribute in increasing amounts to tax revenues? Can it show a decrease in school drop-out rate, in crimes against persons and property, in drug abuse? Can it provide equally effective services at lower cost? In a sense, interest in fiscal responsibility is equal if not more than equal with interest in social responsibility. Yet while some of this concern might have been unavoidable no matter what the history of community mental health center activity had been during the past decade, these questions might very well have been addressed a few years ago when resources were more plentiful.

Most important is the danger that the concern with costs may limit our fundamental knowledge at its current inadequate level. As public funds are tied more and more directly to the provision of services, less money will be available to extend our knowledge. Every question that has been raised about the organization and character of mental health services requires resources in order to be answered, and there is a staggering gap between what is known and what needs to be known regarding the provision of effective psychiatric care and the prevention of mental disorders. The potential of the community mental health movement has not yet been realized and there is some chance that the mental health center may be supplanted before its potential is ascertained. But to the extent that the emphasis on cost effectiveness requires mental health centers to document the consequences of their efforts, mental health programs may be put on much stronger empirical foundations.

And as we begin to identify the outcomes of our programs, our gaps in knowledge will become increasingly apparent. With these gaps revealed, it may become easier to defend the need for resources for the continuation of both basic and applied mental health- and mental illness-related research.

REFERENCES

American Psychological Association. Stress-illness relationship advanced by researcher. *APA Monitor,* 1973, **4,** 8.

APHA. *Mental Disorders: A Guide to Control Methods.* New York: American Public Health Assn., 1962.

Bethel, H., and Redick, R. W. *Provisional Patient Movement and Administrative Data: July 1, 1970–June 30, 1971.* Statistical Note #60. Washington: Survey and Reports Section, Biometry Branch, NIMH, 1972.

Bloom, B. L. A census tract analysis of socially deviant behaviors. *Multivariate Behavioral Research,* 1966, **1,** 307–319.

Bloom, B. L. An ecological analysis of psychiatric hospitalizations. *Multivariate Behavioral Research,* 1968, **3,** 423–463.

Bloom, B. L. The ecology of psychiatric hospitalizations for acute and chronic brain syndromes. *Journal of Gerontology,* 1969, **24,** 48–54.

Bloom, B. L. Prediction and monitoring of resource utilization in a community-oriented mental hospital. *American Journal of Public Health,* 1970a, **60,** 2257–2268.

Bloom, B. L. Changing patterns of hospitalization for psychiatric disorders. *Public Health Reports,* 1970b, **85,** 81–87.

Bloom, B. L. *Community Mental Health: A Historical and Critical Analysis.* Morristown, N.J.: General Learning Press, 1973.

Blum, R. H. Case identification in psychiatric epidemiology—methods and problems. *Milbank Memorial Fund Quarterly,* 1962, **40,** 253–288.

Bureau of the Census, U.S. Dept. of Commerce. *U.S. Censuses of Population and Housing—1960: Census Tracts: Pueblo, Colorado. PHC(1)-123.* Washington: USGPO, 1961.

Bureau of the Census, U.S. Dept. of Commerce. *Detailed List of Spanish Surnames. 1970 Census General Coding Procedures Manual. Attachment J-2.* Washington: Mimeographed, 1970.

Bureau of the Census, U.S. Dept. of Commerce. *1970 Census of Population and Housing; Census Tracts: Pueblo, Colorado. PHC(1)—168.* Washington: USGPO, 1972.

Clausen, J. A., and Kohn, M. L. Relation of schizophrenia to the social structure of a small city. In B. Pasamanick (Ed.), *Epidemiology of Mental Disorder.* Washington: AAAS, 1959.

Clausen, J. A., and Kohn, M. L. Social relations and schizophrenia. In D. Jackson (Ed.), *Etiology of Schizophrenia.* New York: Basic Books, 1960.

Cohen, B. M. and Fairbanks, R. Statistical contributions from the mental hygiene study of the Eastern Health District of Baltimore. *American Journal of Psychiatry,* 1938, **94,** 1153–1161.

Conley, R. W., Conwell, M., & Willner, S. G. *The Cost of Mental Illness, 1968.* Statistical Note # 30. Washington: Survey and Reports Section, Biometry Branch, NIMH, 1970.

Cooper, J. E., Kendall, R. E., Gurland, B. J., Sartorius, N., & Farkas, T. Cross-national study of diagnosis of the mental disorders: some results from the first comparative investigation. *American Journal of Psychiatry,* 1969, **125**, 21–29.

Crandell, D. L. and Dohrenwend, B. P. Some relations among psychiatric symptoms, organic illness, and social class. *American Journal of Psychiatry,* 1967, **123**, 1527–1538.

Cumming, E. Primary prevention—more cost than benefit. In H. Gottesfeld (Ed.), *The Critical Issues of Community Mental Health.* New York: Behavioral Publications, 1972

Denner, B. and Price, R. H. (Eds.). *Community Mental Health: Social Action and Reaction.* New York: Holt, Rinehart and Winston, 1973.

Dohrenwend, B. P. Social status, stress, and psychological symptoms. *Milbank Memorial Fund Quarterly,* 1969, **47**, 137–150.

Dohrenwend, B. P. Psychiatric disorder in general populations: problem of the untreated "case." *American Journal of Public Health,* 1970, **60**, 1052–1064.

Dohrenwend, B. P. and Chin-Shong, E. Social status and attitude toward psychological disorder: the problem of tolerance of deviance. *American Sociological Review,* 1967, **32**, 417–433.

Dohrenwend, B. P. and Dohrenwend, B. S. The problem of validity in field studies of psychological disorder. *Journal of Abnormal Psychology,* 1965, **70**, 52–69.

Dohrenwend, B. P. and Dohrenwend, B. S. *Social Status and Psychological Disorder: A Causal Inquiry.* New York: Wiley and Sons, 1969.

Dohrenwend, B. P., Egri, G., & Mendelsohn, F. S. Psychiatric disorder in general populations: a study of the problem of clinical judgment. *American Journal of Psychiatry,* 1971, **127**, 1304–1312.

Dunham, H. W. Anomie and mental disorder. In M. B. Clinard (Ed.), *Anomie and Deviant Behavior.* New York: Free Press, 1964.

Dunham, H. W. *Community and Schizophrenia.* Detroit: Wayne State University Press, 1965.

Dunham, H. W. Theories and hypotheses in social psychiatry: an analysis of the evidence. In J. Zubin and F. A. Freyhan (Eds.), *Social Psychiatry.* New York: Grune and Stratton, 1968.

Dunham, H. W. Discussion. In E. H. Hare and J. K. Wing (Eds.), *Psychiatric Epidemiology.* London: Oxford University Press, 1970.

Dunham, H. W. Sociocultural studies of schizophrenia. *Archives of General Psychiatry,* 1971, **24,** 206–214.

Eaton, J. W. and Weil, R. J. *Culture and Mental Disorders.* Glencoe, Illinois: The Free Press, 1955.

Essen-Möller, E. Individual traits and morbidity in a Swedish rural population. *Acta Psychiatrica et Neurologica Scandinavica,* 1956, Supp. No. 100.

Faris, R. E. L. and Dunham, H. W. *Mental Disorders in Urban Areas.* Chicago: University of Chicago Press, 1939.

Gove, W. R. Societal reaction as an explanation of mental illness: an evaluation. *American Sociological Review,* 1970a, **35,** 873–884.

Gove, W. R. Who is hospitalized: a critical review of some sociological studies of mental illness. *Journal of Health and Social Behavior,* 1970b, **11,** 294–303.

Gove, W. R. Sex, marital status and suicide. *Journal of Health and Social Behavior,* 1972, **13,** 204–213.

Gruenberg, E. M. Community conditions and psychoses of the elderly. *American Journal of Psychiatry,* 1954, **110,** 888–896.

Gunderson, E. K. E. Epidemiology and prognosis of psychiatric disorders in the naval service. In C. D. Spielberger (Ed.), *Current Topics in Clinical and Community Psychology,* Vol. 3. New York: Academic Press, 1971.

Gunderson, E. K. E., and Arthur, R. J. Prognosis for psychiatric patients in naval service. *Military Medicine,* 1967, **132,** 704–712.

Hafner, H. and Reimann, H. Spatial distribution of mental disorders in Mannheim, 1965. In E. H. Hare and J. K. Wing (Eds.), *Psychiatric Epidemiology: An International Symposium.* London: Oxford University Press, 1970.

Hagnell, O. *A Prospective Study of the Incidence of Mental Disorder.* Stockholm, Sweden: Svenska Bokförlaget Norstedts-Bonniers, 1966.

Hollingshead, A. B. and Redlich, F. C. *Social Class and Mental Illness: A Community Study.* New York: Wiley and Sons, 1958.

Hudgens, R. W., Robins, E., & Delong, W. B. The reporting of recent stress in the lives of psychiatric patients. *British Journal of Psychiatry,* 1970, **117,** 635–643.

Hughes, C. C., Trembly, M. A., Rapoport, R. N., and Leighton, A. H. *People of Cove and Woodlot.* New York: Basic Books, 1960.

Jaco, E. G. Incidence of psychosis in Texas—1951–1952. *Texas State Journal of Medicine,* 1957, **53,** 86–91.

Jaco, E. G. *The Social Epidemiology of Mental Disorders.* New York: Russell Sage Foundation, 1960.

Karno, M. and Edgerton, R. B. Perception of mental illness in a Mexican-American community. *Archives of General Psychiatry,* 1969, **20,** 233–238.

Karpinos, B. D. Results of the examination of youths for military service, 1968. *Health of the Army,* Supplement, 1969, **24,** 1–107.

Klee, G. D., Spiro, E., Bahn, A. K., & Gorwitz, K. An ecological analysis of diagnosed mental illness in Baltimore. In R. R. Monroe, G. D. Klee, and E. B. Brody (Eds.), *Psychiatric Epidemiology and Mental Health Planning.* Research Report #22. Washington: American Psychiatric Association, 1967.

Kohn, M. L. Social class and schizophrenia: a critical review. In D. Rosenthal and S. S. Kety (Eds.), *The*

Transmission of Schizophrenia. Oxford: Pergamon Press, 1968.

Kramer, M. A discussion of the concepts of incidence and prevalence as related to epidemiologic studies of mental disorders. *American Journal of Public Health,* 1957, **47,** 826–840.

Kramer, M. Epidemiology, biostatistics, and mental health planning. In R. R. Monroe, G. D. Klee, and E. B. Brody (Eds.), *Psychiatric Epidemiology and Mental Health Planning.* Psychiatric Research Report #22. Washington: American Psychiatric Association. 1967.

Kubie, L. S. Pitfalls of community psychiatry. *Archives of General Psychiatry,* 1968, **18,** 257–266.

Langner, T. S. and Michael, S. T. *Life Stress and Mental Health.* New York: MacMillan Co., 1963.

Leighton, A. H. *My Name is Legion.* New York: Basic Books, 1959.

Leighton, D. C., Harding, J. S., Macklin, D. B., MacMillan, A. M., & Leighton, A. H. *The Character of Danger.* New York: Basic Books, 1963.

Lemkau, P. V., Tietze, C., & Cooper, M. Mental hygiene problems in an urban district: description of the study. *Mental Hygiene,* 1941, **25,** 624–646.

Lemkau, P. V., Tietze, C., & Cooper, M. A survey of statistical studies on the prevalence and incidence of mental disorder in sample populations. *Public Health Reports,* 1943, **57,** 1909–1927.

Lemkau, P. V. The epidemiological study of mental illnesses and mental health. *American Journal of Psychiatry,* 1955, **111,** 801–809.

Levy, L. and Rowitz, L. *The Ecology of Mental Disorder.* New York: Behavioral Publications, 1973.

MacMahon, B. Epidemiologic methods. In Clark, D. W. and MacMahon, B., *Preventive Medicine.* New York: Little, Brown, 1967.

MacMahon, B., Pugh, T. F., & Ipsen, J. *Epidemiologic Methods.* Boston: Little, Brown, 1960.

Malzberg, B. *Social and Biological Aspects of Mental Illness.* Utica, New York: State Hospital Press, 1940.

Manis, J. G., Brewer, M. J., Hunt, C. L., & Kerchner, L. C. Estimating the prevalence of mental illness. *American Sociological Review,* 1964, **29,** 84–89.

Mechanic, D. Problems and prospects in psychiatric epidemiology. In E. H. Hare and J. K. Wing (Eds.), *Psychiatric Epidemiology.* London: Oxford University Press, 1970.

Mechanic, D. Social class and schizophrenia: some requirements for a plausible theory of social influence. *Social Forces,* 1972, **50,** 305–309.

Mendel, W. Brief hospitalization techniques. In J. Masserman (Ed.), *Current Psychiatric Therapies.* New York: Grune and Stratton, 1967.

Meyers, J. C. *Women in divorce and after.* Unpublished Manuscript, 1972.

Michaux, W. W., Katz, M. M., Kurland, A. A., & Gansereit, K. H. *The First Year Out: Mental Patients after Hospitalization.* Baltimore: Johns Hopkins Press, 1969.

Mishler, E. G. and Scotch, N. A. Sociocultural factors in the epidemiology of schizophrenia. *Psychiatry,* 1963, **26,** 315–351.

Mulford, H. A. and Wilson, D. W. *Identifying Problem Drinkers in a Household Health Survey.* Public Health Service Publication No. 1000, Series 2, No. 16. Washington: USGPO, 1966.

Pasamanick, B. What is mental illness and how can we measure it? In S. B. Sells (Ed.), *The Definition and Measurement of Mental Health.* Washington: USGPO, 1968.

Phillips, D. L. and Clancy, K. J. Response bias in field studies of mental illness. *American Sociological Review,* 1970, **35,** 503–515.

Phillips, D. L. and Segal, B. E. Sexual status and psychiatric symptoms. *American Sociological Review,* 1969, **34,** 58–72.

Pugh, T. F. and MacMahon, B. *Epidemiologic Findings in United States Mental Hospital Data.* London: Churchill Ltd., 1962.

Rogers, E. S. Man, ecology, and the control of disease. *Public Health Reports,* 1962, **77,** 755–762.

Ryan, W. *Distress in the City.* Cleveland: Case Western Reserve Press, 1969.

Sarbin, T. R. A role-theory perspective for community psychology: the structure of social identity. In D. Adelson and B. L. Kalis (Eds.), *Community Psychology and Mental Health: Perspectives and Challenges.* Scranton: Chandler, 1970.

Snow, J. *Snow on Cholera.* New York: Commonwealth Fund, 1936.

Srole, L., Langner, T. S., Michael, S. T., Opler, M. K., & Rennie, T. A. C. *Mental Health in the Metropolis.* New York: McGraw-Hill, 1962.

Stokes, J., III and Dawber, T. R. Rheumatic heart disease in the Framingham Study. *New England Journal of Medicine,* 1956, **255,** 1228–1233.

Taube, C. A. *General Hospital Psychiatric Inpatient Units, 1969–1970.* Statistical Note #44. Survey and Reports Section, Biometry Branch, NIMH. Washington: DHEW, 1970.

Taube, C. A. *Admission to Outpatient Psychiatric Services, 1969 by Age, Sex, and Diagnosis.* Statistical Note #48. Survey and Reports Section, Biometry Branch, NIMH. Washington: DHEW, 1971.

Taube, C., and Cannon, M. S. *Whom are Community Mental Health Centers Serving?* Statistical Note #67. Survey and Reports Section, Biometry Branch, NIMH. Washington: DHEW, 1972.

Terris, M. (Ed.). *Goldberger on Pellagra.* Baton Rouge: Louisiana State University Press, 1964.

Tyron, R. C. and Bailey, D. E. *Cluster Analysis.* New York: McGraw-Hill, 1970.

Wagenfeld, M. O. The primary prevention of mental illness: a sociological perspective. *Journal of Health and Social Behavior,* 1972, **13,** 195–203.

Warren, R. L. Mental health planning and model cities: "Hamlet" or "Hellzapoppin." *Community Mental Health Journal,* 1971, **7,** 39–49.

Wechsler, H., and Pugh, T. F. Fit of individual and community characteristics and rates of psychiatric hospitalization. *American Journal of Sociology,* 1967, **73,** 331–338.

Witkin, M. J. *Private Mental Hospitals: 1969–1970.* Survey and Reports Section, Biometry Branch, NIMH. Washington: DHEW (Pub. No. HSM 72-9089), 1972.

Witkin, M. J., and Cannon, M. S. *Residential Treatment Centers for Emotionally Disturbed Children: 1969–1970.* Survey and Reports Section, Biometry Branch, NIMH. Washington: DHEW (Pub. No. HSM 72-9022), 1971.

WHO Technical Report Series. *Epidemiology of Mental Disorders.* No. 185. Geneva: World Health Organization, 1960.

Zola, I. K. Culture and symptoms: an analysis of patient's presenting complaints. *American Sociological Review,* 1966, **31,** 615–630.

APPENDIX A

Pueblo Psychiatric Epidemiology Project— Inpatient Form

Instructions: Complete this form for every psychiatric inpatient who lives in the city or county of Pueblo at the time of admission. If you cannot complete the entire form, complete as much of it as you can.

Name of Reporting Agency _____

1. Patient's Name _____

2. Patient's Address _____

   _____

   _____

3. Patient's Home Phone Number (indicate if no phone) _____

4. Patient's Sex (check one)

   1. _____ Male

   2. _____ Female

5. Date of Admission _____

6. Hospital Case Number _____

7. Age at Admission _____ years

8. Diagnosis (provisional or final) _____

   _____

347

9. Hospitalization History (check one)

    1._____First admission to any psychiatric inpatient unit

    2._____Previously admitted elsewhere for inpatient care but first admission here

    3._____Previously admitted here for inpatient care

10. How long have you lived at your present address_____
                                         Specify time unit

11. How long have you lived in Pueblo County_____
                                         Specify time unit

12. Do you live in a (check one)

    1._____apartment

    2._____one-family house

    3._____two-family house

    4._____three-family house

    5._____rooming house

    6._____mobile home or trailer

    7._____other (please specify)_____

13. Regarding your home, do you (check one)

    1._____own it (including making mortgage payments)

    2._____rent it

    3._____occupy it without paying cash rent

    4._____other (please specify)_____

_____

14. How many rooms do you have in your living quarters (do not count bathrooms, porches, balconies, foyers, halls or half-rooms)

_____

15. About when was your house originally built (check one)

    1.＿＿＿1967 or later

    2.＿＿＿1965 or 1966

    3.＿＿＿1960 to 1964

    4.＿＿＿1950 to 1959

    5.＿＿＿1940 to 1949

    6.＿＿＿before 1940

16. Do you have complete kitchen facilities (sink with piped water, a range or cook stove, and a refrigerator) (check one)

    1.＿＿＿yes, for this household only

    2.＿＿＿yes, but also used by another household

    3.＿＿＿no

17. Is there hot and cold piped water in your building (check one)

    1.＿＿＿yes

    2.＿＿＿only cold piped water in my building

    3.＿＿＿no piped water in my building

18. Do you have a flush toilet (check one)

    1.＿＿＿yes, for this household only

    2.＿＿＿yes, but also used by another household

    3.＿＿＿no

19. Do you have a bathtub or shower (check one)

    1.＿＿＿yes, for this household only

    2.＿＿＿yes, but also used by another household

    3.＿＿＿no

20. How many passenger automobiles are owned or regularly used by members of your household, including company cars kept at home_____

21. Number of people living in your household (including patient and babies, relatives, lodgers, servants, or anyone else who lives here most of the time_____

22. Relationship of patient to head of household (check one)

    1._____head of household

    2._____wife of head of household

    3._____son or daughter of head of household

    4._____brother or sister of head of household

    5._____father or mother of head of household

    6._____other relative of head of household

    7._____not related to head of household (please explain)_____

    _____

    _____

23. Education of patient (check one)

    0._____no formal education

    1._____some grade school (less than six years)

    2._____graduated from grade school or junior high school (six to nine years)

    3._____one or two years of high school (ten or eleven years)

    4._____graduated high school

    5._____attended or graduated trade school or business college

    6._____one to three years of college

    7._____graduated college

    8._____did some post-graduate work

9._____completed post-graduate work or professional school

24. Current marital status (check one)

1._____single (never married)

2._____married (living together)

3._____married (separated)

4._____divorced

5._____widowed

6._____other (please specify)_____

25. Marital history (check one)

1._____never married

2._____married once (never separated)

3._____married once (separated one or more times)

4._____married once, now divorced

5._____married once, now widowed

6._____remarried, following divorce

7._____remarried, following widowhood

8._____other (please specify) _____

_____

26. Length of current or most recent marriage _____
Specify time unit

27. If remarried, length of first marriage _____
Specify time unit

28. If female, number of living children_____

29. If female, how many babies have you ever had, not counting stillbirths_____

30. What is your usual occupation_____

_____

31. What job were you holding just before coming here_____

_____

32. Employment history last year (check one)

    1._____did not work at all *and* did not look for work

    2._____did not work at all *even though* was looking for work

    3._____worked 13 weeks or less

    4._____worked 14 to 26 weeks

    5._____worked 27 to 39 weeks

    6._____worked 40 weeks or more

33. Name of respondent (if other than patient) and relationship to patient_____

34. Length of hospitalization

    1._____between 1 and 7 days

    2._____between 8 and 14 days

    3._____between 15 and 21 days

    4._____between 22 and 30 days

    5._____between 31 and 60 days

    6._____between 61 and 90 days

    7._____more than 90 days

Pueblo, Colorado Psychiatric Epidemiology Project Data Collection Form

Instructions: Please complete this brief form for every patient who meets ALL of the following criteria:

1. Admitted to your agency anytime between Sept. 1, 1969 and August 31, 1971
2. Resident of Pueblo (city or county) at the time of admission
3. NOT hospitalized for a psychiatric disorder during this episode of care

NOTE: If a patient was admitted more than once during the two year data collection period, complete a form for each admission.

* *

1. Name of Reporting Agency _____

2. Patient's Name _____
                Last   First   Middle

3. Patient's Address _____
                Number   Street

4. Patient's Sex: Male _____ Female _____

5. Date of Admission _____

6. Age at Admission _____
                   Years

7. Diagnosis (APA Nomenclature) _____

8. Diagnosis (Check most appropriate choice)

   A._____Psychoneurosis or Psychosomatic Disorder

   B. _____Personality Disorder (including Alcoholism and Drug Abuse)

   C. _____Functional Psychosis

   D._____Acute or Chronic Brain Syndrome

9. Outpatient History (check one)

   A._____First admission to any outpatient unit

   B. _____Previously admitted elsewhere for outpatient care but first admission to your agency

   C. _____Previously admitted to your agency for outpatient care

10. Date of Discharge_____

INDEX

Mental hygiene clinics, 30–31, 87, 91
Mental retardation, 29, 46
Mental Retardation Center, Colorado State Hospital, 99–100
Methodological details, 43–65
  census tract cluster scores, 58–65
  extent and nature of missing data, 57–58
  sources of data, 50–57
  study definitions, 45–49
Mexican–Americans, 197, 198
Meyers, J. C., 305
Michael, S. T., 36
Michaux, W. W., 262
Midtown Manhattan Study, 36–38, 285, 286
Midtown Treatment Census, 290
Military services, mental disorders in, 29
Minority status, as a stressor variable, 312–316
Mishler, E. G., 293, 322
Mobility, 176, 179, 306
Mulford, H. A., 285
Multiple episodes of care, 257–275
  diagnostic stability, 269–273
  prevalence and agency participation, 260–266
  single patients contrasted with multiple episode patients, 274–275
  three or more episodes, 266–269

National Institute of Mental Health, 88, 93, 235
National Mental Health Act of 1946, 87
Neighborhood characteristics, admission rates and, 145–164
New Haven, Connecticut, 33–34
Nursing homes, 28, 106, 113
Nursing visits, 71, 76

Occupation, 166–170, 179, 222
Outpatient facilities, 28, 43, 44, 115, 116
  private, 30, 47, 48, 117
  public, 48, 91, 333
  See also Facility, type of

Parkview Episcopal Hospital, Pueblo, Colorado, 104–105
Pasamanick, B., 284
Patients
  changing character of hospitalized psychiatric, 121–144
  contrasted with general population, 165–183

additional comparisons, 175–177
  social disequilibrium, 168–173
  socioeconomic affluence, 166–168
  young marrieds, 173–175
contrasting 1960 and 1970 study periods, 130–144
marital disruption as stressor variable, 298–305
minority status as stressor variable, 312–316
service statistics versus household surveys, 280–287
social isolation as stressor variable, 305–312
Spanish surnamed, 56–57, 166, 167, 179, 185–201, 215, 312–317
  length of episodes of care, 239–242
See also First admission inpatients; First admission outpatients; Psychiatric care; Readmitted inpatients; Readmitted outpatients
Personality disorders, 46, 127, 128, 130–137, 142, 146, 155, 159, 160, 191, 193, 224, 230, 249, 270–274
Phillips, D. L., 287
Porter, R. A., 321
Prevalence measures versus incidence measures, 287–296
Prevalence rates, 34, 35, 37
Preventive intervention, social disequilibrium and, 316–326
Price, R. H., 143
Private inpatient facilities, 28, 47, 57, 116
  expanding role of, 29–30
  See also Facility, type of
Private outpatient facilities, 30, 47, 48, 117
  See also Facility, type of
Psychiatric care
  length of episodes of, 235–256
    factors associated with, 236–244
    length of consecutive, 250–256
    public and private inpatients, 244–250
  multiple episodes, 257–275
    diagnostic stability, 269–273
    prevalence and agency participation, 260–266
    single patients contrasted